AMERICAN FASHION

QUADRANGLE/THE NEW YORK TIMES BOOK CO.

AMERICAN FASHION

The life and lines of

Adrian

Mainbocher

McCardell

Norell

Trigère

EDITED BY SARAH TOMERLIN LEE FOR

THE FASHION INSTITUTE OF TECHNOLOGY

Library of Congress Cataloging in Publication Data

Main entry under title:

American fashion.

Bibliography: p.
1. Costume designers—Biography. I. Lee,
Sarah. II. New York. Fashion Institute of
Technology.
TT505.A1A44   746.9'2'0922 [B]   75–8295
ISBN 0–8129–0524–5

CONTENTS

FOREWORD

The Fashion Institute of Technology is a vast career college. In its twenty-five year history, it has produced thousands of graduates to work with expertise in the fashion industry. Yearly increasing thousands of day and night students are learning the skills of fashion: design, production, promotion, merchandising. F.I.T. is a dynamic center of creative accomplishment.

How appropriate now for this institution, just as it is moving into its expanded new campus, to reach out and celebrate in its initial publishing project the stellar creative forces in the great American fashion industry . . . the largest industry in New York state and the third largest in the United States.

In this volume is the record of the first five decades of true American Fashion. The only biographical series that we know of which singles out individual designers, discovers their background, inspiration, influences—the drama and trauma of making fashion (and fame).

Of the many brilliant American talents flowering between 1925 and 1975 we begin with Adrian, Mainbocher, McCardell, Norell, Trigère. A New Englander, a Middle Westerner, a Southerner, a Naturalized Citizen . . . each talent, each personality, each product highly individual. Here, as well, begin the patterns of the burgeoning retail and manufacturing industry and the often thrilling evidence of the support of a talented press.

Each designer has costumed his or her America with a unique palette, sense of time, place, occasion, and view of women and their role. Fifty years of fashion which reveal a particularly fascinating aspect of this civilization. We hope this compilation of designer's work will be a source of delight as well as a reminder to those of us who have already witnessed these fashions. Particularly we hope it will spark the flame of tomorrow's talent.

William J. Lippincott, *President*
The Educational Foundation for the Fashion Industries

INTRODUCTION

The American Fashion community, before World War II, was a colony of France as truly as America was England's before the Revolution. True, there was an independent outpost in Hollywood, but people wrote that off as pure "costume," not fashion. Meanwhile, the American genius for organization and manufacture, promotion and distribution was building a powerful empire.

But the inspiration and authority was in Paris and nowhere else. When the collections were ready, the New York manufacturers, the retailers, the editors migrated as regularly as any flight birds toward their nesting ground in season. The dictates of the Paris Couture were exquisite, delicious, NEWS, carrying their own mandates. Its influence was so pervasive that even in this book, devoted to American Fashion, four of the five designers prepared themselves in the schools and workrooms of Paris and the fifth traveled in his earliest years from a New York design establishment to each collection—not to buy but to absorb.

When World War II stemmed the flow of imported fashion news and imported originals, American fashion creativity, from sportswear to grand couture, came into full flower and recognition. American designers championed as their own American girls and the contemporary woman.

From "Paris Says," the watchword became the bravura "Why don't you . . . ?" The outpouring of American Fashion was a yeasty mix: Hollywood siren glamour, precise town tailleurs, the most playful playclothes ever seen. Made to size, any size. Sometimes startlingly inexpensive as McCardell's wartime popover ($10) or as much of an investment as a 1972 Norell mermaid sheath ($5,000). American design—confident, resourceful, adventurous—in total harmony with life, the time, the place—became a prime unshakable force.

While a wealth of supporting descriptive and pictorial material exists, it is so dispersed as to be largely unavailable to the student and the public. And because of the moment-to-moment nature of newspaper and magazine coverage and the seasonal essence of fashion, its reportage has seldom been viewed as the consistent output of creative individuals whose cachet continues and whose talent with color, surface, and silhouette often equates with high art.

The board of the Fashion Institute's Educational Foundation has long felt that a publishing program centered on individual designers —their backgrounds, sources of inspiration, theories, experiences with manufacturers and retailers and the press—would be a great inspiration for young student designers. In fact, such a publishing program would have wide interest far beyond the school room, even beyond the producing centers of American fashion.

We are fully aware that within one volume we could only make a beginning. We could not salute all who deserve a permanent record; we have had to choose five to make a start. This volume was conceived initially as a single monograph to be followed into an infinity of creative talents. As it is, *American Fashion*, with five subjects and nearly one thousand illustrations, will later divide like an amoeba into single paperbacks.

Our authors are editors and a fashion curator-historian, all authorities especially informed on their individual designer. They have often gone far beyond their assigned subject because of the scope of their knowledge and experience and have acted as general research advisers throughout—"remembering" and tracking down particularly valuable photographs. Nowhere else in book form are there records of photographs interpreting a given designer's work and development. At the very time American fashion was soaring, so was fashion photography. Color film and engraving techniques advanced its pace to fit the time schedule of fashion reportage . . . but even without color, fashion photography achieved new brilliance. Design often became Fashion in the camera's eye.

It is this visual treasure which our authors have searched out over five years. Louise Dahl-Wolfe has given us selections from her priceless collection, as has Horst, who also supplied us with rare photographs by Hoyningen-Huené. The riches of John Rawlings' photographic estate were given to us as well as several marvelous photographs by Edward Steichen. Bill Cunningham has given us his super fashion show reportage. We are deeply in the debt of John Engstead for total Adrian fashion coverage; to Joseph Simms for his vast accumulated library of Adrian costumes in movie stills; to Toni Frissell, Irving Penn, Milton Greene, Richard Avedon, Peter Fink, Kay Bell Raynal, for highly prized and particular turning-point photographs. We are grateful to Charlotte Erickson for releasing the great gouache and line drawings of her father, Eric; to Madame Bouché for her husband's drawings which, with those of Count René Bouët-Willaumez, have stirred three decades with their authority and elegance. Our gratitude especially to Condé Nast and to Hearst for their enthusiastic cooperation giving permission to reproduce their editorial illustrations from the pages of *Vogue* and *Harper's Bazaar,* as well as to *Life* and *Look,* to *Architectural Digest,* and to the families of Adrian and McCardell who contributed their pictures and their memories.

Sarah Tomerlin Lee

Editorial Director
Educational Foundation
The Fashion Institute of Technology

AMERICAN FASHION

ADRIAN

BY ROBERT RILEY

CONTENTS

PREFACE

Nowadays, the Hollywood of the twenties and thirties has become a camp cult. Undoubtedly many of its pictures and many of its customs were ludicrous and pretentious in the extreme—the inevitable result of a commercial enterprise struggling with an art form. However, that antic facade should not conceal the fact that many of Hollywood's workers and some of its chiefs were creative artists. Some of these succumbed to their commercial environment; others disregarded it and by their efforts enriched America's popular culture. Such a one was Adrian.

He was a man who wrote his signature very clearly on his generation. When the movies began to fade, he moved into the fashion business and established his mark there with equal force. Such dynamic personalities usually leave behind them a trail of satellite disciples. Adrian's legacy, on the contrary, was a large number of friends with whom he had lived a rich and complex life.

Bernadine Szold, Tony Duquette, his sister Beatrice Leventhal, Paul Gregory, Woody Feurt, Eleanor Lambert and a host of others have most generously shared their memories of Adrian.

Luther Davis, Sheila O'Brien, Norman Norell, Charles LeMaire, Anna Crouse, Eleanor Pinkham, Al Nickel have told of Adrian and show business. Nan Martin, Harriet Frank, Kitty Sully, Adrian's models; Evelyn Byrnes, then buyer for Marshall Field; Sam Bergstein, his production man; Louis Wheeler and Warren McCurtin then of the Gunther-Jaeckel venture have told of Adrian and the fashion business.

Several institutions have opened their archives for research: among them the Los Angeles County Museum of Art, the Theatre Department of the Museum of the City of New York, the Library of the Motion Picture Academy, and Metro-Goldwyn-Mayer itself.

Special thanks must be rendered to Joseph Simms, an Adrian fan, who has done indefatigable research on his subject and shared every contact and each piece of information with me.

And finally to Janet Gaynor Gregory, who has borne my questions with courage and answered them with candor, I can but say I am grateful for the help.

Robert Riley

HOLLYWOOD PARTY, 1937

Adrian, costumer to Joan Crawford, *opposite*, and the rest of the MGM stars, gave parties of the first magnitude. In the snapshot, *above*, the host is bareheaded, Janet Gaynor in a straw boater, and Bernadine Szold turbanned.

Wherever he was—in the jungles of Brazil or throwing a Hollywood party—the man had an air of quiet elegance. The long-boned body was relaxed. The lean hands moved precisely, without waste. From the dark and narrow head, with its great beaked nose, brown eyes were turned directly on you. If he wanted to, he could transform an ordinary greeting into candid friendship.

This Sunday afternoon in 1937, Adrian was giving a party. Although holidays generally held no particular significance for him, they provided convenient dates for gatherings of friends. He enjoyed great varieties of people, and they in turn enjoyed him. No one came to an Adrian party just to be seen there or to advance himself socially or financially in Hollywood. They came knowing they would find bright people, stimulating conversation and a sense of special occasion.

The setting was a former Spanish Mission horror house of stucco and overwrought ironwork that Adrian had gutted and remodeled. Now his guests passed from bright sunlight into airy rooms with blue shadows, wide couches, and everywhere explosions of flowers. Through tall French doors he led them into the patio, where sunlight filtered through an oversized pepper tree. In a curlicued wire cage as high as the rooftop, flocks of finches, macaws, and bright parakeets fluttered, squawked, and sang. A matching cage enclosed plum trees and a large family of antic monkeys. Adrian had designed this as a backdrop for people.

Hedda Hopper, who had lately turned from acting to writing a daily gossip column, held center stage. Margaret Sullavan, Hollywood's version of the-girl-next-door, sat cross-legged in her slacks, surrounded by several devoted admirers and her producer-husband, Leland Hayward. Writer Thornton Wilder reminisced about show business and was roundly kissed by dancer Ann Pennington because he remembered her "Peekin' Knees" number in the *Follies*. Amid the vivid shirts and dresses and hats, Thomas Mann and his family sat in gray wool and sad Teutonic dignity. Dorothy Parker listened intently to their few words.

Suddenly, at precisely the right dramatic moment, Constance Collier strode through an open window. It was a *grande dame* entrance from Pinero, and Adrian could not help applauding.

Not all his guests were the kind who made dramatic entrances or rated space in Hedda Hopper's column. Also present was the dry-witted Yankee, Miss Cook from Naugatuck, a friend of Adrian's mother; Ruth Hawkes, who bravely managed to keep her wits as she presided over Adrian's disorganized antique shop; a newspaper editor just returned from covering the explosive political situation in Europe; a designer of airplanes; the widow of Hollywood pioneer Jesse L. Lasky.

It was an international guest list that recognized no occupational boundaries. Ilona Massey and Hedy Lamarr stood together speaking careful German; Odette Myrtil joined them in staccato French. In the shadows of a wisteria, the shy British voice of Aldous Huxley remarked that if one omitted the sun, this party was really not too different from those of his native Bloomsbury. In what appeared to be an accidental collection of arms and legs, he sprawled in a deck chair. Beside him sat Janet Gaynor, her wide brown eyes missing nothing.

Collection of Bernadine Szold

This gathering of the pleasant and powerful had been assembled by a comparatively young man. Adrian was then only thirty-four. For the last dozen years he had worked in Hollywood studios. The chief product of the Hollywood dream factories was their unutterably glamorous stars, the idols of millions. Everyone, it seemed, wanted to imitate Jean Harlow's allure, sing Bing Crosby's songs, and dance like Fred Astaire. All the skills of Hollywood's writers, directors, photographers, and publicists were directed to building a star whom the whole world would dream about and pay their money to see.

Adrian had an indispensable role in creating Hollywood glamour. As chief designer at MGM he dressed that studio's brightest stars: Greta Garbo, Joan Crawford, Norma Shearer. In the shifting galaxy of movie heaven, he seemed part of a fixed constellation. His credit line, "Gowns by Adrian," had already appeared in almost two hundred pictures.

Yet it was not Adrian's dazzling success that made one eager to be invited to his house. The truth was, he gave good parties. Moreover, he was a kind man who tolerated none of the superficialities of Hollywood protocol, and people liked to be around him. They sat down to an exquisite dinner with impeccable service, but Adrian's easy manner made it as companionable as a picnic. If conversation flagged he could galvanize his guests with unexpectedly blunt or prodding questions. He was a good listener, genuinely interested in people.

Basil Rathbone most elegantly recited a scatological limerick. There were bursts of laughter, gusts of conversation, and quiet pauses. Rosa Ponselle, Marguerite Namara, Gladys Swarthout—three celebrated Carmens of the day—eyed the silent piano and sighed contentedly. With three prima donnas present, they knew that it would probably remain silent.

There was a performance that evening, however. Adrian and Fanny Brice dragged out a box of magic tricks. To their own obvious delight and the evident boredom of those who had seen the tricks before, they made flags change colors, rings mysteriously link and unlink themselves, cigarettes appear and smoke come out of unlikely places. The effort Miss Brice expended in making three glasses pass through a scarf exhausted her, and left the remaining audience limp with laughter.

At last, one by one, the cars left the driveway. Monday was a working day and shooting began early in the morning. A handful of guests lingered. Alice Longworth stood up. Adrian smiled.

"Please don't go. I've wanted to talk to you—seriously talk to you —ever since you came. You know Africa. Even as a youngster I've dreamed of going—"

The two stepped out into the dark patio—the president's daughter whose tongue had seared three decades of diplomats, and the milliner's son from Naugatuck, Connecticut, who dressed Hollywood's dream girls. On and on they talked. The others listened quietly.

That was in the year 1937.

The fun and games of Adrian parties were sometimes preserved in photographs. The conversations—spiced with the mordant wit of Hedda Hopper, shown above right— have unfortunately vanished.

NAUGATUCK, 1903

Photographed at age 5, Adrian is obviously the milliner's son. During his school-days he chose to emulate the drawings of Aubrey Beardsley. Not a bad choice as can be seen by the boy's decorative panel of leaves in the wind.

tion of Mrs. Clarence Leventhal

In March of the year 1903, Adrian Adolph Greenburg was born in Naugatuck, Connecticut.

Eight years before, young Gilbert Greenburg had braved Helena Pollak's stern German-Jewish father and announced that he wanted to marry Helena. Consent was finally won, on condition that the young couple remain in Naugatuck and take over the management of the family millinery shop. As Helena had worked as a designer for the celebrated New York firm of Lichtenstein, and Gilbert had recently given up his job at Gunther, the furrier, they happily assumed the responsibilities of a shop and a marriage. As the years passed, both projects prospered.

About the turn of the century, after generations of gentility, Naugatuck was becoming a booming industrial town. There was to be seen, among its carriages and trolley cars, an occasional sleek Locomobile, or a more frequent Ford or Reo. The advent of the automobile brought high hopes, for autos run on rubber tires and the U.S. Rubber Company was Naugatuck's chief industry.

Many of the local ladies' huge "motoring" hats, anchored with veils, came from the millinery shop on Church Street. The wealthy wives and daughters brought in their swatches, leafed through the fashion magazines, and placed their orders. At least once a month, Helena or Gilbert would board the train for New York and bring back French ribbons, willow plumes, velours, and straw in the latest colors. They worked hard. Before their last delivery was made and the shop lights turned off, it was often dark, well past suppertime, and their children were long abed.

Helen Johnson ran the Greenburg house and looked after Adrian and his older sister, Beatrice. A warm Swedish woman, she scolded and laughed and dried their tears. While she helped Beatrice with her homework or her sewing, young Adrian pasted together elaborate constructions of felt and lace and scraps he had gathered from the shop. On the rolls of paper used for wrapping ribbons, he drew an endless procession of animals and people. Despite attempts to contain the boy's artistry, his drawings appeared on the wallpaper, the flyleaves of books, on practically every available blank space.

When he was five, Adrian started kindergarten. Beatrice led her brother down the long flight of steps to the red brick schoolhouse at the bottom of the hill. For him, Miss Hartland's class was a bonanza. Here he found limitless paint and paper and pencils, and an almost endless opportunity to use them.

One spring afternoon, while waiting for Beatrice to call for him, he gathered pieces of colored chalk and eyed the four blackboards around the room. He set to work. First there appeared an elaborate calliope, puffing curls of musical steam; next followed carriages of dazzling circus performers drawn by hyperactive horses; a line of draped and tasseled elephants; a scarlet-coated band; cage after cage of zebras, lions, tigers, and more fancifully decorative beasts pranced around the classroom. Miss Hartland was astounded. For four days she did not erase the blackboards and they became the pride and wonder of the lower school. It was Adrian's first public success.

He had inherited his facility, since both of his parents were adept at drawing. Before she became embroiled in the millinery business, his mother had painted graceful flower pieces. His father did rather dashing caricatures for the publications of the local Elks and Masons. The boy had a compulsion to draw, and his own idea of how to do it. Aside from a session with his mother on the mixing of colors, Adrian had no formal training and firmly resisted any that came his way in school.

Adrian's schoolmates esteemed him as a kind of artist-in-residence and called on him for dance posters, yearbook covers, and opinions on matters artistic. At the age of twelve he undertook to illustrate the horror tales of Edgar Allan Poe. His drawings, in the erotic style of Aubrey Beardsley, were somewhat advanced for decorous Naugatuck, but his peers thought them splendid.

Adrian did not avoid but did not seek out the world of the all-American male. He never cared for organized athletics, and he looked at animals as subjects for drawing, not hunting. Like many middle-class sons of the day, he was brought up in a house of women; his father, the head of the family, was not supposed to concern himself with the children. This Victorian hangover undoubtedly generated conflicts within the growing boy but it also gave him an enduring interest in and an intuitive understanding of women.

From his father he inherited a brilliant gregariousness and a love of learning. At an early age, Adrian had read extensively in Greco-Roman history and mythology. A special treat was the infrequent

At an early age Adrian took to pen and ink to express his world. In the self-portrait, *right,* he battles one of the dragons which menace every child. But not every child could imagine a balloon-skirted showgirl complete with aigrettes and jewelled and ribboned shoes.

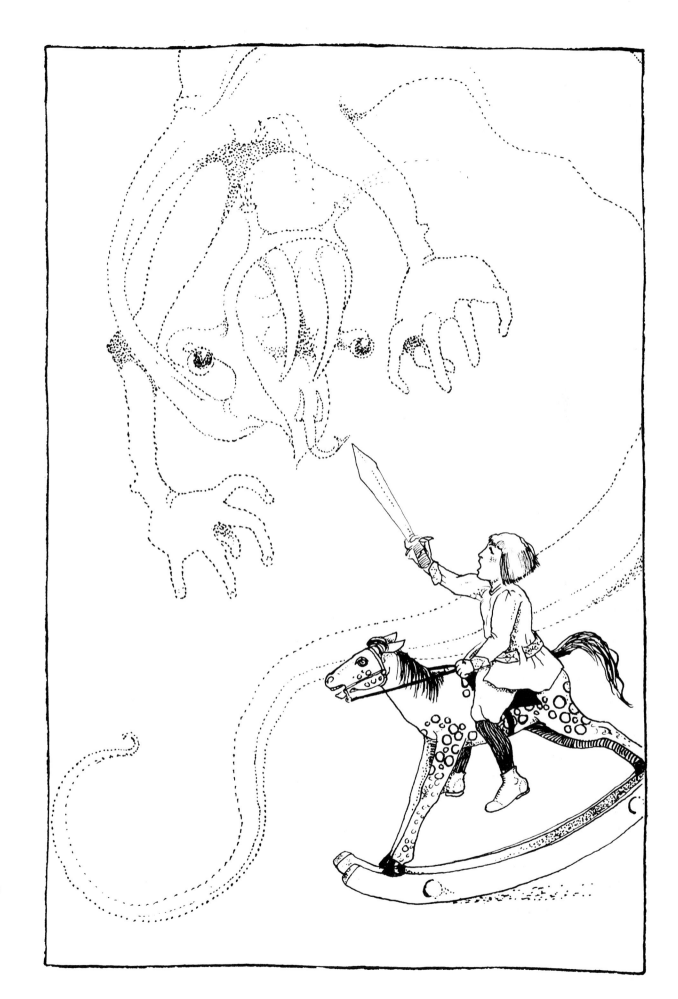

visits of Rabbi Lewis Brown, for then he and his father and the rabbi would argue all manner of subjects, and bedtime would be forgotten.

But the visits of Uncle Max were magic. Max Greenburg was a scenic designer and his presents to the boy were discarded models of theatre sets. Adrian spent hours cutting, pasting, painting, filling castled halls or parlors with furniture and characters in costume. He had entered that reckless world where imagination was reality; Naugatuck and Frederick Street vanished, at least for the afternoon.

The Greenburgs were far from authoritarian parents. They had lived with authority in their own youth and they did not want to pass it on to their children. When Beatrice decided that she wanted to go to New York to study dancing with Vernon and Irene Castle, they thought it a splendid idea and sent her with their blessing. Now, however, with high school graduation approaching, some decision had to be made about their son. Adrian's multifaceted nature and talents puzzled them. His abilities as an argumentative speaker suggested a possible career as a lawyer. Mr. Greenburg went to New Haven to look at the Yale Law School.

Adrian solved the problem for them. He decided that he was going to an art school in New York, and he was very firm about it. So in the fall of 1921 Adrian was enrolled in the Parsons School of Fine and Applied Art and his mother saw him settled in Mrs. Hausman's brownstone rooming house in the East Fifties.

Postwar New York did not particularly frighten or fascinate Adrian. He had seen the city before, on buying trips with his parents, and on visits to Beatrice and her dancing classes. School was his serious work, but it soon proved to be a disappointment. There were slide lectures on the history of art; four hours a week of drawing from a plaster cast; drawings to be made of draped fabrics; tests on the identification of colors on a chart. Adrian accomplished these mundane assignments quickly and competently. His teachers, at a loss, resorted to giving him the same assignments again in slightly different form. Adrian's interest faded. To him this was art without fun or reason. As a result, his midyear marks were disastrous.

Beatrice, now established in Naugatuck as a dancing teacher, came down to help. They went to tea dances at the Plaza and the Ritz. They saw Marilyn Miller in *Sally*. Alicia Howell assured Beatrice that Adrian was one of her most talented students. Mrs. Wicks confessed that she was so impressed with his sketches that she would rescue them from the wastebasket in her classroom. Fellow students, George Stacey and Eleanor LeMaire, were fervid in their belief that Adrian was the most brilliant of their class. But the next set of marks was no better than the first. The authorities summoned his parents for a conference.

Discussion led to a decision on the part of the school officials: Adrian would be more challenged if he attended the Paris branch of

In his student days at Parsons Adrian was preoccupied with the exotic costumes so prevalent in the Broadway revues of the early twenties.

Parsons. His parents were alarmed at the idea of "that city," but they courageously agreed, and made the necessary arrangements.

While waiting for the fall, Adrian had his first taste of the working theatre. Robert Kallock, designer for the famed couture house of Lucille and a lecturer at Parsons, had suggested him as designer at the Gloucester Playhouse, a pioneer summer theatre which produced art plays requiring ambitious and artistic sets and costumes.

Adrian spent the summer in an organized delirium of scene paint, dye pots, and sewing machines. Florence Cunningham ran the Playhouse and the lives of her young protégés. Taking Adrian in hand, she pointed out that the bourgeois name of Greenburg would get him nowhere. After all, Leon Rosenberg had become Bakst, and Romain de Tirtoff called himself Erté; why shouldn't he be just Adrian? So Adrian Adolph Greenburg—who did not mind joining such distinguished company—became Adrian.

Not unexpectedly, Adrian's father was very upset by the change. He felt that the Greenburg name was perfectly respectable. He did not like what this change implied to him: that his son was becoming fancy, that he was trying to avoid a Jewish name. It was pointed out that he himself had changed from Greenburgh to Greenburg, using brevity as an excuse. That, the father stated, had nothing whatsoever to do with the case.

The upshot was that the son borrowed the father's first name, and in the fall of 1922 Gilbert Adrian sailed for France and the school in the Places des Vosges.

Collection of Mrs. Clarence Leventhal

JACK FROST   adrian

NOTE—
MR SHORT THESE SKETCHES HAD TO
BE MADE IN A GREAT RUSH AS I
HAD HARDLY STARTED THEM WHEN
MRS VALENTINO TOLD ME TO START
WORK ON THE NEW PICTURE. THE
FORE PLEASE REALISE TECHNIQUE HA
TO BE FORFITTED TO GET YOU THE IDEAS I

Miss McCormack

PARIS TO BROADWAY TO HOLLYWOOD, 1922

Adrian's last Broadway job before his first Valentino picture was a revue for Hassard Short. As seen by the note on the sketch, *left*, Adrian's spelling was shaky but his Snowflake number scored a sound success in *The Greenwich Village Follies*.

Adrian's marks did not improve in the pink-bricked classrooms of the Place des Vosges. But the past summer's theatrical work and Florence Cunningham's interest had changed him. He had a new assurance, every sense was sharper; he felt that he was boiling with talents and anxious to use them all.

Student life in those postwar days was freewheeling, friendships were easy, and wherever you turned there was something curious or lovely or crazy. Such were the huge costume balls which lit the Paris social scene. The Bal du Grand Prix, held each year in the Opera House, was the most popular, elegant, and merriest event of them all. The young, the raffish, the artists, everyone but the properly respectable flocked to it. Parsons students considered it part of their education.

Each moment they could snatch from schooling was devoted to the planning and making of their costumes. As his costume model, Adrian chose a fellow student, a tall, long-faced exotic girl who was known by the simple name of Honor. Making use now of Helen Johnson's sewing lessons and the practical advice of his concierge, he cut and stitched her costume, and what could not be stitched, he pasted.

For the Bal, celebrated couturiers dressed the most notable beaux and beauties. The grand staircase of the Opera was a perfect background for their fantasies. In a blaze of spotlights and fanfares, the Queens of Sheba, or the Nile, or Cathay were carried in on litters. Sinbad and his sailors supported an almost nude Scheherazade. The American movie queen, Pearl White, entered to great applause, dressed by Worth to represent an electric light bulb.

The parade of the comic, the ludicrous, and the beautiful went on for hours. The audience sweated and applauded, and applauded again to impress the prize jury. They roared as four huge slaves carried a platter on which sat Erté himself, dripping with pearls, his hair and body powdered white, his eyes rimmed in glittering blue. Adrian and Honor, standing together at the bottom of the stairs, were frankly dazzled.

"Excuse me," said an American voice behind Honor. "Would you tell me who designed your costume?" Honor turned toward Adrian. He looked down at a rather small, sad-faced man.

"We are looking for a costume designer for a revue I am doing in New York this fall. Perhaps you would—"

"Where are you staying?" Adrian interrupted.

"We are at the Crillon."

"Would you like me to show you some sketches tomorrow morning at eleven o'clock?"

"Why, yes," the man replied, "that would be fine. We'll expect you. My name is Irving Berlin."

Adrian appeared at the Crillon to interview Mr. Berlin and his director, Hassard Short. He asked them questions: What kind of revue did they have in mind? What kind of numbers? Who was to be featured? He discussed his sketches and money and credits, and emerged from this rather one-sided conference with an agreement to design costumes for the next *Music Box Revue*.

Here at last was good reason to abandon his so-called education. After just four months in Paris he sailed back to New York and Mrs. Hausman's rooming house.

Adrian soon discovered that Broadway was not waiting for him, nor was the *Music Box Revue* to be his special passport to fame. Irving Berlin had never intended to rely solely upon the untried talents of a young designer. He took Adrian's first batch of sketches to consult with the prolifically successful costume designer Charles LeMaire. "Very nice," said LeMaire, "very, very nice drawings. But, you know, a lot of these just won't work as costumes."

The result of this judgment was that Adrian's contributions to the *Music Box Revue* of 1923 were decidedly minor.

Half a dozen revue numbers, no matter how successful, are hardly a designer's meal ticket. Adrian lugged his portfolio to the producers' offices. He hung around the costume makers in the hopes of dressing a nightclub act or a state fair pageant. They occasionally doled out such bread-and-butter jobs to young designers like Emmet Joyce, Mark Mooring, or Norman Norell, for their services were cheap. He even entered a contest to design a costume for a female impersonator known as The Creole Fashion Plate. He won the contest, his name appeared in the newspapers, but publicity did not produce the jobs he needed.

Adrian looked forward to the New York visits of his parents and

Collection of Mrs. Clarence Leventhal

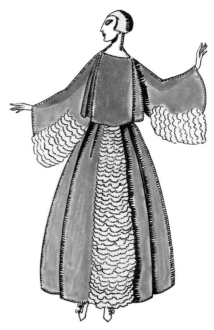

Like all art students of his day Adrian imitated, *from top to bottom*, the dramatics of Jimmy Reynolds, the sophistication of Benito, and the manners of Pierre Brissaud. He was obviously more sure of himself and less imitative in his visions of stage extravaganzas, *opposite*.

16

notie Selve —?   Rough   Whiai
                                  Suggestion

- Orchids -

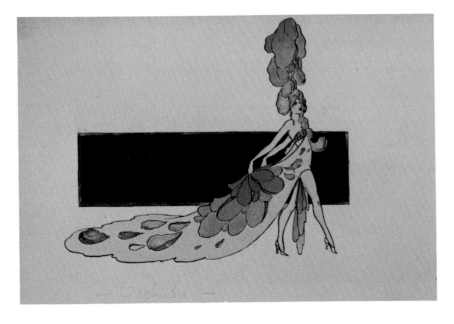

- Orchids -

Collection of Mrs. Clarence Leventhal

sister. He enjoyed them, and they also meant dinner at a restaurant. Beatrice was engaged to a young man in the real estate business, Clarence Leventhal. Seven years older than Adrian, he took a fatherly interest in the boy. Often they dined and went to the theatre together when Clarence was free. But for Adrian there were lonely evenings and discouraging days, and there seemed no way to use his talents.

However, Irving Berlin had not forgotten him. He told his fellow producer, Charles Dillingham, about the new young designer and asked Adrian to leave his portfolio in Dillingham's office. The next day Mr. Dillingham reported to Adrian that Charles LeMaire had said the sketches were not the kind of things he wanted.

Adrian strode the few blocks to LeMaire's studio. He banged through the door.

"You," he said in chill anger, "you seem to be very anxious to keep me off Broadway."

LeMaire was startled. "That's not true at all," he soothed, "You do nice sketches. But the trouble is you don't design what people need —what people want. You design to suit yourself."

Adrian's reaction to this well-meant advice was to slam the door on his way out.

Nor had Hassard Short forgotten Adrian. He and John Murray Anderson were now the brains of the *Greenwich Village Follies*. Anderson was undoubtedly the king of revue directors. He had also adopted some imperial manners: While interviewing Adrian, the director lay soaking in his black marble bathtub, sketches scattered about the puddled floor. Fortunately Anderson liked the sketches, and Adrian did many of the costumes for the next two *Follies*. For the next *Music Box Revue* there were many more Adrian costumes. Flamboyant producer George White bought some of his more startling ideas for the *Scandals*. Jobs began to pile up.

Across the river from Broadway was the Paramount Pictures studio in Astoria. Their greatest star, Rudolph Valentino, was making a picture there, and nothing was going well. At the bottom of their trouble was a wealthy, mystic-minded, and determined woman: Winifred Shaughnessy De Wolf Hudnut, who called herself Natacha Rambova.

Several years earlier she had married the famous Latin lover, and ever since had guided his career through her "mystic" powers. Everything about *The Sainted Devil* displeased her: the story, the players, the sets, the director. For once her astral bodies were right. *The Sainted Devil* was a dreadful picture.

On Broadway Adrian designed almost anything theatrical—the ideas for production numbers, *opposite*, a cover for the Equity Ball, sketches for a brochure advertising *The Clinging Vine* with Peggy Wood.

The only redeeming feature of the project was Norman Norell's costumes, but Miss Rambova hated the designer's crabbed little sketches and would have no more of them for their next picture. At this propitious moment she was shown some of Adrian's most imposing drawings, and she was enchanted. She summoned the young man: Would he care to go to Hollywood to design the costumes for Mr. Valentino's next picture?

Natacha Rambova was a striking woman with alabaster skin and jet hair. She trailed her chiffon tea gown over the filthy Astoria studio floor. At her side strode the gracefully feline Valentino, the world's most glamorous movie star. Adrian felt as though he had been touched by the gods, but he managed to keep his voice calm as he accepted their offer.

In a last-minute flurry of arrangements and good-byes, he finished up his jobs, packed his bags, and joined the trek to Hollwood. The Valentino retinue included maids and valets, a cook, a business manager, a publicity agent, innumerable pieces of luggage, three trunks of tea gowns, and Natacha Rambova's monkey. The Valentinos were most gracious to their new designer, but the monkey adored him. He slept in Adrian's berth and refused to be ousted.

For the small-town Yankee, Hollywood was bliss. The bright sun-baked colors, the constant air of drama, the fact that he had steady work, his own office and workroom, induced a state of euphoria.

With his first paycheck he bought a white suit and a black cape lined in red satin. He rented an apartment on Highland Avenue, pasted silver tea papers on the walls, and bought a handsome bombé desk. He had to await several more paychecks before he could add to the furnishings, and it took considerable time before he had the courage to wear the white suit and the black cape, even separately.

Although he met people easily, Adrian was essentially a loner. Many Hollywood climbers wanted to claim the new Valentino designer, but he had a quick side step. One of the first friendships he made was with an older couple who lived in the next apartment.

Mr. and Mrs. Burrows had lived in California years before the flood of movie money. They liked the shy young man who would appear with a grin and a bag of groceries or a length of silk for Kathleen to sew. They became surrogate parents to the twenty-one-year-old Adrian. It was a relationship which lasted all their lives.

Producer Natacha Rambova was in trouble. She had written and produced *The Hooded Falcon* for her husband. Everyone, including Adrian, had done their best by the picture, but after $80,000 had been spent, all their efforts proved useless. *The Hooded Falcon* died and was abandoned. Natacha, determined to rescue their fortunes, returned to New York to make arrangements for another picture, ironically titled *What Price Beauty?* Left to themselves, Valentino and Paramount made *Cobra*, which was released with the usual fanfare and eaten up by the Valentino-hungry fans. It marked the first screen appearance of "Costumes by Adrian."

When Valentino boarded the train for New York and his next picture, Adrian took a gamble and stayed behind. He had no job, but he had an offer from Sid Grauman to design the stage prologue for the première of Chaplin's *Gold Rush*.

It was an important première, and Grauman's ornate Chinese theatre would be filled with every bigwig in the business, a captive audience for Adrian's fireworks. Grauman liked the sketches and gave him *carte blanche*. The prologue was a smash hit.

The next morning there were seven job offers waiting for him on Sid Grauman's desk. Now that his gamble had paid off, Adrian wanted to choose carefully. Which producer would give him the most leeway, the best chance to use his imagination? He decided on Cecil B. DeMille.

In all fabulous Hollywood, DeMille's was the gaudiest fable. His pictures were sensational money-makers, nor was that their only sensation. In superheated footage, Gloria Swanson, attended by maids who waited with towels of chinchilla, took a bath in an onyx pool of rosewater before a stained-glass window three stories high. Or Lillian Rich retired for the night on a gilded swan bed, with diamond-studded sheets and a blanket of ermine tails. These sybaritic settings were often used by DeMille to point out the unlikely moral that wickedness does not pay.

Now, needing a super-morality, he settled on the Bible and the story of Jesus for what was to be his most spectacular creation. He put Adrian to work on a DeMille version of the King James version, to be titled *The King of Kings*.

Jacqueline Logan played a surprisingly luxurious Mary Magdalene. For her and her attendants Adrian designed embroidered velvets, tasseled veilings, fabulous—and sometimes real—jewelry, and a sumptuous bouffant skirt of leopard skins. Before shooting, DeMille staged a dress parade of every costume to be worn by stars or extras. Any dress insufficiently extravagant would be ruthlessly eliminated. DeMille, who never boggled at the cost of anything so long as it was on camera and could astonish the audience, found in Adrian a sympathetic pupil.

The King of Kings was released to suitably reverent reviews in 1927. In October of that same year, Warner Brothers released *The Jazz Singer* in which Al Jolson sang, so that all could hear, "Sonny Boy." There was no need for reviews—the public embraced it with delight. The "talkies" had been born.

SILENCE AND SOUND, 1927

MGM

Collection of Joseph S. Simms

From his studio drawing board Adrian produced an avalanche of sketches so that his actresses might have the choice of many suggested costumes. For *Camille* there was not only a wide choice of sketches, but several costumes were actually made up before settling on this cloudy black net embroidered with shooting stars worn by Greta Garbo. Her Armand was Robert Taylor.

The next two years were a virtual reign of terror. Many of the crowned and decorative heads of Hollywood fell, because their voices did not match their faces. Corinne Griffith, Colleen Moore, Pola Negri, Emil Jannings, Vilma Banky, and the Talmadge sisters accepted cash settlements for their otherwise useless contracts.

Hastily the studios were being rebuilt for sound. Panic-stricken movie moguls wondered what to do with them. For some obscure reason they all fixed on musicals. Mary Pickford donned top hat and tails to tap-dance. Janet Gaynor survived a gigantic Fox musical comedy in creditable style. To everyone's surprise, it was discovered that Gloria Swanson and Bebe Daniels could sing.

During these years of upheaval DeMille evolved a script called *Madam Satan*, in which a lushly costumed party is held aboard a zeppelin in flight. He decided to take this musical morality play to MGM as an independent producer. Being independent was not easy under the autocratic rule of Louis B. Mayer. Though secretly hated when he was alive, and posthumously reviled, Mayer was an extraordinarily able businessman. He also had a quick and larcenous eye for talent. He soon spotted Adrian in the DeMille entourage and signed him to a contract.

Among the several designers on the MGM lot was David Cox, who picked the plums, such as Ruth Chatterton in *Madame X*, and the first all-talking, all-singing, all-dancing *Hollywood Revue of 1929*. Adrian's first important MGM picture, and his first for Greta Garbo, was a disinfected version of Michael Arlen's *The Green Hat,* rechristened *A Woman of Affairs*. It was a perfunctory film, designed to present once again the popular love team of Greta Garbo and John Gilbert. However, since the script had omitted their trademark of lingering horizontal kisses, and the studio had not yet wired them for sound, the public by and large passed this one by.

Enthusiasm, however, came from an unexpected source—the Seventh Avenue garment business. Designers and sketchers rushed to the Capitol Theatre to see Garbo's crepe coat and dress inlaid with ombré bands; her slinky satin dinner gown with casual scarf tossed across her shoulders. But the costume that bugged their eyes was Garbo's slouch hat and loosely belted trench coat, entirely lined in bold plaid wool. These marvels of casual elegance were blazoned in *Women's Wear Daily,* and plaid linings and trench coats appeared in hundreds of showrooms.

Three more silent Garbo films followed within a year's time. Then Norma Shearer, the queen of MGM, ordered Adrian designs for her talking film, *The Divorcée.* When the popular Joan Crawford, dressed by Adrian, garnered glowing notices for her clothes in *This Modern Age* and *Possessed,* the young designer found the plums were now falling into his lap.

Toward the end of 1930, the Baroness von Kraus demanded an interview with Louis B. Mayer. Her title was genuine enough, but the forward young baroness was better know as Betty Adler, wife to Paul Adler of Seventh Avenue's famed sportswear house. She bluntly told Mayer that he was harboring a genius, that Adrian could make a fortune in the wholesale garment business, and that she could see to it. Mr. Mayer promised to give the idea some thought. His thinking led to the hope that, by some business tie-up, the garment business might be persuaded to pay a part of his increasingly expensive designer's salary. He directed Adrian to investigate Seventh Avenue. This was like asking a seagull to investigate an airplane—they both could fly, but by entirely different means. Adrian knew nothing about the wholesale market. However he did remember that in his shopping tours with Greta Garbo there had been a helpful merchandise manager at Bullock's-Wilshire, a discreetly humorous and knowledge-able man named Woody Feurt. When he consulted him, Woody Feurt invited Adrian along on his next New York buying trip.

Together they visited Seventh Avenue's eminent names: Herman Florsheim, Rentner, Nettie Rosenstein, Mangone, Patullo, Zuckerman and Krauss. Wherever they went, they were known and welcome, and many deals were proposed. Each had its special attractions, and the money was staggering. Adrian was most uncertain which to take.

Finally Woody advised, "Don't take any of them. You don't need the money any more than Louis B. Mayer does. You will work yourself to death doing two jobs, and you will worry yourself to death because you won't be able to control the clothes they make in your name. Forget it."

Adrian did forget the proposals, but as the train took him back to Hollywood, he thought a great deal about Woody Feurt and the wholesale workrooms he had seen.

Collection of Joseph S. Sir

Adrian first won the notice of the MGM Publicity Department when Norma Shearer selected him to do her clothes for *The Divorcée.* But the costumes which gained the most attention were for Garbo in *Mata Hari.* Much of their success can be credited to Miss Garbo, *opposite,* who wore the bizarre creations with great authority.

Adrian's own workrooms were part of the huge stucco barn known as Wardrobe on the MGM lot. Beyond the office lobby, beyond the shadowy caverns of costumes hanging in indexed rows, was a clearing of bare boards, bright hanging bulbs, women bending over their sewing machines, embroiderers at their frames chattering in Spanish. Against the wall, padded dress forms bearing famous names stood in silent rows. Over the years Adrian had organized a superbly efficient factory which produced an enormous volume of work, precisely, without fuss, meeting implacable deadlines with calm professionalism. Here he ruled benevolently but firmly.

Walled off from this active kingdom was Adrian's studio. He worked

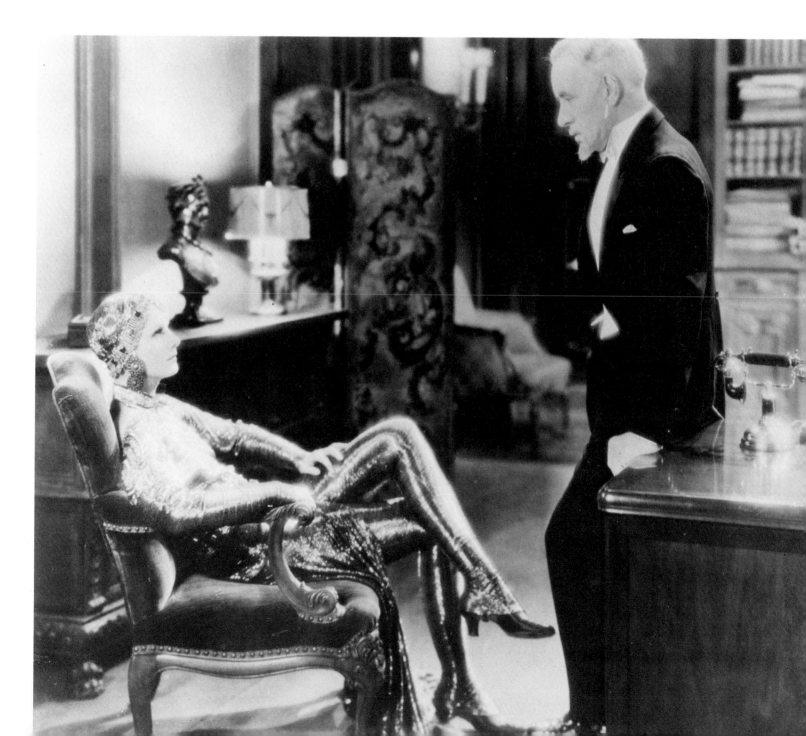

MGM

in a comfortable yellow chintz chair surrounded by books and paints, a drawing board, and the fifty to seventy-five sketches he produced each day. In the thirties, he was partial to a New England-California-Classic scheme of decoration. The tall shuttered windows were heavy with ruffled net. Neoclassic columns framed vast expanses of mirror. A platform was crowned with spotlights so that the gown being fitted could be lit as seen by the camera. Everything was neat and pale cream except for great loops of color on the carpet where Adrian shook out his paint brushes.

It was hard to lure Adrian out of his studio for any reason—for conferences, luncheon, or any other official, time-consuming function. He was perpetually busy. Yet one of his favorite studio luncheon companions was Greta Garbo, for she fascinated him. He found her uniquely self-involved, disconnected from other people, a woman who lived solely in the present, without future or past.

At the insistence of Ouida and Basil Rathbone, he had once persuaded her to accompany him to a costume ball. He provided her with a flowing black velvet gown, a medieval jeweled skullcap, and a black velvet mask. Their entrance at the Rathbone ball created electric curiosity, but Garbo headed for the most remote corner of the ballroom and would talk to no one, not even her hostess. Together she and Adrian sat, surveying the gay and sometimes very handsome parade of costumes. In fifteen minutes she had seen enough. Miss Garbo was ready to go home.

As an actress, Garbo fired the designer's imagination. For her there seemed to be no limits; she would wear any costume which amused her as though born to it. Taking full advantage of her daring, he produced costumes for *Mata Hari* bizarre enough to make almost any other actress look like a cooch dancer; but Garbo gave them authority. He liked to emphasize the fine strong drawing of her head. For *Mata Hari* he designed an austere cap which completely hid her hair and outlined her skull. For *As You Desire Me* and *The Painted Veil* he devised odd little pillbox hats to draw attention to her mobile face. These were quickly copied by millinery manufacturers at all price levels.

There were four thousand costumes to design for Adrian's most elaborate production, *Marie Antoinette*. To prepare himself, he haunted the museums and libraries of France. Although he had no interest in producing "authentic" costumes and refused to be hampered by history, he wanted to immerse himself in eighteenth-century life, to smell it and feel it, and to think like any eighteenth-century man. Once rooted in the period, he could unleash his dramatic imagination. Also, in France he was close to the source of French elegance. With a hand only slightly less lavish than Louis XVI's, he bought Lyons velvets, eighteenth-century gilt braid, diamante buckles, feather and embroideries, fans, patch boxes and laces.

Opposite. Any woman can wear anything, Adrian said, if you watch out for the proportions. Norma Shearer's head and shoulders were superb, but her long waist and shorter-than-ideal legs presented a problem. His solution, shown here being fitted by assistant Hannah Lindfors, lifted the waist well up on the rib cage to make her legs seem longer; extended the shoulder line to minimize the waist; underlined her handsome face with an exclamatory ruffle.

Below. Though he made his wholesale collections on skyscraper models, Adrian dressed many small women. For his wife he designed Oriental pants—not too full, a broad shouldered jacket—not too long, a waistline—not too curved, and Janet Gaynor's scant five feet seemed inches taller.

John Rawlings
Vogue

Garbo's incredibly mobile face fascinated Adrian. He liked to draw attention to it with eye-catching head gear such as the plumed bonnet for *Camille* and the jewelled skull cap for *Mata Hari*. Her close fitting caps in the last picture were widely copied by the American millinery business. Miss Garbo's glaring co-star is Lionel Barrymore.

MGM

29

Adrian's pencil was as sharp and as ac-
curate as the dressmaker's scissors, as can
be seen by comparing the sketch and the
realized costume for Garbo in *Anna Karenina*.

Opposite. Camille was probably Garbo's
greatest role. Looking as though she had
just stepped out of a Constantin Guys
sketchbook, she breathed a vibrant reality
into the old play which even MGM's paper
daisies could not dim.

Collection of Eleanor Lambert

MGM

31

Adrian's *Marie Antoinette* costumes possessed a drama that dazzled the audience. The embroideries glittered, the headdresses towered, trains and fans and canes and swords flashed and fluttered.

As the flighty French queen, Norma Shearer had thirty-four costume changes and eighteen different wigs. With the patience of a female Job, she stood for hours of fittings, wearing at her own insistence the proper wig, hat, shoes, gloves, jewelry, and fan. She was an indefatigable worker, and carefully considered every smile, tear, and hair ribbon. When Adrian's queen, frothing in white ostrich plumes, faced her rival, the black-spangled DuBarry, it was not "authentic" dress, but it was a superb theatrical vision. Unfortunately, the actual drama in *Marie Antoinette* did not match that of the costumes.

For Adrian, the function of a costume went beyond its appearance on the screen; it could help an actress realize her role. Underneath Greta Garbo's *Camille* costumes were yards of extravagantly pleated and ruffled silk organdy in which she billowed and swished with all the luxurious raciness of a Constantin Guys courtesan. For a feeling of floating femininity in *The Gorgeous Hussy*, Joan Crawford wore thirty yards of silk organza in a delicate cutout pattern, each cut edged by hand with buttonhole stitching. The coronation robe in *Queen Christina* rustled sumptuously, as it should have, since a single embroidered panel cost the studio $1,800.

The money men raged at Adrian's extravagance. The directors and cameramen and timekeepers complained bitterly because he insisted on fitting his actresses first thing in the morning, before the day's shooting had tired them. He also insisted on punctuality, and his actresses sometimes gave vent to their outrage when they arrived

MGM

Of all Hollywood costume pictures, none was more sumptuous than Norma Shearer's *Marie Antoinette*. It was also Adrian's most dazzling spectacle on which he lavished furs, feathers, laces, and embroideries more gorgeous than any that flighty queen could have worn in her days at Versailles.

MGM

For MGM Joan Crawford played melo-drama, comedy, song and dance, and costume drama. Above she is President Jackson's *Gorgeous Hussy* among some of Adrian's most successful period clothes.

late for a fitting and were told that the appointment had been canceled. Not even Jeanette MacDonald's sweetest tones could persuade Adrian that star status rated another chance.

Nor was Louis B. Mayer immune to Adrian's stern judgments. Toward the end of 1934 Hollywood was buzzing over the announcement that Norma Shearer's next picture was to be *Romeo and Juliet*. Then one day the *Motion Picture Herald* reported from London that George Cukor had signed Oliver Messel to design the sets and costumes. Newspaper in hand, Adrian called on Louis B. Mayer and told him that he admired George Cukor and Oliver Messel, and of course Shakespeare. Then he added, "I'll design the picture. Don't think that I'm just the MGM workhorse, because I'm not. I'm the MGM designer, and since *Romeo and Juliet* will be an MGM picture, I'll design it."

After studying the contracts, Mr. Mayer was able to make a judgment of Solomon: the designing chores of *Romeo and Juliet* would be divided between Adrian and Oliver Messel.

There was one person who made Adrian visibly apprehensive—Joan Crawford. Like many another star, she had approval of wardrobe

MGM

Right. Crawford was filmdom's most popular and most durable star. She had boundless vitality which Adrian clothed in some of his most electric costumes, such as this abstract black and white photographed on the set of *Grand Hotel* and, on the facing page, a dazzler of solid bugle beads for *The Bride Wore Red.*

34

MGM

Adrian had an eye for strict tailoring and well understood that a masculine touch could be perversely feminine. Therefore he tailored a lamé trench coat for Joan Crawford and a tweedy suit for the romantic Jeanette MacDonald, shown here with Clark Gable in a scene from *San Francisco*.

written into her contract. Of the many sketches submitted to her, he managed to fix her volatile attention by coloring his choice in her favorite shade of blue. But fittings were nerve-racking. As sleeves were being pinned, she gestured and chatted with friends. A telephone was always at hand for gossip or the reciting of grocery lists. She would often be on the set to block out action for the next scene, trailed by unhappy fitters trying to take a hem length. Adrian attempted to stem the tide of Crawford energy, and failed. Yet he soon realized that he was not dealing with bitchy temperament, but rather with an actress of undiluted intensity who was forever on camera.

Many other stars earned Adrian's admiration or irritation: Jeanette MacDonald, furbelowed and lacy, was the all-American romantic; Myrna Loy, the erstwhile oriental menace, was transformed into a triumphant sophisticate; Luise Rainer, the leading lady, shyly aggressive, arsenically sweet; Jean Harlow, the comic sexpot. For them the

On the facing page, Bill Cunningham records the Adrian costumes on exhibition at the Metropolitan Museum of Art in their spectacular show called Glamorous and Romantic Hollywood Design. Top row, *left to right,* is a Garbo costume from *Anna Karenina,* Gladys George's Dubarry gown from *Marie Antoinette,* the brown velvet *Anna Karenina* dress for Garbo, and, in the background, *The Gorgeous Hussy's* red velvet for Joan Crawford. On the second row, Lenore Ulric's cockade trimmed velvet for the horse auction scene in *Camille,* Garbo's costume for the same scene, and Anita Louise's riding habit from *Marie Antoinette.* These costumes are from the collection of the Fashion Institute of Technology.

MGM assembly line turned out a staggering number of pictures; Jean Harlow alone averaged three films a year.

Adrian designed the clothes for all the important pictures, for that matter any picture he really wanted to do, while Dolly Tree worked on the others. His workroom assistants, who were both devoted and skillful, had to handle the enormous volume of work. Hannah Lindfors cut and supervised the modern clothes; Inez Schrodt was responsible for period costumes and trick outfits like a Cowardly Lion or a Tin Woodsman; a singularly creative Mexican, Mrs. Cluett, produced the embroideries.

There were dozens of workers, no union, and labor was cheap. In the depth of the depression, the studio could hire skilled needle-women and tailors for $15.85 to $21 a week. Gossip had it that Hannah Lindfors earned $125 a week; it was hard to believe such a fabulous figure.

For most of his MGM years, Adrian earned one thousand dollars a week. As recognition and honors came his way, he was urged to ask more, but he refused. He wanted no more pay and no more responsibility. He came to work at ten in the morning and left at four in the afternoon; those hours were the studio's time. The rest of the day was his, and that was the way he wanted it.

MGM

Below. Larger-than-life extravagance was a successful Hollywood recipe served here by Jean Harlow in *Dinner At Eight* wearing Adrian's bugle beaded negligee cuffed in 22-inch ostrich fronds.

Opposite. Equally successful were extravaganzas like *The Great Ziegfeld* where showgirls carried spears atop 30-foot columns and Harriet Hoctor danced among lions. Just above is Luise Rainer as Anna Held, Mr. Ziegfeld's star and wife.

MGM

PRIVATE DESERT, 1935

The interior of Adrian's Sunset Strip Antique shop in one of its more orderly moments. Opposite is a scene from the Fox production *Daddy Long Legs*, starring Janet Gaynor and Warner Baxter, in which Miss Gaynor first wore Adrian clothes.

To those who did not know Adrian, he might have seemed a forbidding person. There was about him an air of New England self-control, a look of austere simplicity. He did indeed possess the Yankee virtues. They lived side by side with the other more self-indulgent aspects of his nature.

Paradoxically, his self-indulgence drove him harder than any Puritan conscience. His home was filled with evidence of his compulsive and impulsive search for perfection. The silky opalescent finish on a table required months of painting and rubbing and waxing. The constant acquisition of Burmese temple bells or the sudden purchase of fifty crystal paperweights kept him broke. In his bedroom stood a huge Mexican clock, complete with twittering birds, waterfalls, and blooming flowers, which had cost him a sprained back and months of chiropractic treatment after he had lugged it back from Mexico City.

Although he was not physically active, and spurned even such sports as swimming and tennis, he had a dazzling amount of energy. At the studio he might be working on as many as five pictures at once, and still have the stamina to tend to his antique shop on Sunset Strip and to decorate for such diverse private clients as Claudette Colbert, Harpo Marx, and Saks Fifth Avenue. In addition, there were intense periods of concentrated painting. He was always reading up on some new subject of interest. He enjoyed giving parties and dinners and could be relied upon to fete visiting celebrities like Lady Mendl, or to accommodate two hundred guests for Easter breakfast.

In carrying such a heavy schedule with apparent ease, he was aided by an eye and mind which could immediately discard the nonessential. With this convenient grace, he produced paintings, costumes, rooms, and dinners of an opulent simplicity. Though dinner might very well be bread and gravy served on pewter plates, it would be a

most exceptional gravy and the very best pewter. His bills were astronomical.

The garish splendors of Hollywood were not always for him. To escape, he bought a working ranch shack in the desert of Palm Springs. For water, there was a hand pump; for light, kerosene lamps; for toilet facilities, mugs, jugs, and an outhouse. The shack sat on the floor of the desert, shaded by towering pepper trees and surrounded by jagged blue mountains; it was private indeed. The guest list was restricted to those who could live the primitive life and provide their own amusement.

Many were willing to brave the rigors, not the least of which was the long drive with Adrian from Los Angeles to the desert. He enjoyed driving at breakneck speed while pointing out distant features of the landscape to his nervous guests, and very little that was not directly on the road in front of him escaped his notice.

On one trip, Hedda Hopper and Bernadine Szold clutched each other in terror as Adrian slammed on the brakes and leapt from the car to inspect a passing snake. Nor were they reassured when he identified it as a deadly sidewinder. His interest in animals had continued unabated since the time he drew circus parades on the blackboard. He now doodled animals, painted animals, caricatured his friends and staff as animals. He liked all kinds of animals except toads. Toads he considered badly designed.

The ranch was ideal for painting, and the chicken house served as both bedroom and studio. Here were leisure and quiet, and Adrian took advantage of them to experiment, to indulge his fancies. He was an expert at the process of painting. His skill was at the command of his décor-loving eye. Together they rearranged the realistic objects of the world to suit themselves. The arrangements might be boisterous or lyric or antic, often laced with his deceptively sly humor.

In his playful mood Adrian adored jokes. He could assume an entirely convincing Chinese accent with which he trapped his friends into absurd telephonic adventures involving smuggled treasure and international spies. Some victims retaliated: One April Fool's Day his long-suffering staff arranged with the studio commissary to serve him a salad of artificial leaves. Adrian devoured it with gusto to the last shiny green olive.

Undoubtedly he was a complicated man, but his affection for his family was simple and clear. When his father and mother retired, he persuaded them to move to the Coast. He was both amused and deeply touched when his father paid him the tribute of changing his name from Mr. Greenburg to Mr. Adrian.

Adrian's feeling for his mother was particularly strong. After his father's death, he made an apartment for her in his Bella Vista home. Friends like Kathleen Howard took her to lunch at Hollywood's watering holes, where she would stare at the celebrities. She seemed

Collection of Joseph S. Simms

"I look like a camel," said Adrian and in his doodles the rest of his staff looked like frogs or ostriches or elephants, but Hannah Lindfors was always the neat cat. Here she does on-the-set pressing for Norma Shearer in *Private Lives*.

MGM

to grow smaller as she grew older and would hover on the edges of Adrian's parties like a charming shadow. His sister's visits helped to recreate the family circle for her, for then the three of them would have family gossips, go on special visits to the studio or drives to the ocean. When his mother died, Adrian felt abandoned.

Adrian had a deeply spiritual side to his nature and from the time he first went to New York he began studying different philosophies. He explored Christian Science, and read deeply in many religions, such as the writings of Swami Prabhavanandha and Ernest Holmes, author of *The Science of the Mind*. He found the life of the spirit engrossing, and his reading extended into myths, folklore, and legends. Orthodoxy did not interest him, new concepts did. In the middle of the night he would telephone a friend to read a paragraph or a chapter, as if he had found a new idea and the world could not wait to hear it.

Endlessly curious about people, he was able by means of his unfeigned interest to draw out the most timid. His own candor was a source of delight and occasionally, embarrassment. At times, however, he beat an unexpected retreat. Once, at dinner, the writer, Katherine Anne Porter, turned on her persistent questioner.

"All right. You like the truth. Tell me what is the one thing you have done in your whole damn life which you are most ashamed of?"

Adrian stared at her. "I cannot answer that," he admitted.

Although generally impatient of evasions, and liking and expecting candor in himself and others, there would come a time in his closest relationships when he set up an emotional barrier. Almost no one passed beyond it.

Over on the Fox lot, toward the end of 1930, Janet Gaynor was to revive *Daddy Long Legs*. A Cinderella incarnate, she had gone from extra girl to overnight stardom in *Seventh Heaven, Sunrise* and a string of silent classics, and had been honored with the first Academy Award. Now she had not only weathered the talkie era, but had performed brilliantly and was the highest paid star in Hollywood. This was a tribute both to her popular appeal and the fact that she had the mother wit to be her own business manager.

Very few details of picture-making escaped her, as for example, her costumes for *Daddy Long Legs*. When she suggested changes, the designer, knowing she had had an appendectomy a month before, asserted that she had lost her figure, and quit. The twenty-four-year-old star was infuriated. She stormed into producer Sol Wurtzel's office to demand new costumes and a new designer. When Sol Wurtzel asked her whom she wanted, she replied without hesitation.

"Adrian."

Mr. Wurtzel called his rival, Louis B. Mayer, and told him, "I have a star here wants to borrow your designer. How about it?"

Louis B. Mayer said he would ask Adrian, and the next day word

43

came through that the matter could be arranged.

In working with him, Janet Gaynor was charmed by Adrian's directness and his workmanlike approach. After the picture was finished, she wrote him a note of gratitude.

Four years later, after her divorce from Lydell Peck, Janet Gaynor and Adrian found themselves on the same guest lists and at the same dinners. Both good talkers and good listeners, they eventually became good friends.

Janet was far from the popular concept of a flamboyant movie queen. A small intense woman, she—like Adrian—had a complex nature. She had just lived through a suffocating marriage, and was trying to avoid any similar entanglement. Adrian, who did not follow the familiar Hollywood pattern of gregarious celebrity, often withdrew into jealously guarded solitude to ensure his emotional independence. Theirs was a somewhat fearful and wholly cautious relationship at first.

Both were also cautioned against each other. Jeanette MacDonald, remembering inflexible fitting schedules and Adrian's exacting details, warned Janet, "Don't ever marry him. Let me tell you—he's a tyrant!—He's a regular Tartar!"

However, despite advice, they did elope one day in 1939 and were married in Yuma. None of the press was there. Janet's chauffeur of twelve years was best man.

Now Adrian closed the door on his old life. Whatever his needs and whatever Janet's needs may have been before, they now found them answered in each other. Theirs was a close, engrossing, and private marriage.

Yet being a movie idol, worshipped by a public more numerous than members of any one religious faith, held personal hazards as well as monetary rewards. For a movie star to appear on the streets could be dangerous. Her adoring public would snatch at hair, clothes —any souvenir to prove that their idol existed. Being married to a star was, in many ways a new existence for Adrian. One day, sitting in Janet's intimidating limousine, complete with armed chauffeur, he growled, "I feel just like Pal Joey."

The year 1940 brought rumors of war as well as the highest birthrate in American history. For Janet's pregnancy, Adrian devised a crisply colorful smock over a slender skirt, the front cut away to accommodate the expanding belly. It was photographed by *Vogue* and created an instant sensation in the press. Janet became the envy of countless young wives who had to wrap themselves in that dreary maternity uniform of black crepe with detachable white collar. In fact, the publicity about Adrian's smock outweighed the notices of the birth of their son, Robin.

As the fan magazines would have it, they were now to live happily ever after. However, that sort of rainbow promise stirred Adrian's

Photographed for *Vogue* are the expectant parents of the child who turned out to be Robin Adrian. Janet's crisp smock, designed by her husband, is still sold in an infinite variety of fabrics in the maternity departments of today's stores.

Yankee irony: An ecstatic interviewer's questions on fashion provoked his acid reminder that in this year of threatening war, Schiaparelli-designed gas masks were available to the sufficiently affluent. Publicity on Joan Crawford's divorce from Franchot Tone brought forth one of his ghastliest puns: "At last," he observed flatly, "she's footloose and Franchotfree."

Despite a calm and happy life at home, Adrian was not convinced that all was for the best in his most glamorous of all possible worlds.

Luis Lemus
Vogue, 1940

FADE-OUT, 1940

Two of the last big moneymakers of the thirties: sophisticated comedy in *Idiot's Delight* starring Norma Shearer and Clark Gable, and sophisticated bitchiness with Rosalind Russell, Norma Shearer, and Joan Crawford in *The Women*.

In the months before his marriage, Adrian had been, as usual, busy. Among other assignments, his schedule included Joan Crawford's two annual films; an all-star version of *The Women*; *Idiot's Delight* for Norma Shearer; a Jeanette MacDonald musical; and costumes for *The Wizard of Oz*.

With *Wizard* there were special problems, since it was the first color film he had tackled. There were also special delights in getting to know the horde of midgets hired to play Munchkins. Their private speech, their separate world, their dignity and their biting humor fascinated him. On the set, Adrian's tall form was forever to be seen squatting or bent over like a jackknife so that he might converse on their three-foot level.

In 1940, Adrian added to his customary Crawford, MacDonald, and Shearer features three films for Louis B. Mayer's new star, Greer Garson, as well as *Philadelphia Story* and *Woman of the Year* for Katharine Hepburn. Judy Garland, Hedy Lamarr, and Lana Turner starred in an incredibly elaborate musical, *Ziegfeld Girl*. This confection was replete with showgirls, Busby Berkeley dance routines, backstage romance, and Adrian costumes which looked like caricatures of his earlier work for the Follies. The whole production was smothered in frills, an over-eager attempt to excite an apathetic box office.

For the first time since the advent of sound, the picture business was in trouble. Weekly attendance, said the Gallup Poll, had shrunk from eighty-five to fifty-five million. It was radio entertainment, analysts said, that kept the moviegoer at home. Undoubtedly the tense, realistic drama of the Nazi invasion of Poland and Edward R. Murrow's reporting on the Battle of Britain were riveting. For the moment, not even Bingo, free dishes, and double or triple features

could compete with world events. A chill air of retrenchment settled over Hollywood.

Louis B. Mayer grumbled about rising production costs and the outrageous salaries he paid his stars. Clark Gable was earning $7,000 a week. Greta Garbo would not consider less than $250,000 a picture. Mayer's own salary was just short of a million dollars per year.

So budgets were trimmed and a tight MGM ship was ordered to sail close to the fiscal wind. Fiscal reality was the order of the day, and cinematic reality was to be the prescription for a sick business.

Reality was to be imposed even upon the great Garbo, who was half-way through *Two-Faced Woman*. She was no longer to be remote and dramatic, but as "real" as any supermarket housewife. The patent impossibility of deglamorizing Greta Garbo resulted in exasperated production conferences, front-office interference, rejected scripts, and discarded sketches.

In his dozen years at MGM Adrian had never met such frustration, and he was plunged into gloom. Mr. Mayer suggested that perhaps

Judy Garland, *opposite*, as Dorothy in that enchanting classic *The Wizard of Oz*, backed by Bert Lahr, Jack Haley, and Ray Bolger. Judy Garland, *below*, with Hedy Lamarr and Lana Turner bedizened for the "You Stepped Out of a Dream" sequence in the soon forgotten *Ziegfeld Girl*. Both were costumed by Adrian.

MGM

49

Two Adrian sketches for *Two Faced Woman*. On the back of the one upper left he had scribbled "Miss Garbo wants to wear this in the night club scene." She did not get her wish.
Opposite, showgirl Harriet Bennett is dressed in an orchid vine for *Ziegfeld Girl.*

he had been working too hard, that a rest might change his point of view. But Adrian's point of view had already changed. He saw that Hollywood would never again be as it had been in the thirties; that an age which he had had some part in creating was indeed coming to an end.

But *Two-Faced Woman* was not at an end, nor was its impossible problem nearer a solution. Garbo's clothes were half-finished, but no one would take the responsibility of approving them. One afternoon, in gloomy anger, Adrian ripped up his sketches and walked out of MGM.

When *Two-Faced Woman* was at last released, the reviewers called it "absurd," "empty," "embarrassing," "in fact, *Two-Faced Woman* does everything it can to destroy Garbo." Adrian's judgment had been upheld by the press. The impact on Greta Garbo was unfortunately devastating too, for she never made another film.

Adrian had no intention of retiring. He could not afford to, and he did not want to. Still only in his thirties, he felt that itchy ambition of the designer. Ever since the Seventh Avenue trip with Woody Feurt ten years earlier, he had thought about having his own business.

What he had done for movie stars, he could do for ordinary mortals. He had a worldwide reputation, so raising money should be no problem. Since the Nazis had occupied Paris, the American market had been cut off from that inspirational city of fashion. Perhaps this would be just the right moment to launch a business. The first thing to be done, he decided, was to talk to Woody Feurt again.

Tactfully, Woody Feurt pointed out the pitfalls of the dress business: the size of the investment needed, the long time lapse before there was a chance of breaking even, the plethora of existing businesses, and the probable difficulties that a wartime economy would make for them.

Adrian interrupted, ''Woody, I just can't do it without you. What do you say?''

Woody said that there were new government restrictions in the works which would make new businesses impossible; that a manpower draft would undoubtedly cripple the clothing industry for a struggling new firm.

Adrian smiled at Woody. Woody sighed and acknowledged defeat.

MGM

John Engstead

Model Bess Dawson smiles a greeting to the
black tie audience of Adrian Ltd.
From the first Adrian collection, a gingham
coat studded with sequins.

BIG BUSINESS, 1941

In almost every collection, among the imported woolens and silk brocades, such as the models are wearing, *above*. Adrian would show at least one American gingham. He considered it as elegant as sables.

At its birth in 1941, Adrian Ltd. was dogged by disasters. Nothing worked. It was impossible to get the lease on a new building; the fabrics ordered suddenly became unavailable; good seamstresses, tailors, and pattern makers were nowhere to be found.

In his desperate search for headquarters, Adrian was introduced to an ardent prohibitionist by the name of Lloyd who owned what had once been the chic restaurant, Victor Hugo. Rather than see liquor served on his property, the eccentric landlord had closed his establishment. Adrian, who coveted the austerely stylish building, talked for many days with Mr. Lloyd. Adrian's strong point was that dressmaking is a teetotal operation. At last Mr. Lloyd saw the light, a ten-year lease was signed and the new business had a potential home.

Adrian immediately summoned his one-time Parsons schoolmate, Eleanor LeMaire, from New York and gave her the job of transforming a restaurant into a salon. Her plans were slow in coming, but once he had looked them over, he did not have to look again. He left her entirely alone to do her work, for he had work of his own to do.

The first job was to recruit a skilled staff. Since they were not to be found on the West Coast, Woody went to New York to see whom he could pirate away from there. He lured Herman Florsheim's bookkeeper. Then from his old friend, Mme Eta, he drew a fabric man and a contractor. Eta bowed before Hollywood money and released them graciously. But Louis B. Mayer charged angrily that he was being robbed when Adrian extracted his ex-assistant, Hannah Lindfors, from MGM.

As the staff was being collected, fabric had to be shopped for in earnest. Cadwallader prints, and Chardon and Werk crepes were ordered. The fabric houses were delighted to work with a creative designer who respected their ideas. With Pola Stout he left a standing order for her woven "compositions," varicolored blocks and squares and stripes of worsted to be worked into suits and coats. The fabric houses were only too willing to allow the new firm credit, but the best fabrics naturally cost the most money, and Adrian's bills mounted quickly.

Back in Beverly Hills, Woody and Adrian watched as carpenters, plasterers, and electricians swarmed through the future salon. Woody opened a fresh batch of bills.

"By the way," he asked, "How is the salon going to look? What did you tell them?"

"I told them I wanted it to look floating—kind of ethereal."

"Well, there's nothing ethereal about the bills for Dorothy Liebes' draperies, and the estimates for Tony Duquette's decorations don't float much. And the electricians are held up again. The fixtures haven't arrived."

Nor had many of the fabrics arrived, and tailors and seamstresses sat with nothing to do. But they had to be paid. And rent on idle factories had to be paid. For the first time in his life Adrian developed a case of cold feet.

To keep his workers busy and bring in some cash, he undertook the costumes for a Carole Landis movie. While the film was in production, Woody Feurt was on the road lining up business. Many stores were interested in Adrian's new venture and eager to sample the line, but Woody was not interested in samples. If their infant business was to survive, it had to be on a sturdy diet of exclusive franchises and contracts to buy. If a store wanted the Adrian line exclusively in their city, they would have to contract to spend a minimum of ten thousand dollars per collection.

Stanley Marcus signed, Mrs. Best of Seattle signed, followed by William J. Block of Indianapolis, and—after some persuasion by Woody—Elizabeth Fairall of Garfinckel's. In a short time Adrian Ltd. had an impressive set of contracts, but no clothes and no place to show them. Woody and Adrian coldly appraised the chaotic collection, the upheaval in the salon, the list of missing fabrics, the mounting bills, the diminishing cash, and decided on drastic action. No more expensive delays. Ready or not, the spring collection must be shown to the buyers in January.

Phone calls to New York produced a few more fabrics. Samples were pushed through the workroom. Advertising space was secured in *Vogue* and *Harper's Bazaar,* and the few finished clothes were photographed for publicity. Given good fortune, Woody and Adrian decided, they could make a go of it. Then the Japanese bombed Pearl Harbor.

Adrian managed to avoid the hysteria that followed that fateful Sunday by working interminably. Work was no longer kept within the boundaries of the MGM ten-to-four schedule. Unlike the movies, where his clothes had been a result of cooperation between designer, director, and actor, this business depended wholly on his decisions, and there was no time for retakes.

As the deadline for the January show neared, it became clear that certain key fabrics would not be delivered, that the magazine ads were a hotchpotch that could not be changed, and that the "ethereal floating" salon was bogged down in plaster dust, months from completion.

So the first showing of Adrian Ltd. had to be held in the patio of Adrian's home. The tables were gaily decorated and lights flickered through the pepper tree. Janet was a charming hostess, and the charmed buyers applauded warmly. But Adrian was bitterly disappointed. He knew the clothes were not right and the presentation was makeshift. It was, for him, humiliatingly unprofessional.

Fortunately, the buyers and the press were not so stringent in their judgment. Bonwit Teller signed a contract. Many stores overbought their originally timid quotas. *Vogue* scheduled three full pages of photographs with a sequin-studded gingham coat in color. But Adrian was not consoled. He was determined that the next collection, for fall, would be shown in the salon in just the way he wanted it. Nothing would be rushed or half done. That collection would be his real test.

His ideas poured forth. Everything went into this collection: suits, dresses, coats, cocktail dresses, at-home dresses, dinner dresses, ballgowns. Though many of the clothes looked simple, the cutting and shaping were staggeringly intricate. Lean, severe suits had sweeping curved seams from neck to hem. Often they were sparked with cubes of fabric like a Mondrian painting, or dangled tabs and crests of medieval splendor. Slim dresses that skimmed the body were draped, fringed, or blazed with embroidery. One dinner dress wrapped the model in a slinky black sarong to the floor, while above the waist she appeared quite nude behind wisps of lace. Adrian christened this dress, "It's Not True."

Woody kept a calculating buyer's eye on Adrian's fancies. He would drop by the designing room with a word of gossip, and sometimes a word of advice. "That little dress you did for Carole Landis when she was poor—" (almost all Hollywood heroines were poor in the first two reels) "you know, the one with the surplice neckline and the diamond-shaped midriff. We could use that on the line." So it too was added, christened "A Black Dress," and marked in the wholesale book as #346.

Every morning Hannah brought Adrian her beautifully precise muslins for changes and fittings. Mr. Peters presented his suits. Adrian would smile approval, rip off a collar and reset it, or cry out at an overfancy touch of tailoring, "Damn it! Don't make it better than I've drawn it!"

The June showing for store buyers was mobbed, an unequivocal

Three tailored Adrian beauties from his first collection photographed for *Vogue* by John Rawlings.

success. Both Marshall Field and Bonwit Teller took all day to write very substantial orders. But for Adrian the testing ground was to be the customers' showing, two months later. They would be his ultimate judges, the people who would wear his clothes.

Still more ideas were poured into the new collection: dresses by a custom dressmaker, too intricate or too subtle for factory production; suits which a custom tailor would stretch and shape to the customer's body. Until the last moment—the last dress rehearsal with the models—Adrian's mind teemed with new thoughts, new clothes. The work-rooms were in a state of controlled frenzy.

Under a blazing August sun the salon was given its finishing touches. Dress after dress had a final pressing, then hung ready on its rack. The invitations were sent, the ads okayed, the seating list revised for the nineteenth time. The programs had been delivered, and printed on their covers was: Adrian Presents His First Collection for the Fall and Winter of 1942. In his designing room Adrian sat exhausted, staring blankly at the dusty palms. He slowly chewed a piece of gum, his stomach tense with excitement.

That night the limousines lined up early before the stark facade of Adrian Ltd. Guests stepped across the sidewalk into a soaring space of blue and pink. Light-ringed rooms shimmered with color caught in huge mirrors and gilt-threaded draperies. On a stage, two slender columns loomed before a shifting electric sky.

Backstage, Hannah and her corps of dressers waited silently by the racks of clothes. The models were in their first outfits. Adrian had inspected them and now stood by their side, listening to the growing sounds of the audience. Suddenly his face paled, sweated. He ran down the hall, slammed the door, and was ignominiously sick.

In the salon, Janet and Woody were greeting the guests with hand-shakes and kisses all around. Lady Mendl, accompanied by her Pekinese, settled down on a couch that perfectly matched her blue hair. Carole Landis and Joan Fontaine looked their ornamental best. Margaret Sullavan and Leland Hayward, on a couch front and center, waved to Barbara Hutton and Cary Grant, on a couch across the way. Woody checked the long lines of chairs and their occupants and stepped backstage to give the signal.

Adrian was now in tight control of himself and everyone else. The lights in the salon dimmed. The stage glowed. As the music swelled, the audience fell silent. Adrian snapped his fingers and Lucienne strode out between the columns in the first suit of the collection, "Gallant Lady." She paused for a moment to look out over the room. There was a crash of applause. Adrian snapped again and Ann followed in "A Gay Bolero." Applause again and a shrill "Bravo!"

As suit followed suit and dresses followed coats, Woody glanced along the rows of chairs. The customers were writing in their black-and-white programs. They looked up for "Oriental Patchwork" and

The openings at Adrian Ltd. were star-studded parties. Just below Janet Gaynor plays hostess to Reginald Gardiner and Clifton Webb; Adrian relaxes with an old studio chum, Clark Gable and his then wife, Lady Ashley; Janet Gaynor greets two important customers, Loretta Young and Claudette Colbert.

wrote; glanced at "Dinner with a Dash of Gold" and wrote. Trim, boyish Harriet brought down the house with "Where's the USO?"

In all, sixty-one pieces were shown, and there was a standing ovation as "Opera Season" ended the show. Adrian was hugged and pummeled and kissed. Barbara Hutton waved her program with twenty numbers checked to try on. In a rush to call in their stories, three reporters snatched at a single phone. Lady Mendl, who well knew the difference between mere excitement and the enthusiasm that means money, tapped Adrian on the shoulder. "I hope you like it," she said. "You are a success."

Adrian did like it. The success of Adrian Ltd. was stupendous. The orders rolled in and, much sooner than Woody's cautious prediction, the money followed. The clothes checked out of the stores almost as soon as they were unpacked. Number 346—the "Black Dress"—appeared on every order. Season after season it was cut in an uncounted number of fabrics. Marshall Field alone sold one thousand in three months. When most factories were closed for the season, #346 kept the machines busy. The dress became so ubiquitous that Woody forbade his wife to wear it and Adrian thought it such a bore that he never had it photographed.

When Hannah's sample room was not busy, her staff turned out custom orders. Wealthy clients came from Pasadena, Santa Monica, and Malibu, and measurements arrived from as far away as Chicago, New York, Seattle, and Palm Beach. Joan Crawford, Norma Shearer, Greer Garson, Loretta Young, and other members of the movie colony now happily paid for their Adrian costumes. Millicent Rogers and other fashionables made their appointments at the salon. "Buggsy" Siegel's girlfriend, Virginia Hill, was so grateful for her Adrians that she sent enormous bottles of perfume to the entire staff.

These were the years of awards and prizes in the fashion business; Adrian gathered his share. From the Fashion Critics' Award on up and down the prestige scale, he accepted each honor courteously and seriously. Any committee could be sure that he would put on a

John Engstead

bang-up show and say something interesting, even controversial. He worked on his public appearances with the diligence of a movie star.

Adrian's California success story was echoed in the showrooms of Seventh Avenue. Adrian copies appeared everywhere. Some manufacturers, incapable of duplicating the intricate seaming, sold a freakish padded shoulder that they called "The Adrian Silhouette." Others, without bothering to use his name, took his ideas and sold them as their own "originals." His print designs were stolen and marketed in cheaper versions. Manufacturers of buttons, belts, and embroideries peddled their products with the story that "Adrian has bought it for his new collection."

Not unnaturally, Adrian became almost paranoid on the subject of copying. As a result, he rarely allowed publicity shots or sketches of his clothes, and, for his advertising pages he used such outrageously theatrical confections that no one could copy them.

Woody, who was well versed in all the tricks of the trade, spent much of his time as security guard and policeman. Every sketch, every pattern, every trimming, every employee who might be bribed was carefully watched. Also he combed the lists of customer orders, matching them with news reports of their social engagements, so that none might see her dress on another's back. If his vigilance somehow slipped, Woody glimpsed Hell right beneath the pink carpet.

An important part of Adrian's emotional makeup was an awesome sense of dedication to design. Sikorsky helicopters intrigued him quite as much as Schiaparelli's hats, though he was quick to admit that he understood hats better than helicopters. When Schiaparelli visited Hollywood in the mid-thirties, Adrian hastily organized a fashion show. Clothes by Omar Kiam, Travis Banton, and other Hollywood designers were modeled by Joan Crawford, Kay Francis, Carole Lombard, and other movie stars. The showing was both a compliment to "Schiap" and a statement that American designers deserved attention. Unlike the French, said Adrian, Americans lacked many of the conditions for doing good work, not the least of which was recognition from the public and the press.

At the beginning of the war, with France in captive isolation, Adrian took every public opportunity in articles and interviews to urge American designers to make an all-out effort. Now was their chance, he declared, to work out their own solutions to the special problems of American life. The wartime press reported on the American designers at length, for there was no other available copy. In the years following, many new designer names began to appear on dress labels.

This lasted as long as the war. Then in the Paris collections of 1947, Christian Dior presented his "New Look." As a change from the square-shouldered, lean-hipped shape, Dior's round shoulders, corseted waist, and long swinging skirts made a press sensation. Mrs.

John Engstead

A slim, mannish suit with brass buttoned jacket in hunting pink which was copied all over the "junior" market and sold for about one tenth of its original price.

Chase of *Vogue* and Carmel Snow of *Harper's Bazaar* proclaimed the New Look the only look, and their considerable prestige soon brought the stores and manufacturers around to their position.

Adrian was furious. Not only had he been declared démodé, but the small importance earned by American designers had been dictated out of existence. His anger was highly articulate. Sensing controversial copy, the press and radio pitted Adrian against Mrs. Chase, and arranged a broadcast debate between Adrian and Christian Dior. Mrs. Chase said that Adrian should know that fashion can change, and Christian Dior said that he believed in femininity. Adrian, on the other hand, said that women would not be dictated to, that corsets were barbarous, and that long skirts were uncomfortable relics.

Nonetheless, American women did cut out their shoulder pads, lace in their waists, and wear skirts that brushed their ankles; and the editors agreed that Adrian had had his day.

Adrian was hurt but far from crushed by this fashionable uproar. He was, in fact, looking at greener fields. Louis Wheeler of New York's Gunther-Jaeckel had flown to California with a very interesting proposition. The old fur firm, where Adrian's father had once worked, was anxious to dramatize its entry into the dress business. They needed some grandiose, publicity-laden gesture: What could be better than duplicating the Adrian salon in their store and presenting his entire collection in New York, just as it was shown in Beverly Hills?

The offer could not have been better timed; Adrian grabbed it. Almost before Wheeler had time to return to New York, Eleanor LeMaire moved into his store followed by the carpenters, painters, and upholsterers. There were minor details for Adrian to settle, such as the existing New York contract with Bonwit Teller, but all fell quickly into place. To challenge the fashion critics on their own home ground filled him with a sense of combative anticipation.

Adrian opened the collection in New York on a chill March day in 1948, and the police were called to control the crowds. There had to be four showings. At each, over three hundred people jammed the salon and the models tripped their way through the aisles. Wheeler had bought the collection for forty thousand dollars at wholesale. On the first day, his customers ordered three times that amount. In the evening Adrian telephoned Woody in Beverly Hills. "I told you so," he said.

As a touch of spring atmosphere for the show, a hurdy-gurdy man with a monkey had been hired. The way the monkey took to show business quite won Adrian's heart. He bought him. On the train back to the Coast the monkey occupied a drawing room of his own. Adrian had made a similar trip twenty-five years before.

THE SUITS
An Adrian suit was the civilian uniform of the American woman during the hectic days of World War II·when she needed a single costume appropriate for all occasions—morning, noon, and night.

John Engstead

65

John Engstead

In some of his suits Adrian manipulated stripes with a geometric precision and intricacy which would be virtually impossible to reproduce in today's factories.

67

68

John Engstead

POLA STOUT

Pola Stout's beautiful rectilinear compositions in fabric inspired some of Adrian's grander gestures: *left to right,* model Kitty Sully in a sweeping Bedouin cape, Bess Dawson in an unusual sleeved stole, Nan Martin in a melange of stripes of various sizes and colors.

John Engstead

John Engstead

CONTRASTS

Adrian's talents covered a wide range. He could turn his hand to the severely architectural shaping of this velvet wrap as well as to misty floral taffetas, *opposite*. He designed these warp prints and they were made for him by the prestigious old silk firm of Bianchini.

Photograph by

The most satisfactory Adrian customer was a woman who could play many parts. She could be cast either as a Dramatic Personage hooded in velvet or, *opposite*, as an innocent Romantic Belle clouded in net and flowers.

John Engstead

Rawlings
e

John Engs

COATS

This simple coat created a sensation and was much copied in the wholesale market. It was the first use of a fabric which was to become ubiquitous in the 1950s—Lesur's "Poodle Cloth."

Right. The gray-paned yellow wool coat flares from an enormous wedge collar. Each panel is shaped on the bias and each plaid is matched precisely, which makes it something of a mathematical marvel.

Below. This coat too created a stir in the fashion business primarily because, in a day of swirling "pyramid" coats, it was refreshingly slim.

John Engstead

SPAIN

A side trip to Spain filled Adrian with Hispanic fervor and a multitude of ideas for his collection. Outstanding were his new capes and undulating flamenco ruffles.

John Engstead

Other Spanish ideas from that startling collection were almost literal translations of *Goyescas* costumes, yet Adrian made them seem fresh, contemporary.

ANIMALS

His long-standing fascination with the Animal Kingdom provoked some of Adrian's liveliest fantasies: A jaguar print, a rooster hat, a cobra brocade, and a stallion rampant on an evening dress which he showed when he won the Coty Award.

John Engstead

PERSIANS

For his glittering Persian collection Adrian devised embroideries as fabulous as any worn by a caliph's favorite. These he used lavishly on capes and coats and dresses for high voltage glamour.

BEADS

The beaded dinner dresses from Adrian Ltd. were designed to sparkle even when the conversation lagged. The singular embroideries and their unusual placements strongly influenced the Seventh Avenue wholesale market and brightened a decade of American dinner tables.

John Engstead

GOTHIC

The extravagance and the purity of medieval art appealed to Adrian probably more than any other period. In every collection some Gothic detail would crop up: A hooded suit, an almoner's pocket, or a wedding scene which could have illuminated a missal.

John Engstead

IDEAS

Adrian seemed to have an inexhaustible supply of ideas which could encompass chic confectionery like the milkmaid dress worn by Mrs. Paul Kullsman, or modern masterpieces of dressmaking like the dress and cape of abstract shapes and the vibrant disharmonies to be found in a Braque painting.

Genevieve Naylor

Photograph by

SCULPTURE

Consciously or unconsciously, every dress-maker is a sculptor. Fabric is their clay, their medium for achieving three-dimensional shape. Louise Dahl-Wolfe's sensitive camera recorded the Adrian sculpture opposite for *Harper's Bazaar*. John Engstead, who photographed every Adrian collection, caught the rough-hewn velvet sleeves above.

91

STARS

Adrian's best clothes were not meant for secondary roles. They took center stage and held it. Here are two of his stars frothing in stellar organdy: Ilona Massey and Ingrid Bergman.

93

PAINTED JUNGLES, 1948

Collection of Joseph S. Simms

Even after his African trip, Adrian's pictures were far from a literal recording of that continent, but more an extension of his childhood fantasies and movie travelogue remembrances. They were also technically excellent paintings.

In a dull period, an editor could always enliven the women's page with an Adrian interview. He was incredibly good copy: His views were serious which immediately made them unusual in the fashion business, and he had humor, so that the editor did not have to strain for "the light touch." Unfortunately for the editor, a question on fashion might also be met with, "I don't know. I haven't been thinking about clothes lately. I've been painting."

Twice each year, for a period of three months, Adrian would design his collections. Then his concentration on clothes was fierce and single-minded—no parties, no books, no telephones. After the collection was launched, he would emerge refreshed, ready to rejoin the human race. The truth is, clothes were not the consuming passion of his life. He was too curious about the world and the people in it, and the extraordinary impulses which drove them to do extraordinary things. He refused to restrict his life to the world of fashion.

When Adrian was a boy of twelve in Naugatuck, a Saturday afternoon movie had been a travel feature called *African Hunt* by Paul J. Rainey. Ever after, the shots of animals coming to the water hole had remained with him. For years he had sketched elands and elephants and zebras and giraffes as he remembered them, set against plains of grass and sky.

He determined to test his memory. After showing the 1948 spring collection, he and Janet packed safari clothes and painting gear and set out for Africa. Despite gloomy guides who predicted a great deal of rain and very few animals, the weather proved clear and the animals were plentiful. Seven lions roared all night outside their tent. Adrian was awestruck, "My God, it's just what I thought it would be."

In March of 1949, the prestigious Knoedler Galleries on New York's Fifty-seventh Street exhibited Adrian's canvases. The viewers saw

extraordinarily beautiful animals, as in the decoration of medieval missals; tall-trunked palms ending in feathery leaves; handsome black people, reminiscent of a Benin frieze; and vast spaces that made one think of the beginning of the world. The reviews were kind; the public was kinder. They bought a great many pictures. "He is a romantic realist," said actor and art dealer Vincent Price in summing up the exhibition.

The same words could be a neat summation of Adrian, the man. He was indeed a romantic. To him, drama was as necessary as breath. Despite the pressures of the dress business, he was easily lured into costume projects for the theatre or the movies. Leland Hayward persuaded him to dress the national company of *State of the Union*. That same year he clothed Eugenie Leontovich, appearing with Basil Rathbone in a melodrama called *Obsession*. The critics liked the clothes, although the play did not last the week. When MGM decided to remake an old musical called *Roberta*, retitled *Lovely to Look At*, Adrian was the logical man to hire. For that production—set in a dressmaking establishment—Adrian did a twelve-minute fashion show, using Tony Duquette's backgrounds. It brought the audience straight up in their seats. Twelve minutes is a long sequence on film. Only a romantic would dare fill it with a fashion show; only a realist could carry it off.

In the spring of 1952, as he was working on his fall collection, harsh reality felled Adrian with a heart attack. His physician, Dr. Alter, was visibly concerned. He ordered his patient to remain in bed, cut off from the world; no business, no visitors, no telephone, a complete rest for months. But knowing that Adrian was anxious about the collection, the doctor wisely allowed him one brief outing. An ambulance brought Adrian to the salon, where from a wheelchair he checked the clothes and directed the rehearsal. Then the ambulance took him home.

Not only was Janet dismayed at the threat to her husband, but she now had to pick up the pieces of their family life: to create a new atmosphere of calm; above all, to protect him from anxious friends and the curious world. Since he was a man with so many ties to so many people and so many projects, her watchdog role was critical.

Friends rallied around with tactful and unexpected offers of help. The affairs of Adrian Ltd. fell on Woody Feurt's shoulders, and the business prospered as usual. But the future had to be faced. Adrian was not going to be able to work for months. Hiring a substitute designer presented an impossibility. Their ten-year lease on the salon was up and a new one would have to be negotiated. As the days of the lease ran out and the alternatives seemed more and more implausible, Woody and Adrian finally determined to close the business.

The buyers who gathered on the day of the showing all knew of

From the fashion show sequence of *Lovely To Look At,* one of Tony Duquette's fantastic sets and a bevy of Adrian showgirl gowns.

Adrian's illness. Over the years many of them had become friends. In the salon there was an air of anxious silence. The lights dimmed, and Woody stepped forward to announce that the fall collection of 1952 would be their last. Everyone had expected some sort of announcement, but now they were dismayed and saddened by the knowledge that an exciting decade had come to an end. When Janet came on stage to read Adrian's customary few words of greeting and explanation of the collection, many eyes blurred.

It was as briskly successful a collection as ever before, and the salon was kept busy far into the months of autumn. Then the final steps had to be taken. One day Janet and Woody unlocked Adrian's designing room, sorted through the papers and tore up the sketches. Dealers crowded into the salon. The couches, the Dorothy Liebes drapes, even the pink carpets were rolled up and loaded into trucks. When everything had been sold, the last shipment made, the last form signed, Woody handed over the keys, and Adrian Ltd. was finished. Lying on his bed in the quiet house, Adrian turned the page on that chapter of his life.

As his patient improved, the doctor gradually allowed telephone calls and visits. By the fall Adrian was up and around, yet his lack of energy and the rigid limits on his activities annoyed him. At last Dr. Alter prescribed a trip to escape the tensions and depression of the last months. Instead of the usual therapeutic ocean voyage, Janet and Adrian decided to revisit the quiet, vast stretches of land in the Canyon de Chelly. For two idyllic months a Navajo trading post was their headquarters, and the trader's family and the Indians became their friends. With their son Robin, they roamed the canyon. The soaring cliffs, the sudden beauty of a peach tree in leaf, the dignified and kind people were more healing than any medicine. The nearest doctor was a hundred miles away in Gallup, but Adrian was not anxious. This was a time to lie fallow and slowly renew himself. He savored a sense of peace as the three of them sat on the rim of the darkening canyon and the sound of sheep bells drifted upwards. He and Janet did not want to abandon this life for the world beyond.

Providentially, one day the mail included an invitation to a film festival in São Paulo. Brazil would be at its best at that time of the year. Adrian longed to see the jungle and above all, they could be quiet.

On the trip, Janet was watchful, hiding any sign of anxiety but barely containing herself as she watched Adrian carrying heavy luggage through porterless airports. It was a long flight to São Paulo. It was happily uneventful.

Having put in an appearance at the film festival, Adrian looked about for trips further inside Brazil. He found a friend who knew someone who lived far in the interior in a place called Anápolis. The twice-removed friend was Joan Lowell Bowen, who twenty years

before had hoaxed the literary world and made a fortune with her autobiography of a salty life she had never lived. The prospect of seeing jungle wildlife in such merry company was irresistible to Adrian. The next day they were off.

Anápolis, in Goias Province, was a four-hour flight from São Paulo. Here they found a small jewel of a town, set in a lacework of streams, bordered by jungle. Monkeys chattered and macaws flashed and screamed in the forests. Butterflies in blinding colors sunned themselves on the rocks. White ginger blossoms spiced the air. Within twenty-four hours the Adrians were asking the price of land.

One morning, bumping along in the Bowen jeep some forty miles from town, they came upon a valley that had lately been a coffee plantation. A rounded hill looked down on swelling fields; a stream carved bright loops through the jungle; flocks of parrots scattered across the sky. Here the Adrians decided to build their dream house. Before they returned to California, the dream had started to become reality.

The months back in the States were haunted by the memory of their jungle land. Reports on the progress of their house kept them in a state of anticipation. But when at last they were able to return to Brazil, instead of rushing to Anápolis by plane, they decided on a typical Adrian reverse play—they would drive the thousand miles from São Paulo to their home. Joan Bowen and Dr. Fleury joined them as guides and, despite predictions of fierce rains, the four set out to see the country at close range.

After the first day, the road no longer existed. In its place were washed out bridges and huge holes filled with water. Gentle people of all colors, from pale gold to black, gathered about the car to gaze in wonder at *Janeta, Janeta artista*. For his birthday Adrian was presented with a baby macaw. He fed the bird with a spoon as they inched their way through central Brazil. It was, perforce, a leisurely trip, a chance to savor the intoxicating airs of their new country.

As they turned into their own road and saw their house, they were enchanted. To Adrian it seemed a miracle. His first architectural venture was serenely dramatic, just as he had drawn it. The large, high rooms were spread around an inner garden. An enormous raised green marble fireplace seemed to float in the cavern of the living room. The kitchen gleamed. In the bedrooms, skylights looked out on the stars. Beside the terrace a pink kapok tree was in bloom. The setting could not have been improved upon; it was an Adrian production.

There remained a great deal to take care of. Their furniture had not yet arrived. There was the planting to do. There was no electricity and no telephone. From Anápolis came the chief of police, the town bankers and their families, country neighbors who were politely curious about the new house and the famous movie star who lived in it. On some days, Joan Bowen dropped in, but at night there was no one within miles, no sound except the hornlike braying of toads.

Adrian was worried. Although nothing had been said, he wondered if he had buried Janet, if his jungle idyll might not turn into a lonely nightmare for her. But then one day he wrote to Bernadine Szold,

Janet rode five miles on horseback—loved it and had no fear. I was so delighted and proud of her. . . . The big adventure is on again— here we go—where it will lead we do not know, but if following adventure through green beauty takes you anywhere—we'll follow.

Several years followed in peace and contentment as their farm grew and prospered. Banana trees shot up beside their road. Coffee fields spread far. Each morning just before dawn, Antonio headed for market, the truck loaded with figs, pineapples, bananas and coffee, chickens and pigs, and eggs and vegetables. One happy day Juan, the overseer, announced that the farm was paying for itself.

Their first guests were their old friends Mary Martin and Richard Halliday, who lost no time in buying themselves a neighboring *fazenda*. Manchester Boddy, Rosalind Russell, the Burdens, Noel Coward, Diana Vreeland, and Clifton Webb lent an international air to the jungle guest list.

Robin flew down to spend his summer vacation, bringing young Heller Halliday to stay on the new ranch with her parents. Robin's friend Sammy Ribiero came up from São Paulo to spend a few weeks. The boys were invited to play soccer with the Anápolis team and the place sometimes overflowed with young people.

But often at the Adrians' Fazenda Amazona, there was no one. Janet painted and gardened. They rode. Adrian started to work on a book. Days shimmered in the crystal air and velvet nights stretched tranquilly before them. They felt as though they had been planted in the earth and were beginning to grow again.

Each fall they returned to Los Angeles to see Robin back to school, to catch up with friends and the affairs and gossip of their other world. Then, as winter came, they flew back to the jungle. On one memorable occasion they carried a diesel generator which Adrian then reassembled from sketches he had made and his memory of what the electrician had told him.

It was in Los Angeles in 1958 that an old friend, screenwriter Luther Davis, lured Adrian into returning to work. Davis had written the book for a musical version of *Grand Hotel*. The Civic Light Opera was slated to give it a deluxe production in their new theatre, with Paul Muni starred as Kringelein, Joan Diener to do the Garbo role, Ter-Arutunian to do the sets—and an impressive budget for costumes.

Adrian first cautiously consulted Dr. Alter, who pronounced him fit. Producers Edwin Lester and Eleanor Pinkham assured him that their scheduling would match his tempo. He read the script, listened to the music, listened to the outline of the production numbers.

Sketch for the prima donna's entrance in *At The Grand*.

Collection of Eleanor Pinkham

Before he started to sketch, he asked Davis for a biography of each person on stage and the reason they were in the hotel. Davis's inventive sketches intrigued him. He plunged ahead. He sketched, he shopped for fabrics, he supervised fittings. Theatre people and their talk excited him once again. "It's like being let out of a cage," he exulted. "I'm not designing something to sell or something that women will buy. I just want to knock the audience's eyes out."

Al Nickel and the Western Costume Company had contracted to make the costumes. They brought them in under budget and without alteration, and they were magnificent. The show girls in their evening gowns were breathtaking. The dancers, swirling and dipping in their waltz costumes, drew an ovation. But neither Paul Muni nor music nor costumes could breathe life into Vicki Baum's old story. The world had changed since 1932. In 1958 *At the Grand* seemed irrelevant.

But Adrian and Janet had had a beguiling taste of the theatre again. After the show closed, they held a small dinner party in their Melrose Street apartment for the Lesters and Eleanor Pinkham. Adrian thanked them for being so pleasant to deal with. *At the Grand* had been, he said, a very gratifying experience; so much so, in fact, that he and Janet had decided to come out of retirement. They were going back to work.

Soon thereafter, Janet was announced for the lead in *Midnight Sun* on Broadway and Adrian had drawn the season's musical prize—*Camelot*. It could not have been a more auspicious beginning for their new careers.

Robin was going back to school in Switzerland, so Janet flew with him to New York, where the two of them could spend a few days together before her rehearsals began. Adrian holed up in the Los Angeles apartment, surrounded by books on Arthurian legends, prehistoric myths, and medieval illustrations. No contract had been signed; in fact, the script was not yet complete, but Adrian was anxious to get started. Using *The Once and Future King*, from which *Camelot* was being adapted, he devised his own continuity and his own characters.

He had never been over-anxious about a job before, but *Camelot* for some reason represented a special challenge. He was distinctly nervous. Dr. Alter called almost every day, and even put him in the hospital overnight for tests. Since Adrian was not above dramatizing a scratch, his malaise could assume grand proportions. Yet when he started to work on his sketches, they flowed. It seemed that all the tabs and loops and strong patterns he had been designing all his life were just a training ground for *Camelot*. His enthusiasm for myths had found a home in the Arthurian world of the Green Man and cabalistic magic. These were some of his happiest creations, his most apt ideas. He worked far into the night.

Then the night of September 13, 1959, he suffered a devastating attack. He was rushed to the hospital. Janet was telephoned in New York. In a panic, she and Robin caught the first plane out. There were no friends to meet them at the airport. The limousine was waiting. As they sped to the hospital, Janet asked about Adrian, but the chauffeur could tell them nothing. At the hospital they hurried to the reception desk. The attendant called a doctor. It was he who told them that Adrian was dead.

Costume sketch for Merlin in *Camelot*.

The Adrian family poses for passport photos for their family friend, *Vogue* photographer John Rawlings.

THE PRO, 1959

Vogue

Sketch for Garbo's traveling cloak in *Camille*.

The columnist F.P.A. once remarked that there were only two categories of mankind, the hosts and the guests. He might have added a third—the critics who tell us which host gives the best parties.

In his life, Adrian was very much a host—not only in the literal sense to those who attended the parties he enjoyed giving, but in the larger and more figurative sense, host to the many he entertained and influenced by his work. In the dozen years he worked for MGM, his designs were sources of wonder to a huge international audience of women who tried as hard as they could to imitate the Adrian brand of glamour. Other loyal and imitative fans were the Seventh Avenue designers who used to hasten with their sketchbooks to the latest Adrian picture. Although they had to sit through some dreary Hollywood dramas, they were inspired by Joan Crawford's ruffled shoulders or Greta Garbo's organdy shirtwaist, and they translated them into American ready-to-wear outfits.

During the decade of Adrian Ltd., particularly during the war years, he was one of the American designers capable of making an individual statement. His influence was felt in every showroom and store in the country; his trim suits and slinky crepe dresses were reproduced in every price bracket. To judge by his imitators, he was the most influential designer in their copybooks. For them, he took the place of Paris.

And yet, he received scant notice from the established critics. They did not even bother to write that his clothes were bad; instead they chose to ignore them. Carmel Snow of *Harper's Bazaar*, who never attended his showings, sent her reluctant alter editor, Diana Vreeland.

Vogue's Mrs. Chase attended when it was convenient, but discouraged any overt enthusiasm for Adrian in her editors. Because he was good copy, both magazines would give him editorial space to air his views on costuming, preview his sketches for *Camille*, photograph

his home, or report on the safari to Africa; but there were few editorial credits for his clothes. These few were often dumped into a departmental grab bag titled "The California Market," or given secondary placement and perfunctory photography. Undoubtedly the friendship and admiration of photographer John Rawlings and his editor-wife gave Adrian his best *Vogue* coverage. He did break into the pages of *Harper's Bazaar* with the aid of the impeccably social and decorative modeling of Millicent Rogers in her Adrian wardrobe. But the usual coverage was meager, just sufficient to keep an advertiser happy.

For almost forty years the words of Carmel Snow and Mrs. Chase had ruled the world of fashion. Both women had been educated in the subtleties of French couture, and they were exceptionally sharp observers. Adrian's theatrics appalled them. During the war years, they felt much more of an affinity for Hattie Carnegie's echoes of Schiaparelli and Balenciaga, and featured them in their pages. After the war they returned with enthusiasm to the Paris milieu, the fashion world with which they were most familiar and which they considered impregnable.

Now that Carmel Snow, Mrs. Chase and Adrian are gone; now that the swift revolutions of our times have wiped out the kingdom of the chic; and now that the authority of the fashion magazines is questioned, one might wonder if Adrian's influence was not more prophetic than it appeared at first. The popular success of his clothes was certainly a concrete challenge to their editorial authority. The fact that his business flourished despite the magazines' patent disapproval again suggests that by ignoring Adrian the editors were also closing their eyes to reality.

Adrian was no revolutionary, nor was he a conservative. He looked neither forward nor back. He lived, without nostalgia, in his own time. Nothing he did blazed new trails for the future. He simply solved the problems of the moment. It pleased him that he, Claire McCardell and other American designers during the war had made their own design statements, and been recognized for them. He felt that a future for American design was at last being established. When the war ended and the *status quo ante* reappeared, he was understandably angry, baffled, and filled with a sense of failure.

He was a man who, most often, got his own way. He insisted quietly. He did not hesitate to demand a great deal of the people around him. Because he worked hard to produce his brand of perfection, because he never settled for the dull and safe, everyone wanted to be included in his projects. It was part of the unmistakable personal glamour of the man, and it attracted to him a crazy quilt of friends. He took chances on people, on his costumes, on almost everything he did, not so much from a love of gambling as from a serene, well-founded self-confidence.

John Engs

104

When it came to money, he was just short of being reckless. Though he earned a great deal, there was never any money at hand. His antique shop and his home were stocked with splendid and expensive objects. For years, he stalked a magnificent Grinling Gibbons overmantel, a massive wood carving of nesting birds, twining flowers, pineapples, and bees. When at last the price had come down to what he considered a reasonably few thousands of dollars, he bought it. It now sprawls across the narrow chicken-house bedroom in Palm Springs where one is forced to duck beneath its scrolls to go to the bathroom. The year before he bought the carving, he had lost money trying to sell a new kind of face cream; that same year, according to his accountant, the antique shop had been a more than usual disaster. "But this I've got," he said to Hedda Hopper. "The Grinling Gibbons is paid for. Whatever happens I could live here for the rest of my life and be perfectly happy."

Fortunately, with coolly practical Janet at his side, he never had to put this fiscal theory to the test.

He often disregarded what many considered "appropriate" or "in good taste" in order to create a special dramatic effect. Those who lived by rigid standards of "good form" were outraged. They were shocked at his attempts—quite mild by our present standards—to add excitement to his own wardrobe, for example, with ties that matched shirts that in turn toned in with the offbeat colors of his suits. Had they only seen him in the dusty little desert house, in his gray suede shorts, green Tyrolean jacket, and square-toed slippers with silver buckles.

Everything was done for effect—his effect. As Charles LeMaire had said, he designed to please himself. His costumes, his dinner parties, his paintings were as much an extension of himself as the ideas he could express so persuasively. The paintings, the ideas, the costumes, the dinners were all of a piece, a part of the man. He gave himself to each of them completely. He was a man who had no hobbies.

He conceived most everything in terms of theatre. The houses and rooms he designed were backdrops for drama. Each dinner party had a cast of characters. Each person had a story to be discovered. His best clothes were meant for the dramatic moments of life, for dramatic gestures. To judge by their popularity, a great many women enjoyed taking center stage.

No man, of course, can belong everywhere. On their way to the theatre one evening, Adrian, Janet, and Noel Coward stopped by at a New York friend's cocktail party. Her guests were made up of the polite social set; it was quite a coup for her to present them with a real live movie star, a glamorous designer and a famous theatrical personality. However, the guests were unaccountably disappointed.

Although Noel Coward was at his most charming, they had clearly expected a spate of quotable wisecracks from him. They stared

Millicent Rogers graced the pages of *Harper's Bazaar* looking like a Gibson Girl in garnet velvet. Below is the finale of Adrian's Americana collection.

dumbly at Janet wondering what might be the correct way to address a movie queen, and Adrian was startled by a lady who asked, "Tell me, do you *really* know Greta Garbo?"

When at last the three were able to escape politely to their car, Noel Coward exploded with relief, "God! It's good to be back again with the pros!"

History may or may not take the trouble to judge Adrian, but if some day it should be looking for him, that is undoubtedly where he will be found—among the pros, that collection of clowns and geniuses who have lived by their own rules, and whose skills have created an epoch.

Each designer has his favorite period. The Middle Ages was Adrian's happiest inspiration. With fine disregard for exact time, he robbed the seventeenth, the thirteenth, and whatever century he chose, for details, shapes, and patterns. To the right are some of his sketches for the lords and ladies and warriors of Camelot, brashly handsome and theatrically perfect.

When Janet Adrian presented much of his work to American museums, these sketches were given to the Theatre Collection of the Museum of the City of New York where they are now preserved.

Vogue

3 Thursday

To My Friend Meeur
From C.
CM

Mainbocher

BY DALE McCONATHY

CONTENTS

1

MAINBOCHER AT 83: A PORTRAIT

The famous portrait, sketched by Eric, that hung in Mainbocher's office.

I don't believe that dressmaking is an art but I do think that dresses are an important part of the art of living, just as important as food, surroundings, work and play.

Mainbocher
June 1971

Mainbocher is one of the last of the great snobs—an eighteenth-century French cardinal who somehow got himself born on the West Side of Chicago. He is short and stout, with a cap of white hair and steady brown eyes; in spite of his years in Paris and New York, his speech is still surprisingly midwestern. Seeing him, one is struck by both his seriousness—"discretion" his clients call it—and a delightful merriment that can cause him to throw his head back with a singer's laughter, deep and rich, colored by his years of operatic training. His air is distinguished and courtly—there is the flash of a white handkerchief in his jacket pocket, and his polite, graceful nod has the flourish of a bow.

It was this manner, at once worldly and sincere, that won him the confidence of his customers, "his ladies" whom for forty years he so admirably dressed. It was his manner, redolent of the confessional, that caused his clients to confide in him with the greatest trust. Seated in his corner at La Grenouille in New York, signaling for service almost without words, Mainbocher wrapped his guests in a dizzying attention that hypnotically drew them forth.

"He loves gossip although he never broke a confidence," said Diana Vreeland, special consultant for the Costume Institute of the Metropolitan Museum and former editor-in-chief of *Vogue*. "New Yorkers don't have time for that kind of gossip, filled with detail, an accumulation of gossip really, like a novel. But Main loved to gossip because he was a midwesterner. And only Europeans and midwesterners can gossip like that."

Mainbocher's attentiveness and his extraordinary memory for the details of the lives that touched his was a matter of the strictest form for him. But beyond those rules of conduct, he had an unending fascination with the world of women. There are the givers and the takers. Main was always one of the givers, a great personal friend. Main understood the inner lives of his customers; he knew their houses; he knew their families. The cult of Mainbocher often came to include three generations—mothers, daughters, and granddaughters. As Nancy White, the former editor-in-chief of *Harper's Bazaar*, said,

Main had the mysterious ability to make you feel you were the only woman in a room. No matter who else might be seated in a restaurant his eyes never left yours. I don't think I've ever met a man whose manner was so flattering or a man who understood so perfectly the power a man can have over a woman.

This power brought him the richest and most influential of customers, and made him friends that were as devoted to him as to his dresses. His snobbery and sense of his own exclusivity was so great that new customers had to be recommended by already established costumers to gain entry to his salon. His name appeared only on the labels of his own dresses. There were no endorsements, no Mainbocher stockings, bags, shoes, gloves, or jewelry. The business was his and his alone. Others might be in thrall to a textile manufacturer or a perfume distiller. Mainbocher would always be his own man.

Mainbocher and his dresses became a standard against which American women measured themselves. Barbara Paley, the tall, beautiful wife of the president of the Columbia Broadcasting System, one of the most important, if not the most important, arbiters of American fashion since World War II, began to wear Mainbocher dresses as a junior fashion editor at *Vogue*. Her first wedding dress was made by Mainbocher, and the wedding dress of her daughter by that marriage, Amanda Mortimer, was a gift from him.

Gloria Vanderbilt, also an arbiter and the first of the "best dressed" to break the mold of conventional elegance in the late sixties, was terrified by Mainbocher's reputation. Turned away by a *vendeuse* on her first visit because of her black tights, she was formally invited by Mainbocher himself to attend his next collection. She remembers, "He had a way of imparting his authority to those of us he dressed. He made American women women of fashion in a way they had never been before."

Because of his reserve and his bankerlike appearance, Mainbocher's charm was little known outside the select circle of his ladies. His sense of privacy was neither obscure nor strange. Very simply, his personal life was his own. The fashion press, excluded by his very high standards, saw him as a sort of eccentric recluse who might be discovered buried in conversation with the Duchess of Windsor at Pavillon. What were they talking about?

Mainbocher's friends in the theatre maintained that he was the best unpublished critic in the theatre. His views of the opera, the ballet, and the zoo were equally informed and critical. During the twenties and thirties, he had two pairs of seats in the front row of the Casino de Paris. Often, he would attend both the opening night and the second night at the Folies-Bergère. He was, in fact, *le grand spectateur,* that fascinating phenomenon that Henry James had observed some fifty years before among American expatriates. Yet underneath the trappings of twenties sophistication the core remained midwestern—a shy, diffident boy holding back the curtain so that divas could take their bows before Chicago audiences. In time, of course, he became both *entrepreneur* and *spectateur,* but his designs for the stage, though among the least interesting of his work, were always his favorites.

As an editor and later as a couturier, Mainbocher held sway by a highly reasoned taste over a circle of women who could afford the very best for themselves. "Today, when the fashion press attacks the *couture,* they fail to understand the privilege it was to have your dresses so carefully made, fitted with the greatest care," said Diana Vreeland.

Thus, Mainbocher the outsider became an insider of the highest order. His position was the result of his ability not just to exclude people—he would go politely blank—but to exclude anything he found extraneous. What he didn't like didn't exist. Secure in his Fifth Avenue salon, he could dismiss the commercial world of Seventh Avenue with a wave of his hand, making it sound like the furthest reaches of *Ultima Thule.* His enthusiasm was as extravagant as his ridicule, often foolish and short-lived, as was his temper. He was capricious, but grandly capricious.

If one asked him for his version of life, it would surely be the opera —absurd, grandiose, musical, with its own logic. He dressed the ladies and loved the *demi-mondaines.* And he sat up front for all the follies of the past fifty years.

2

THE EARLY YEARS

Mainbocher, *above*, in his fifties.

Horst

ꞁbocher's eternal feminine, *left*.

For Main Rousseau Bocher, born in Chicago on October 24, 1890, the private worlds of Monroe Street have remained at the center of life. Inside, the stiffly starched lace curtains, the glowing gaslights, the shining yellow oak—the domain of his mother. Outside, massed with flowers, the garden—the domain of his father.

"Main," pronounced in the American manner, "Maine," was his mother's maiden name. "Bocher" was a French Huguenot name, pronounced "Bocker" as the Dutch pronounced it when his ancestors migrated from France to Holland to America. His father's father had been a Pennsylvania cabinetmaker who carved furniture with a lightness and grace that was surely French. Mainbocher's father was doubly patriotic—flying the tricolor and the Stars and Stripes on holidays. Mainbocher was fiercely proud of being a descendant of pioneers. "I have two envelopes of genealogy in my mother's handwriting," he said, "one for the Mains and one for the Bochers. Mother traced our ancestry back to the 1640s when our ancestors first arrived in America."

Main Bocher had a sister, Lillian, who shared with him the adventures of growing up on Chicago's West Side. While the Bochers had little money, they loved music and long Sunday walks "admiring nature," and Main helped his father in the garden, "brimming over with pride" when he was asked to deliver a bouquet to one of his parents' friends. "I didn't have fun on those Sunday walks, but I learned from my father his love for flowers. And ever since, I've wanted fresh flowers around me."

At the age of four, Main Bocher made a sort of beginning, sketching a duck in his mother's cookbook. From that point, his mother encouraged his drawing, his father, music. "I can't remember that I was ever interested in dresses in those days," Mainbocher says, looking back. "My sister played dolls with her friends and they made dresses. I do remember once serving as a runner for her, going off to fetch gold stars and tinsel for my sister and her friends to decorate their doll dresses."

And there was Miss McDermott, the mysterious stranger who arrived to sew when his father was traveling, fashion magazines and a roll of pattern paper under her arm, in her black leather bag.

> *a pair of very sharp scissors, a bright tracing wheel, her stubby pencil, a plain black apron . . .*
>
> *There was an absorbing puzzle-solving excitement about the first evening's proceedings. The design finally decided upon was invariably "assembled." There was a bodice idea from one page, a skirt from another, a special sleeve that had pleased my mother right from the start or had been diplomatically praised by Miss McDermott; I realize now they both were quite in love with beautiful sleeves.*

The magic of Miss McDermott stuck in Mainbocher's imagination— the sewing notions laid out on the white spread of his sister Lillian's temporarily vacated bed, the pressing irons "like a family of black ducks," the half-finished dresses.

Years later, he had a Proustian memory of his mother in an almond-green dress, Miss McDermott kneeling behind her, and further back in the room by a green-globed lamp, his sister looking on. His fascination with women had begun. The scene,

> *so Victorian for faraway Chicago, had a wonderful and unsuspected influence in my life.*
>
> *In a cluttered and commonplace room, an ordinary fitting had suddenly been transformed into a thing of beauty . . . a Vuillard: three bent heads, six white hands, figured wallpaper, mixed fabrics and colors, and the peace of simple life going quietly on.*

"I was always talking on Monroe Street about getting to Europe. There was no question of becoming a doctor or lawyer."

Europe to Main was the romantic vision of his father and of the oak-framed sepia photographs of the Colosseum and the Acropolis on the stairs at John Marshall High School. He was water boy for the baseball team. Before the school debates he played Ethelbert Nevin pieces on the piano. For the last two years of high school, he went to the Lewis Institute because it had a dramatics society. He had begun to save his pocket money for the musical Sunday afternoons at the Chicago Auditorium. Holding the curtain for the stars of the Boston Opera Company appearing in Chicago in repertory, Main Bocher had his first experience of the world of opera.

Main Bocher's father died after Main had finished his first year at the University of Chicago. The family was suddenly on its own. For her part, Mrs. Bocher gave china-painting lessons to the neighbors; Main went to work for a wholesale florist and took private art lessons on the side. Later, expecting a small legacy from his father's estate, he switched to the Chicago Arts Academy. He had begun the career that led to Paris.

EUROPE

MAINBOCHER THE ARTIST
Two drawings from the Munich art school
student days, shown in the Paris Salon des
Decorateurs of 1913.

In 1909, Main Bocher left Chicago for New York. Manhattan sailed up before him as he and a friend crossed the Hudson on the railroad ferry from New Jersey. "It was all I had dreamed on Monroe Street that it would be." Mainbocher enrolled at the Art Students League and lived at the Young Men's Christian Association in Brooklyn, "convinced I was in Manhattan."

In the decades before World War I, the Art Students League was teaching the heavily eclectic Beaux-Arts style that was influencing American painting, sculpture, and architecture. Fifth Avenue was lined with American *palazzi* and *chateaux*. The most notable surviving examples of this period are the Frick Museum, the Metropolitan Museum of Art, and the New York Public Library. East on Fifty-seventh Street, three blocks from the Art Students League and adjacent to the Plaza Hotel stood the Vanderbilt mansion, a Fifth Avenue chateau with enormous wrought-iron gates. The most important social event of the season was the opening of the Metropolitan Opera, another of the American palaces.

Main Bocher worked mornings for a commercial lithography firm to pay for his afternoon life classes at the League. In between, he would carry his portfolio of illustrations and sketches from magazine office to magazine office. Some evenings standing room at the opera gave him glimpses of the glittering world of Mrs. August Belmont's "Four Hundred" in their Fortuny and Worth gowns.

His drawings pleased him, but it was opera that compelled him and suggested the wider world he had been seeking. He was being drawn inevitably to Europe. After two years, he persuaded his mother and sister to sell the house on Monroe Street and to take their chances with him in Europe. In 1911, they sailed together on a new ship, the *Rochambeau*.

119

Main Bocher was twenty-one. Summing up that voyage, he has said that he was born again in Europe, that Paris and Munich opened his eyes, that his life had begun. Almost ten years before the Lost Generation of expatriate American artists and writers, Main Bocher had discovered Europe. For six months he studied art at the Königliche Kunstgewerbeschule in Munich, where he often slipped off to the opera and visited the rococo palaces that ringed Bavaria. German art was caught in the swirling, mannered grip of Jugendstil, an outgrowth perhaps of the nineteenth-century revival of the rococo. The Wagner cult in the arts and Mad King Ludwig's extravagant castles gave student life in Munich a heady atmosphere—an atmosphere that drew in those years, among others, Isadora Duncan, the inventor of modern dance, and her family, and Edward Craig, the revolutionary theatrical designer.

Baron de Meyer
Harper's Bazaar, 1932

The straightened shape, a coat punctuated by silver buttons and a black crepe afternoon dress sharpened by a black-and-white dotted crepe blouse, 1932.

120

Lipnitski

THE LONG LINE
Mainbocher's recurrent elongated silhouette in one of its first appearances—a long day dress topped by a fur cape, 1933.

After two years in Munich and Paris, the Bochers returned to Manhattan, only to learn that after their departure three of Main's drawings had been hung in the Paris Salon des Decorateurs. Of course he had to return, and to pay for this he became a tour leader for twenty-one American women and their thirty-three pieces of baggage. Later, settled in London, Bocher cabled his mother and sister to join him. They arrived, unfortunately, just in time to turn around once again and return to New York, as World War I broke out in Europe.

In New York, Main Bocher found he enjoyed a rising reputation. As a favor he designed a dress for a benefit fashion show for Miss Hannah Randolph, a friend from Philadelphia. That design led to a job making fashion drawings for E. L. Mayer, a major wholesale clothing manufacturer, who selected sketches each Saturday. For Main Bocher, the job was merely a stopgap, the source of needed dollars —but it was the beginning of his fashion career.

In 1917, he went back to France for a third time as a volunteer in an American ambulance unit. Once there, he transferred to the Intelligence Corps to trail a narcotics ring supplying drugs to American fliers. He was a sergeant major but he wore civilian clothes, posing as a music student, which he soon became. Demobilized, Bocher returned to Paris to study voice and grand opera.

One day, Main Bocher went to show some designs to Captain Molyneux, the British designer whose Paris *maison de couture* was one of the most influential of the postwar years. Molyneux was interested, but they couldn't come to terms on a price. On the way out, Molyneux's directrice, Anna van Kampten Stewart, "a charming Englishwoman," suggested Bocher apply for a job as sketcher at *Harper's Bazaar*, the American magazine that maintained a Paris office. He began there at $100 a week.

Sketching might have remained only a source of income to support Bocher's voice lessons had he not suddenly lost his voice during a crucial audition in 1921 for an American family living in Paris that had made him their protégé. For three years, Main Bocher could not sing, but his fashion career went on.

4

PARIS, THE TWENTIES, AND *VOGUE*

Hoyningen-Huené

An early distillation of the formula—glamour and mystery compounded of chiffon and roses, 1932.

Mainbocher in his forties, *left.*

People were getting to know me. Baron de Meyer came over to photograph for Harper's Bazaar *and we worked together. Later, Carmel Snow asked to see me and asked me to come on the staff of all the* Vogue *as Paris fashion editor.*

For seven years, 1922–1929, Main Bocher was the Paris fashion editor, then editor of French *Vogue.* French fashion was setting the world standard and Main Bocher's years as Paris editor made the couture collections news. His forecasts, sharply written with a great flair, showed an amazing accuracy. His eye, cultivated as a sketcher, scanned Paris, looking always for the startling or telling detail. Although he had never written professionally before, Main Bocher instinctively knew how to use words. His observations of the celebrities of the twenties who appeared on his pages are memorable, precise, evocative.

Undoubtedly, Main Bocher made a fresh contribution to fashion writing: it was he who invented the phrases "off-white," "dressmaker suits," and "spectator sports clothes." His work on *Vogue* moved the magazine toward the kind of total visual impact that Brodovitch made famous with *Harper's Bazaar* in the thirties. He began by removing the decorative borders framing the illustrations and photographs.

I think the general feeling about my editing was surprise at my independence. I didn't ask buyers for the lists of dresses they had chosen but made my own choices and published them. I was not only getting the magazine out; but I was also writing, even drawing.

Mlle Chanel wouldn't let editors from any magazine in to see her collection except the reporter for the Paris Herald Tribune. *In order to get drawings of the Chanel dresses for* Vogue, *I'd go to the office of Commissionnaire Rosenberg and, as they unpacked the dresses, I'd sketch them on hangers. We were never late with Chanels.*

123

I was very careful to have people working for me who knew something about Paris, how the clothes fitted into the style of life. There was Foxy Gwynn, one of Patou's mannequins and Lillian Fisher . . .

But I suppose my greatest influence was on how the magazine looked. George Huené (the young Baron Hoynigen-Huené) came to me trying to sell me Man Ray photographs that wouldn't have worked as fashion photographs at all. I asked him why he didn't take up photography himself?

Carl Erikson* was living in Rouen when he changed his style of drawing—his wife, Lee Trielmann, was already drawing fashions for me. I sent Erikson to Venice to make some sketches. He'd come to me for work and said all he'd done was "draw super horses but never super ladies." I assured him the same thing that made class in a horse made class in women.

Perhaps Main Bocher's most significant contribution to *Vogue* was the idea for an opening editorial page called "Vogue's Eye-View." For the next fifty years it served to focus and introduce each issue's contents.

Main Bocher's tastes as a fashion editor were exacting. He was a thoroughgoing critic of the styles he viewed. Augustabernard, because of her perfectionism, was a particular favorite. She was hardly a commercial success. Neglecting to pay her bills, she quickly went out of business. The giants like Paul Poiret, with his orientalism and bold colors, and Mlle Chanel, with her déclassée daring, did not interest him. He reported their fashions and reserved his judgment.

I remember Lucienne of Reboux, the milliner. I had been to Lucienne's and seen all around the room the chicest women of Paris waiting for hats. She would cut the hats on the heads of her clients, shape the felt —in all colors—and then the modistes did the sewing.

I greatly admired Augustabernard. It was a great honor to know Mme Vionnet. I knew her before she moved to the rue de Montaigne. I was mad for the wearable part of Mme Vionnet's work. Crazy about Louise Boulanger (Louiseboulanger) who began as one of Mme Cherot's fitters.

On the other hand, I was never moved by what Paul Poiret did. I thought his clothes were expensive expressions of clothing that is more of a costume than a dress.

Interestingly enough, Bocher was unaware of the fashion experiments conducted by the Russian artist, Sonia Delaunay, who, for her shop commissioned textiles and designs by avant-garde artists. The beginning of the boutique and *prêt-à-porter* were not part of his fashion reportage.

The patrons of the *haute couture* of the time were the aristocrats, the rich, and the expensive, well-kept *demi-mondaines*. Main Bocher

---

* Erikson became "Eric," the first fashion artist to break with the literal pattern-book drawing of dresses and . to show women in dramatic impressions of clothes as they were worn.

watched these women carefully, noting their whims, observing their poses, admiring their bravura. One of the most celebrated was Charley Brighton. "She had won me over one night at Patou's (Patou had showings at night). It was the first time I saw a chinchilla coat dragged across the floor. At the races, I saw her wearing sloppy hats and gloves a size too big. She was the epitome of *chic*."

Main Bocher was making $25,000 a year (then, a high salary) as the editor of French *Vogue;* he was enormously successful, enormously influential. Then suddenly in 1929, he resigned to open his own *maison de couture*. "I went into *Vogue* and said I'd be leaving shortly. It was nothing that crept up on me, stealthily and slowly. It was an immediate and very agreeable explosion. It came from the unconscious. The whole idea was born and in twenty-four hours became absolutely upright."

5

12 AVENUE GEORGE V

Fitting one of the dresses for the fall collection of 1930.

With Carmel Snow, *left,* the editor of American *Harper's Bazaar* who became one of his most important American supporters.

Bocher resigned from *Vogue* in June, 1929. In November, 1929, the Great Depression began. Nevertheless with his mother, the Countess Albert de Munn, the Countess Paul de Vallombrosa, Mrs. Gilbert Miller, and himself as stockholders, Main Bocher assembled capital of about $40,000 and set to work to open a salon.

"I went to the Galeries Lafayette and bought muslin, a dummy and lots of pins. When anyone came to visit who was interested in investing in the new business, I hung up muslins of the dresses for them to examine in the dining room which was also our library."

Then he added a finishing touch. In the manner of Augustabernard and Louiseboulanger, Main Bocher contracted his name. Main Rousseau Bocher as couturier became "Mainbocher."

Number 12 avenue George V, Mainbocher's first showroom, was in a residential neighborhood far outside the precincts frequented by most couturiers. (Although Balenciaga and de Givenchy later showed nearby.) Clients climbed to the third floor of an imposing apartment house. Mainbocher had turned the big room where the dresses were shown into a salon filled with flowers, Nymphenburg china, and mirrored mantelpieces. The effect was stunning. Having covered the collections of other couturiers, Mainbocher chose neither to serve champagne nor to play music during his showings.

"I didn't bribe the viewers with food or drink. I wanted them to keep their minds on the clothes. But I did have a marvelous butler serving ice water."

In Paris, Mainbocher was not visible during his collection. He would wait behind the screens placed at one end of his salon, pacing nervously, whispering to his employees, trying to sense the atmosphere of the room.

The first collection of November 1930, however, was not a commercial success. Even so, Mainbocher's reputation was enhanced, puffed along considerably by the fashion press who knew him. Mainbocher, in fact, began at the height of prestige. (By contrast, the two couturiers whom he most admired, Vionnet and Augustabernard, had begun by picking up pins for other dressmakers.) Before long, he overcame the uncertain beginning and gained an extraordinary financial success in comparison with other, larger *maisons de couture.*

Mainbocher had caught on; people were crowding the stairwell to get in. He became the first couturier to impose a *caution* or guarantee of purchase on those who came to view his collection. The *caution,* a business move Mainbocher felt inevitable from his experience as part of the press, was instituted to bar the copiers and tourists. It was priced at an amount equal to the cheapest dress in the collection. In his Paris days, this was $350 or so. Clients had to sign for the purchase of a dress in advance or deposit money. For a former editor, Mainbocher was amazingly severe with the press. *Vogue, Femina, Die Dame, Harper's Bazaar, The New York Times,* and the *New York Herald Tribune* were the only magazines and journals allowed to cover Mainbocher's collections. Even more amazing in a distinguished editor was his denigration of the influence of fashion journalism. He was fond of saying that "The best public relations is word-of-mouth between women, rather than the printed page."

Mainbocher showed four collections a year—more than three hundred dresses for the two main seasons, two hundred for the midseasons. Mainbocher's *maison de couture* first occupied two floors of 12, avenue George V; when it closed nine years later, it had expanded from a salon and workroom to an additional six floors of workrooms in the rear. Business ranged from 16 million francs the first year to 100 million francs in 1939, when Mainbocher bought out his partners at a profit to them.

At the close of the thirties, Mainbocher was employing about three hundred fifty people, fifty selling the dresses under the *directrice de salon,* and the remaining staff in light workrooms or *ateliers,* each supervised by a first and second fitter, the *première* and *deuxième d'atelier.* The first fitters were Mlle Armand, who had been a fitter for Chanel, and Mattie Vramant, who later started the house of France-Vramant.

Fabric was the spur for his designs. Twisting and draping the fabric in his hands, he would "think" his designs, then have them sketched. Mainbocher never employed an assistant designer. Most of his ideas were sketched faithfully by his great friend Douglas Pollard.

In Paris, French and Swiss textile salesmen would visit the salon about two months before the spring and fall openings. Swatches would be chosen and bolts of fabric delivered. The cloth was not paid for when it was chosen, nor was it paid for when it was received. Each month, a manufacturer's agent would arrive and measure the

Benito

EARLY MAINBOCHER
A tribute to Mme. Vionnet and the bias-cut,
1932.

RE-THINKING THE SHAPE
An opaque white crepe evening dress, remarkable for its unmolded hips, 1932.

bolt. The couturier paid only for what had been used. (Mainbocher liked this extraordinary system so much that he would over-order fabric in his New York years to duplicate the freedom he had in Paris. When his salon closed in 1971, his surplus fabric was worth an estimated hundred thousand dollars.) Fabric was his luxury.

> *Embroidery had gotten to be almost dead. I worked with Mitral. We would supply Mr. Mitral with the parts of dresses at the early part of the week and he would drive through eastern France distributing the parts. The sleeves would come from the Vosges, and so on.*
>
> *Brocades and façonnes from Lyons I knew about from an article I had done earlier for Vogue. In the twenties it was still possible to see a husband working at the complicated loom with his wife in the kitchen.*
>
> *Even later, I was very touched by the beautiful fabrics I was shown. I never went out of the house to see fabrics. As my honesty was known, I asked the salesmen to leave me their bags of samples. I didn't want to be influenced by their selling.*
>
> *Bradford Perrier and Ducharme were the only fabric people I saw in person. We profited from my asking for something beyond what was shown me.*
>
> *The fabric firms in those days protected your choices. I would tell the fabric people what I wanted, choose my colors, ask the première what could be done. We were all part of it. Creation was in the air.*

Having chosen a fabric and worked carefully on the idea before it was sketched, Mainbocher did not make many changes in his designs. He was inexhaustibly critical of how the dress was made by his dressmakers, taking apart their work many times before he was satisfied.

Mainbocher became a force. His clothes defined a new breed of women—sure of themselves, their look incredibly and simply elegant. *Haute couture* clung desperately to fashion ideas that stretched back before the First World War. Worth still dressed the most conservative Parisians, Redfern the British aristocracy, and Lelong, Captain Molyneux, and Patou the rich young matrons. Everywhere from New York to Buenos Aires Mainbocher caught fire with what the fashion press called "don't-dress frocks," elegant, simple, semi-formal, "full of good breeding." His style was very influenced by Vionnet's use of the bias cut which made it possible to drape with ease. Mainbocher brought a startling simplicity to his designs.

> *I knew I was growing. I knew I was eliminating superfluous details. My confidence in myself became stronger and I think that I became subconsciously aware of the fact that if I were doing my best that it would be all right.*
>
> *I have never believed in gimmickry, and the changes in the mode then were more subtle than they are today. The changes in the mode came with the birth of a new house, the emergence of a new talent.*
>
> *I never appeared in the salon. I never came out as I later did in New York. I was selling the label of Mainbocher.*

DRESSING DOWN
A white crepe de chine afternoon dress, *left*, with boldly printed train worn by Mrs. Harold Talbot; Mrs. Robert McAdoo in a black polka-dotted chiffon, tied with a scarlet ribbon, 1932.

*Edward S
Vogue*

I had been drinking in a great deal. Paris was the best—the parties, the concerts, the boîtes de nuits. I had many chances to get my own eye in. Fashion then was like an enormous line of playing cards—each a dress. There wouldn't have been anything startling—only subtle changes by which one could get the year.

Long before, when I was still editor of French Vogue, *I was having lunch with Mrs. Kaplan Smith at Claridge's in London (we were having Lanson Onze, my favorite) and she said to me "I wish I could have a wardrobe of your dresses like graduated pearls." That image stuck with me. If the right dresses are put next to one another, they would be like a scale on the piano. Each grows into the other. You see I'm a musician manqué. Music and continuity, that's what my life and work have been about.*

Mainbocher's order book read like a history of the thirties. Film stars bought his dresses; but the duchesses, the countesses, the very rich were his most faithful customers. His trousseau for Wallis Simpson for her marriage to the former King Edward VIII marked the end of an epoch dominated by socially legislated "good taste" and the beginning of a commanding new individuality.

My favorite clients were women, no matter from what country, who knew what they wanted. Women who lived observing, not copying.

I think ladies and grandes cocottes *were the best-dressed by me. The in-betweens who didn't know themselves couldn't wear Mainbocher as well.*

Year by year, fewer clients came to Paris. Once again, a war had interrupted Mainbocher's career. He said of the Paris years that only twenty-two percent of his customers had been American, that most of his clients had been European. Nevertheless, when the war came, Mainbocher sold his salon and left Paris, intending to resume his business there after the fighting was over.

Edward Steichen
Vogue, 1933

FINISHING TOUCHES
Mainbocher's jacket, *above*, in ridged black wool with a swinging back that anticipates his famous topper of the forties, 1933.

A black wool dress, *left*, set off by a white chiffon guimpe and a pleated bertha of black satin ribbon, 1933.

SHOULDER TREATMENTS

A white piqué jacket, *right*, with enormous flounced sleeves worn over a silk organza skirt.

Mrs. T. Reed Vreeland, *left,* as yet a fashion civilian (Diana Vreeland later became fashion editor of *Harper's Bazaar* and editor-in-chief of *Vogue*) shopped at Mainbocher, *Vogue* reported in 1935. Like many of his other customers, she bought his clothes for both day and evening—an unusual tribute to a couturier since most were preferred for either day or evening.

Rene Bouet-Willaumez
Vogue, 1933

Bradley Green

Eric
Vogue, 1934

ERIC'S MAINBOCHER

As the editor of French *Vogue*, Mainbocher had discovered and developed Eric, the most influential fashion illustrator of the century. Because of their collaboration, Eric understood what Mainbocher was about, and his drawings, notably of Mainbocher's fashions of the thirties, are a most remarkable record of the designer's reductionism. Here is an eight page portfolio of Eric's Parisian reportage.

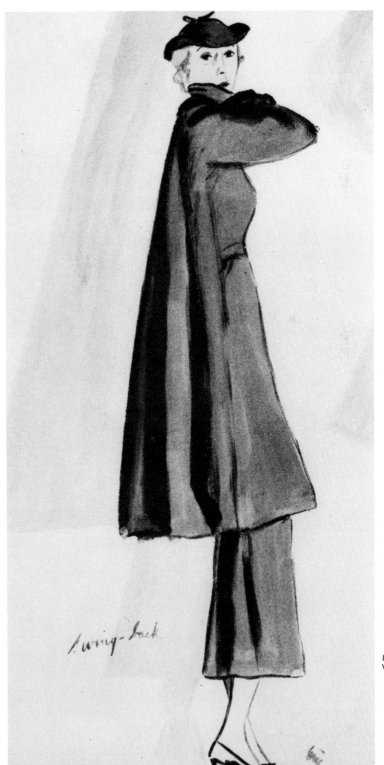

Opposite: Eric sketched his friend fitting a cape-sleeved dress of black wool with red-dotted silk tie, gloves, and hat, 1934. *This page,* an extraordinary swing-back tunic, 1934.

Eric
Vogue, *1934*

Lady Abdy, *left*, in a floor-length "deep dull brownish dregs-of-Burgundy" velvet dress with a buttoned jacket, widened sleeves, and a gold cloth Peter Pan collar, 1933.

Eric
Vogue, 1933

A favored silhouette echoed in a black net gown, with knee-length harem-hemmed satin peplum, 1937.

Eric
Vogue, *1937*

Long wool dinner suits, *left,* with toe-length skirts and short capes on the jackets, 1933.

Eric
Vogue, *1933*

Two dresses from the '38 collection, *right*, one of black serge with a crisp petticoat and organdy at the throat and the other of pleated blue wool.

Eric
Vogue, *1938*

Two black jacketed crepe dinner dress[...] right, formalized with net yokes and [os]trich feather accents.

Mainbocher's forward-looking shaped wa[ist] as reported by Eric, in two town suits, le[ft] one furred and the other pared down [to] fundamentals.

Eric
Vogue, *1938*

Eric
Vogue, 1939

John Rawlings
Vogue, 1939

THE SAILOR AND THE SURAH

Mainbocher revives the diminutive straw sailor and the silk surah. A navy polka-dot dress, *left*, with a full peplum, and full skirt, 1939.

A navy and white surah coat, *right*, worn over a simple dark blue full-skirted crepe dress in one of Munkacsi's earliest fashion action photographs, 1938.

Munkacsi

Harper's Bazaar, *1937*

THE OVERSKIRT

Mainbocher's fascination with the over-skirt—a design to which he returned again and again—was closely linked with his revival of the petticoat and the large skirt. The black bolero and skirt, *left,* are worn over white embossed organdy, 1937.

The simple black satin dress, *right,* has a split skirt that opens on a knee-length underskirt.

Man Ray
Vogue, 1938

Hoyningen-Huené
Harper's Bazaar, *1939*

THE UNEXPECTED TOPPING
The brocade evening jacket, *left,* with capped sleeves and oversize self-fabric gloves.

The gold lamé reefer, a transformation of the workman's jacket. Six square flapped pockets, chamois lining, 1939.

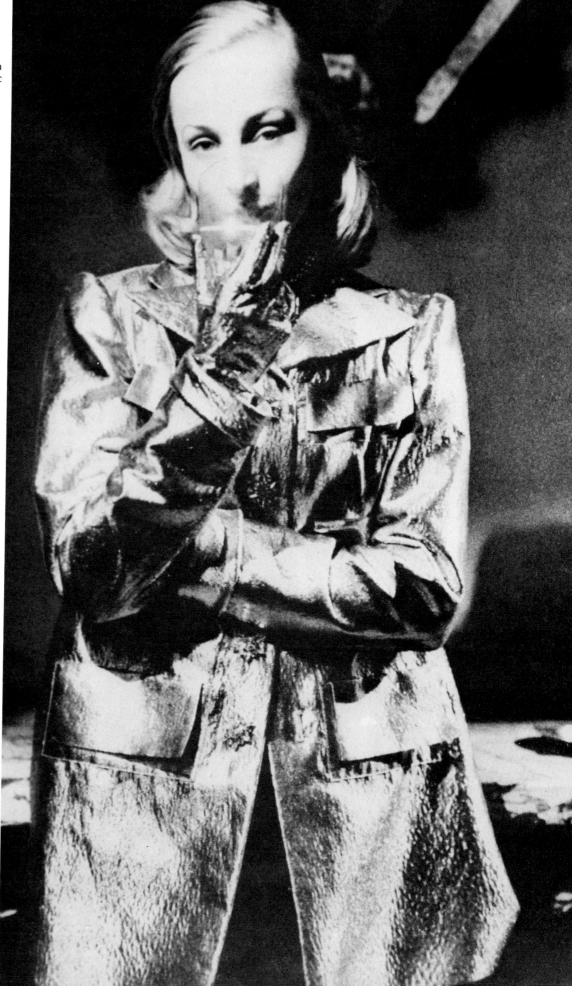

Hoyningen-Huené
Harper's Bazaar, *1939*

THE CORSET

Mainbocher reintroduced the waist and ribcage in his last Paris collection. A pink and silver brocade evening dress with the controversial new shape, 1939.

The revolutionary corset, one of the fashion photographs taken for an Ame fashion magazine before the Nazi oc tion of France, snapped by Horst at A.M. one morning as *Vogue* evacuate Paris studio.

Mrs. Ernest Simpson in 1935.

6

THE DUCHESS AND MAINBOCHER

The Duke and Duchess, *left,* immediately after their wedding, May 12, 1936.

UPI

Perhaps the single most influential figure to wear twentieth-century fashions, the Duchess of Windsor was an early devotee of Mainbocher, introduced to him by Lady Mendl who had become her fashion mentor. The Duchess of Windsor was extremely self-critical and years of analyzing herself and her appearance developed an emphasis on simple shapes and clear colors, immaculate grooming, to offset what she felt were her major faults. As Mrs. Simpson, the Duchess had re-done herself—making herself over as a chic young matron. In many ways, she epitomized the extremes of self improvement that were later to emerge as major motifs of the fashion and beauty industries. Her maxim, "You can never be too thin or too rich," reflected this startling drive. Her eye for detail, her startling memory, and a passion for self-refinement, were the ingredients of her look.

When Cecil Beaton, the photographer-chronicler of British high fashion and society, first met Mrs. Simpson in the early thirties, he remembered her as "somewhat brawny and rawboned in her sapphire blue velvet. Her voice had a high nasal twang." By 1936, when the American divorcee's notoriety was at full flood, the metamorphosis was complete. About a photographic session on the eve of the abdication, Beaton observed that Wallis Simpson was "soignée and fresh as a young girl. Her skin was as bright and smooth as the inside of a shell, her hair so sleek, she might have been Chinese."

Mainbocher particularly admired her self-discipline and over the years found her both the most patient and the most exacting of customers at fittings. He took it as a mark of her seriousness that she could stand for hours during her fittings without complaint.

Many of Mainbocher's most interesting ideas came in answer to the Duchess of Windsor's highly demanding life—notably the simple dress with separate collars, peplums, etc., to be added when luxury

155

was at a low ebb during World War II. The most famous dress Mainbocher made for the Duchess of Windsor was, of course, her wedding dress, perhaps the most widely photographed and widely copied couture dress ever made.

In the spring of 1936, Mainbocher traveled to the south of France where Mrs. Simpson was in seclusion before the wedding and presented sketches of the wedding dress. A fitter went to Candé on six successive Saturdays to finish the dress—a two-piece floor-length gown with a jacket that was not intended to be removed. The line was severe and the effect of the dress was very covered-up with many dressmaker's details, carefully and beautifully rendered with tiny self-buttons at the waist and wrists. The color of the silk crepe dress was a pale blue, that now looks more like gray in the bins of the Metropolitan Museum where the dress is part of the costume collection. Of the color, Mainbocher said, "I named it 'Wallis blue,' a blue of which there was never a sample available to anyone." Nonetheless, the dress was almost immediately in production in the United States.

As a personality, the Duchess seemed to have been created by her marriage. But her effect, carefully calculated and finished, had begun much earlier. Her London apartment at 5 Bryanston Court had already created a stir. She had a knack for unexpected combinations of dinner guests, mixing the Mayfair set and the American colony randomly with health faddists whose theories intrigued her, visiting Hitlerites, and the future Edward VIII, whose presence at her table was kept assiduously from the British public by the newspapers.

A description of her dining room assembled by the decorator, Syrie Maugham, telegraphs her style. A mirror-topped table, large enough to seat fourteen, ruled the room—surrounded by white leather upholstered chairs and crystal vases invariably filled with flame-colored blossoms by Constance Spry. There and in the chartreuse living room with its off-white and beige furnishings people began to talk about Wallis Simpson and her exceptional flair.

She was copied but only later did she become the venerated prototype of fashionable women—a style that was assumed like some magic mantle, whose power might be communicated simply in the wearing.

The Duchess of Windsor, in her apartment at the Waldorf Towers, 1943.

156

Louise Dahl-Wolfe
Harper's Bazaar, 1947

The Duchess had a powerful effect on Mainbocher's imagination. In her person, she reflected many of his favorite feminine attributes—worldly, totally self-made, the creature of a modern fairy tale. Inevitably, his clothes for her embodied his preoccupations. This was particularly evident in two dresses from 1947: A reworking of an Oriental Victorian paisley into a severely cut dress, *above*; and in the austere silhouette of high-necked taffeta dress, *right*, with its elaborate under-structure.

F. Fonssagrives

There was a curious unsympathetic strain in the self the Duchess projected. Her complex preoccupation with surface seemed at once frivolous and perhaps callous to the reporters who charted her every move. But that paradox was the one with which Mainbocher identified. He and the Duchess had much in common. As Americans in Europe and Europeanized Americans in America, their careers seemed to share many motives. It is not surprising that for what became the Duke's favorite portrait of his wife by Horst, *left*, the Duchess wore a Mainbocher or that Mainbocher's tailored look and hers were often synonymous.

With the Duchess, Mainbocher was able to play off his most complicated fashion ironies—putting her public personality against a highly loaded, stand-off simplicity.

1947

Hoyningen-Huené
Harper's Bazaar, 1940

Mainbocher, *above*, photographed on the day of his return to New York by Louise Dahl-Wolfe.

The topper and the long silhouette from the first American collection of 1940.

6 East 57th Street

With 1939 and World War II came the end of Mainbocher's unprecedented success as an American designer in Paris. Again, his mother and sister, who had been living in the relative safety of Monte Carlo, joined him, homeward bound. Mainbocher paid off his staff and spoke of closing temporarily. Seven years later, at the end of World War II, he spoke of returning. He never did.

Mainbocher's last Paris collections had created a storm of controversy. Just as later Dior's New Look, and much later, the Midi raised a furor reaching far beyond the couture, Mainbocher's corselet, a nipped-in waist, radically altered the undefined silhouette of the thirties. This change, linked with the fame of his trousseau for the future Duchess of Windsor, was the beginning of a new phase in fashion, eventually as influential as Coco Chanel's loosely cut, boxy jackets and skirts. His corseted waist, defined bosom, and back draping introduced the Victorian motifs that were to pervade the forties, expressing a nostalgia for a more stable period. He understood perhaps unconsciously, this nostalgic vein brilliantly. It summed up his first memories of dresses, of a past elegance that so appealed to him; and most importantly, it embodied a kind of femininity that stretched back beyond the emancipated twenties and thirties.

As a French-American designer of international reputation, he returned to New York with wide publicity, the first American celebrity in the French fashion world. Reporters wrote eagerly of his views on American women and how they dressed. His Parisian clients—particularly the rich North and South Americans who still had freedom of travel—were pleased to learn that Mainbocher would resume dressmaking in New York.

But Mainbocher had returned to the United States with very little money, and it was only the $100,000 capital raised by Mrs. Baine

Alexandre and a sizable contract with the Warner Brothers Corset Company that allowed him to open at all. His introduction to the mass American public came through the Warner Brothers ads for "The Mainbocher Cinch."

At first, Mainbocher rented a floor in a brownstone house next to Henri Bendel and across from Bergdorf Goodman on West Fifty-seventh Street.

I made the first New York collection working on the floor, behind a little circle of screens that I bought at Macy's. In the midst of my prep-arations and the decorating, my chief fitter quit, jeopardizing the day of the opening. The younger women sat on the floor to see the collection. Everybody made a great effort to come and to judge my reputation on their own.

His first formal salon in New York was as nearly a copy of the old quarters at 12 avenue George V as Mainbocher could make it. It was east of Fifth Avenue, adjoining Tiffany's on Fifty-seventh Street. Off the bank of elevators, plain doors marked Mainbocher, Inc., led directly into the showroom, separated from the desks of the ven-deuses and their assistants by a wall of vast, glassless French windows. The showroom was surrounded by low tobacco felt-covered ban-quettes against beige walls, a pair of Wurzburg mirrors with old glass and rococo frames and a sky-blue ceiling of floating painted white clouds. At three o'clock in the afternoon during the season, an elec-tric switch closed the off-white brocade drapes and the mannequins would leave their *cabines* to show the collection. The three strands of pearls, the pearl earrings and hair-ribbon "hat" worn by the show-room models were standard. The client noted her choice by number on the small mirrored tables in front of her. The minimum two fittings were spaced within the six weeks for delivery.

Mainbocher was most exacting about the performance of his clients during fittings. "The most serious had the intelligence to always wear the same style of underwear." Suits and coats were fitted by tailors in front of the three-view mirrors used by men's tailors. "I taught women to use them for the first time," Mainbocher said. Skirts, blouses, and dresses were fitted by the women fitters. "My clients soon got used to sitting down at some point during the fitting. It was essential for the fit of the dress."

Mainbocher's most direct contact with the public was through the theatre. He had been a great fan of the Boulevard and the Folies in Paris, and the opera was an inexhaustible delight. With *One Touch of Venus,* the musical that starred Mary Martin and began her long, important career in the musical comedy, Mainbocher's clothes intro-duced a luxurious, feminine look that epitomized the casual ease of the rich. In contrast to the styles, really clichés, then prevalent in the movies and theatre, Mainbocher had struck a blow for the elegant individuality that he promoted in his collections. The pale-pink silk

THE CARDIGAN
Mrs. Rodman Wanamaker, photographed in 1942 with her daughter Lynn, wears the jewelled cardigan, Mainbocher's soon-to-be pervasive invention for fuel-rationed wartime nights.

164

Horst
Vogue

Hoyningen-Huené
Harper's Bazaar, 1942

linings for Miss Martin's costumes, never seen by the audience, embodied an idea of expensive comfort that had been lacking previously in American design. (Because he dressed Mary Martin both on and off stage and tied a ribbon around her long neck, she gained a poised polish that epitomized his touch.)

Mainbocher's manner, his exacting values, and open hostility toward Seventh Avenue did not win him many friends. Particular friendships formed in Paris—notably with the editor of *Harper's Bazaar*, Carmel Snow—gave him a play in the fashion magazines that often seemed out of proportion to the space given other American designers. In Paris, he had required that in magazines, photographs or drawings of his models face only other Mainbochers; in New York, he expanded this two-page minimum to four pages. He preempted pages and let no other designer's work be shown with his. Balenciagas might rub shoulders with Diors but not Mainbochers. With each collection, Mainbocher issued a press release as though he were an editor viewing all fashion. For all this he was heavily criticized, but the coverage of his collections in both newspapers and magazines came anyway because of the important influence of his ideas on all levels of fashion.

The following chapters give details of the development of Mainbocher's custom couture and his achievements. Although the thirties in Paris represented the height of his creativity, his American years brought only greater success. (In 1971, the year he retired, his profits were greater than they had ever been before.) Still, as the manufacture of higher-priced dresses, by name designers—Geoffrey Beene, Bill Blass, Norman Norell, James Galanos, Donald Brooks—on Seventh Avenue increased and even Paris succumbed to the demand for ready-to-wear, Mainbocher inevitably became an anomaly. To the end he consistently avoided manufacturing clothes on a wholesale basis.

THE SEPARATES
Princess Paley, Mrs. John C. Wilson, *left*, Mainbocher's premiere vendeuse, shows off his way with wardrobe extenders— dressing up a basic black dress or lining a cardigan. The omnipresent black skirt and white top, *right*, 1942.

Louise Dahl-Wolfe

168

THE SIGNATURE

The Mainbocher look was unmistakable whether in his celebrated design for the WAVES uniform, *left*, 1943, or in his much sought after wedding gowns. The tulle dress shown was made for the wedding of Carmel Wilson, the daughter of his great friend, the *Harper's Bazaar* editor Carmel Snow.

Louise Dahl-W
Harper's Bazaa

Hoyningen-Huené
Harper's Bazaar, 1944

THE SUIT

The Mainbocher suit became the trademark of subdued elegance in the forties. The narrowed beige wool suit, *left*, with beige crepe blouse. Grey wool, *right*.

Hoyningen-Huené
Harper's Bazaar, 1944

By the mid-sixties, Mainbocher's name, closely linked with the extravagances of his most moneyed customers, was seldom mentioned. He had little to offer in the way of the rapid, flashy changes demanded by fashion press. Compared with the styles of the younger designers on Seventh Avenue, Mainbocher's clothes may have seemed monotonous. But they had prevailed for forty years, full of integrity and beauty. For him, the essence of clothing women was personal.

From his first collection in 1930, when he introduced the strapless evening gown, Mainbocher experimented lavishly with evening fashions. His use of fabric was often bold, as in the coral dancing dress of glinting tartan, *opposite*, unexpected cotton shot with Lurex plaid. Mainbocher had great affection for the older, grander fabrics but he was willing to take on the synthetics when they added to the effect.

Louise Dahl-Wolfe

THE WOMEN

In Paris, Mainbocher had specialized in clients who were worldly and used to luxury. While his return to America had begun as an exile from the birthplace of his heart and mind, Mainbocher found he had enormous resources for the austerity of the war years. Although he vociferously resisted the vulgarisms of his countrymen's life, he was drawn to the independence of the women he dressed—a continuity he felt he understood from his pioneer stock. His circle may have been small, his actual influence only slightly greater, but his presence served to certify American fashion and the American woman at a crucial point. That was perhaps the basis for the rapport he set up with the succeeding generations of his clients. They came to him and it was a commerce he ruled mightily. And his stamp of approval, the Mainbocher dress—like the one worn by Mrs. Henry Field kissing her daughter good night on the steps of her Georgetown house—became the emblem of a splendid era and its womanhood.

Joffé
Vogue, 1947

Mainbocher's passion for the theatre found its ultimate expression in this black wool suit, *opposite*, splashed with heavy scarlet paillettes with a skirt—unusual for 1941—fourteen inches off the floor. "A perfect costume for balletomanes," said *Harper's Bazaar*. The suit, recalled Diana Vreeland, then the fashion editor of *Bazaar*, was one of the most beautiful of the decade. In fact, she wore it herself.

Louise Dahl-Wolfe

Black dyed mink, fur new
of importance, here in a late-day
and evening coat by Mainbocher. His ne
the easy, casual shape; the big double collar;

THE LOOK

By the end of his first decade in America, Mainbocher had established his supremacy as a designer. The look was deceptively simple—rich, yet unpretentious. He might dye a mink, *left*, and prescribe its wear for late day. And his finishing touches—the luxurious linings, carefully worked seams and hems, *right*—became a hallmark of quality, the object of status.

Horst
Vogue, 1949

MAINBOCHER'S
SHORT JACKETS

DAY

Mainbocher imprint: jacket to the waistline, just
Above: Double-collar jacket, snug to the ribs
opened here to show the drawstring blouse.
Suit, Oxford grey wool; the silk crepe blouse
a paler grey; both made to order.
Jeweled earrings, both pages, Van Cleef & Arpels.

MAINBOCHER'S CLIENTS

GLORIA VANDERBILT COOPER,
MRS. WYATT COOPER

A member of one of America's most famous and wealthy families, Gloria Vanderbilt Cooper fought to make a life of her own as an actress, writer and painter. Her conversion to Mainbocher was a swift and remarkable one. With as much fervor as she had worn black tights, black sweaters and skirts, Gloria Vanderbilt wore Mainbocher. Her life-style and her extraordinary social prominence were important advertisements for the suitability of the clothes Mainbocher made for her. Her confidence in those clothes led her to greater and greater experiments and Gloria Vanderbilt Cooper was one of the first, as the sixties drew to a close, to wear the eclectic look.

DAISY FELLOWES, MRS. REGINALD FELLOWES
(1890–1962)

Daisy Fellowes epitomized the chic of the thirties. She was most at home in the straight, severe lines of the most extreme *tailleur*. But her taste for simplicity, an almost repetitious attraction to blue and gray, topped off with diamond bracelets, made her a rather eccentric arbiter of fashion. She alone was supposed to have worn the Elsa Schiaparelli lamb-chop hat with aplomb. Because she was witty and had rather a sharp tongue, she tended to terrify even her friends. At the end of the thirties, Daisy Fellowes served briefly as the French editor of *Harper's Bazaar* but she and Carmel Snow quarrelled. Often referred to in the press as "the smartest woman in the world," she was not exclusively Mainbocher's customer but she embodied a certain aspect of high taste that was drawn to his understatement as a foil for jewels or furs or coiffure. A remarkable woman, the author of several books and a grand hostess, she was the daughter of the Duc Decazes et de Gluksburg; her mother was one of the Singer Sewing Machine family. Writing about Daisy Fellowes shorty after her death, James Pope-Hennessy described her as definitely French, a combination of modernity and old aristocracy. About clothes, Daisy Fellowes once said, "Today, when no one can have individual models, it's impossible to wear clothes that are different from everyone else's. We must all wear numbers—Chanel's 36, Patou's 124. But I hope I have sufficient imagination to change what I wear so no one can say, 'Oh, here comes Molyneux's 93!' "

The niece of Alfonso XIII, the last king of Spain, deposed in 1931, and the first wife of the owner of one of Bolivia's richest tin companies, Mme Patino was one of the most glamorous figures of Paris in the thirties, one of the social leaders of the highly influential Latin American continent. Famous for her elaborate parties and her dark good looks, her black hair and white skin, Mme Patino spent extravagant amounts of money on jewels and clothes. She was one of Mainbocher's major customers, buying in depth and indulging his fancy for elaborate fabrics and laces. The habitués of Paris in the thirties, when asked about Paris, invariably said: ". . . And of course, there was Mme Patino." She dressed at Mainbocher.

Man Ray
Harper's Bazaar, 1938

During the forties, Natalia Wilson was the manager of Mainbocher' New York salon, often posing for fashion magazines in his clothes.T daughter of the Grand Duke Paul of Russia, Princess Paley was married to Lucien Lelong, the famous French couturier. Her distinctive beauty, small head, naturally curling hair, and long slender lines we perfectly suited to high fashion. After divorcing Lelong, Princess Pal tried briefly to break into the movies, including one appearance op posite Katharine Hepburn and Cary Grant in *Sylvia Scarlett*. Later, sh married John C. Wilson, the theatrical agent and producer who repr sented both Noel Coward and Alfred Lunt and Lynn Fontanne. She was Mainbocher's *première vendeuse* in America.

Vogue

KATHRYN KING BACHE MILLER, MRS. GILBERT MILLER
(known to her friends as "Kitty")

Kathryn Miller is the last of a generation of American women who had notable reputations as hostesses on both sides of the Atlantic. She was one of the small group of women who invested in Mainbocher's first venture as an American couturier in Paris. The daughter of the remarkable banker and art collector Jules Bache, Kathryn Miller began collecting art as a young woman and her collection of Renoir, Dufy and Goya is one of the finest private collections in the world. Throughout her years as a leader of fashion, Kathryn Miller has been devoted to a simple, uncluttered idea of dress—no jangling bracelets, no beads, dresses with a definitive, quiet line. Married to Gilbert Miller, the highly successful theatrical producer and manager, in 1927, she has maintained—besides a house on Majorca—both a Park Avenue apartment in New York and a house in London, where her famous annual parties are part of a virtually extinct Anglo-American tradition.

Louise Dahl-V

"CEEZEE" GUEST, MRS. WINSTON GUEST
(the former Lucy Douglas Cochrane)

Ceezee Guest was one of the famous debutantes of 1937–38. Her pale blue eyes, pale blond hair and slimness made her one of the great beauties of the years after the war. Her marriage to Winston Frederick Churchill Guest assured her place in the extremely rich, horsey set. In 1962, she appeared on the cover of *Time* magazine. For years, she wore only clothes by Mainbocher, appreciating his beautiful, carefully sewn fabrics. Diana Vreeland said of the dress she wears in this portrait that it was one of the most beautiful dresses she had ever seen.

BARBARA PALEY, MRS. WILLIAM PALEY

Barbara Paley represents the extraordinary triumph of Mainbocher's American years. A junior fashion editor at *Vogue*, she also sometimes modeled the clothes she chose for the magazine. Née Barbara Cushing—the daughter of a famous Boston surgeon, one of three celebrated and beautiful sisters—she found in Mainbocher a teacher who complemented her own quiet, highly refined taste. Mainbocher made the wedding gown for her marriage to Stanley Mortimer. Later married to William Paley, the chairman of the board of the Columbia Broadcasting System, Barbara Paley was named again and again to the list of best-dressed women, came to represent the transition from an aristocratic, moneyed ideal of taste in fashion to an easier, more natural elegance. With her vivid dark eyes, her long neck, her magnificent bearing, and great personal warmth, Barbara Paley reflected the elaborate trust Mainbocher's customers built up around him and the new, more direct relationship he discovered with his clients.

se Dahl-Wolfe

185

MARIE-LAURE, LA VICOMTESSE DE NOAILLES

The daughter of one of France's oldest and most aristocratic families, the Vicomtesse de Noailles was an extravagant patron of all the arts, as famous for her feuds as for her parties. In her salon, a certain sort of chic was promulgated that gave Paris of the thirties its flavor—an aesthetic that somehow linked in her person the seriousness of Gide, the outrageousness of Cocteau, and the studied sophistication of Mainbocher. It was perhaps this mutually shared cerebrality that led her to the American designer. Almost as old as the century, born in 1902, Marie-Laure, her pen-name, ranged widely—insatiable in her experiments with her own work—trying out by turns poetry and painting, even originating a complicated new enamel technique. But her greatest fame was in her help for other artists—and her altogether remarkable appearance.

Hoyningen-Huené

186

ELSIE DE WOLFE, LADY MENDL (1858–1950)

At seventy, Lady Mendl was voted by Parisian couturiers the best-dressed woman in the world. Long a friend of Mainbocher, she was one of his first customers. However, she always left her highly personal stamp on whatever she wore. Lady Mendl was one of the most original and most influential women of fashion in this century. She was the first to tint her hair, every shade from bright pink to vivid green; she was the first to wear accessories that strongly contrasted with the rest of her costume; she turned cartwheels for fun until she was confined to a wheelchair. Tiny, with a brilliantly anarchistic personality, she made her stage debut as Elsie de Wolfe in New York in 1891. However, her greatest fame came as an interior decorator and hostess. Married to Sir Charles Mendl, attaché to the British Embassy in Paris, Lady Mendl's parties at the Villa Trianon in Versailles made her the *grande dame* of Paris. In his charming memoir *The One I Love the Best,* Ludwig Bemelmans remembers Lady Mendl saying to him, during her wartime exile in Hollywood,

> *'For the rest,' I said, looking into that very clear, cruel mirror in my room, 'if I am ugly, and I am, I am going to make everything around myself beautiful. That will be my life. To create beauty! And my friends will be those who create beauty'—and I have held to that every day of my life.*
>
> *And beautiful things are faithful friends, and they stay beautiful, they become more beautiful as they get older. My lovely house, my lovely garden—I could steal for beauty, I could kill for it.*

187

9

MAINBOCHER'S ACHIEVEMENT

Horst
Vogue

"Fashion each season is finding a legitimate place for more and more different fashions . . ." Mainbocher wrote with remarkable prescience in his press release for his spring collection of 1953. His preoccupations, however, remained perennial ones and his superbly tailored suit, *above,* with its short-cropped jacket is timeless in its authority, 1953.

Mainbocher, *left,* photographed in his seventies in his Manhattan apartment with its silver rococo chairs and its proliferation of mirrors, objects, and memorabilia.

Mainbocher's decision to become a couturier grew out of his years as the editor of French *Vogue;* he realized that his critical eye and his feeling for fashion might also serve him as a designer. Although Mainbocher in later years refused to discuss his work in terms of art, he had both in his years as an editor and in those as a designer a definite idea of the woman he intended to dress. The highly innovative designers of the twenties were preoccupied with the style of individual garments, the flair of accessories, and a strongly asserted individuality. Mainbocher believed in an objective good taste, based on good breeding and a highly articulated formality, a rule for every occasion. No situation was unexpected.

Perhaps the real contrast between Mainbocher's role as a designer and the prevailing trends of twentieth-century fashion is his almost total lack of interest in the exotic. The chief exponent of that mode of fashion was, of course, Paul Poiret with what Mainbocher called Poiret's "costumes." In a wider cultural context, this exoticism had been introduced by the Ballet Russe and the orientalism of Leon Bakst; but its content was inherent in the various contrasts introduced in Parisian fashion, particularly the couture.

Mainbocher was not attracted by this eccentricity and his roots as a designer were in the world that Paul Poiret had so openly sought to reject—the sensibility of the Second Empire embodied in the architecture of the Paris Opera, the gowns of Worth, and the Boldini and Sargent portraits of great ladies. For Mainbocher, femininity was epitomized by the lost grandeur of the eighteen-seventies, eighties and nineties, the world of his mother.

But more basic to Mainbocher's career was the essential distinction between the couturier and the designer. Mainbocher was not a designer but a couturier, in the sense of being a dressmaker; he was interested in making dresses for a certain group of women, his clients.

189

The concept of the fashion "designer" evolved in a very different area, related to mass manufacture and the sort of visual and plastic ideas one usually associates with mass culture. Mainbocher was not interested in those ideas and he used the word *designer* only as an inaccurate but workable translation of *couturier*.

Also, Mainbocher's decision to join the couture was made within a very limited but highly lucrative economic system that had surprisingly managed to survive into the twentieth century. Haute couture was patronized chiefly by the rich and, at the point Mainbocher became a couturier, the *demi-mondaine* in particular. The $25,000 annual salary Mainbocher earned as an editor in 1929, though generous, was a fixed one. His choice of couture, within the terms of his experience and contracts, was pragmatically brilliant. He was to make a highly profitable business of what he had been doing all along: telling women what to wear.

As Janet Flanner wrote in 1940, "Bocher's original aim as a dressmaker—which he attributes to his middle western background—was simply to dress women as ladies. He has never discarded his fundamental idea, which perhaps more than anything else has determined the *cachet* of Mainbocher clothes."

When Mainbocher entered the world of the couture it had been vastly altered by the First World War. Before the war, the haute couture produced mainly formal gowns, leaving street dresses and sport clothes to the ladies' dressmaker. Haute couture was not international and only the very richest could afford the elaborate gowns made by Worth and his imitators. This industry, if it may be called an industry, had begun at the court of Louis XIV who, hoping to stablize the nation and rule his nobles, began to dictate fashion down to the last tuck and frill. In spite of the French Revolution, dressmaking continued; fashion dolls, wearing the latest wigs and finery, were sent out of Paris by fast coach to every capital in Europe.

Fashion plates were printed even in the seventeenth century but international journalistic coverage, or fashion reportage collection by collection, began only in the early nineteen twenties. It was started by Henry Sell, a childhood friend of Mainbocher from Chicago, who had been made editor of *Harper's Bazaar* by William Randolph Hearst. *Haute couture* had come to include not only the ballgown but the tennis dress.

The preeminent couture houses in the early thirties—Worth, Paquin, Poiret, Redfern, Callot Soeurs, and Clarint—had very little influence on fashion trends. Their clients tended to be older women who maintained lives of formality more typical of the nineteenth century. These *maisons de couture* did not use cheap materials, were not interested in wearability, and had clients who were willing to pay up to $1,000 for the heavily embroidered and jeweled brocades that were their stock in trade.

THE COAT
One of the first designers to make a coat and dress of the same fabric, Mainbocher favored the large silhouette in outerwear because of the comfort it afforded—often lining the most simple of coats and jackets with fur. Often, he chose men's suiting fabrics for their workability, preferring the shape to make his statement. Always, he gave the coat great importance. The enormous, elongated fur-trimmed coat with matching muff, *right*, from 1938, is one of the boldest statements of this major theme in Mainbocher's work.

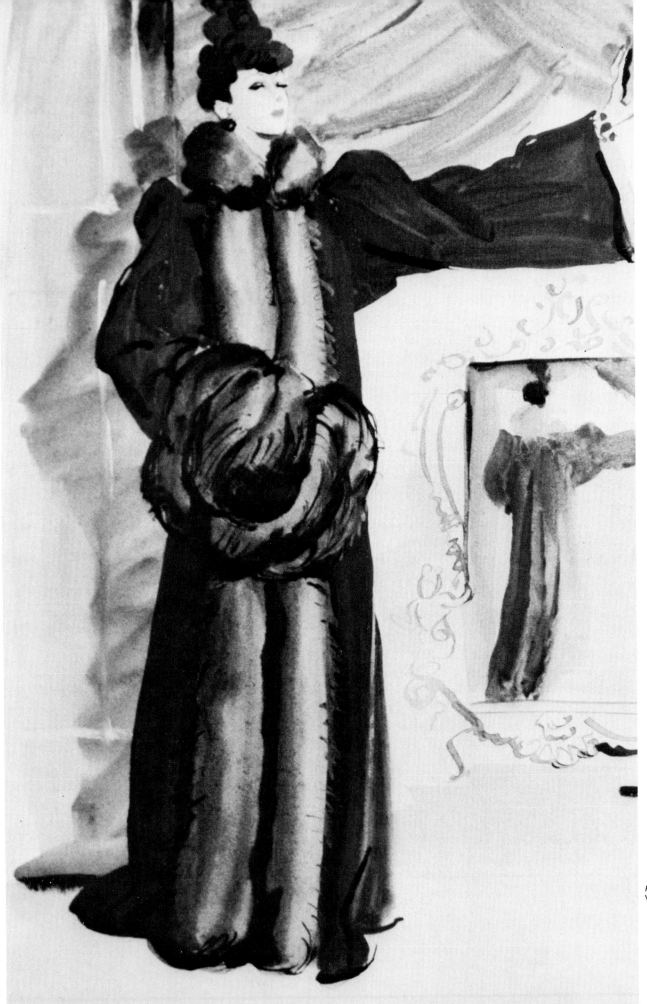

Rene Bouet-Willaumez
Vogue, 1938

In contrast to these old and powerful houses, there were others, fairly conventional but fashionable, who produced tasteful, trustworthy clothes, beautifully cut but not in any sense inventive: Lelong, Goupy, Louiseboulanger, Lyolene, Jane Regny, Bruyère, Martial and Armand, Captain Molyneux, and Maggy Rouff.

Mainbocher joined a third group of houses— individualistic, independent, powerful but not necessarily as financially successful as the larger ones. This group included his admired Vionnet and Augustabernard and also Lanvin, Patou and the two great innovators, Chanel and Schiaparelli.

Of the larger houses, Lelong had the most typical system of management, a system which survives today in most of the couture. Lucien Lelong, the founder, was really the president of a business that employed many designers. The look of the house's clothes was determined by a reviewing board that passed on all the dresses. Lelong was brilliant as a publicist and, as with many houses today, used his perfume to keep his name in the limelight. Over the years, Mainbocher did experiment with a ready-to-wear department attached to the salon, a boutique, and a perfume. But none of these ventures proved successful. Mainbocher clothes were never mass-produced; they could be bought only at Mainbocher.

"Elegant," "simple," "classic," the words, now clichés, most often used to evoke Mainbocher's particular accomplishment, do nonetheless reflect the sensibility that unites all of his work. Because of its self-consciousness, often dogmatic concept, its determined cosmopolitanism, Mainbocher's achievement may seem limited, a brilliant and expensive opportunism. Mainbocher's dresses however are inextricably linked, as symbols, with the affluence of postwar America. For the garment industry and the highly promoted designers who rose to prominence in the sixties, Mainbocher and his work represented a contrary tendency that looked back to a Paris between the wars, fundamentally snob. Mainbocher's definition of couture was too "fashionable," just as "literary," "painterly," and "cinematic," had become terms of disapproval.

"Fashion," in that heightened sense, a cult word that sprang into special use in the rarefied world of photographers and slick magazines was an aesthetic canon that has yet to be adequately explored. Such divergent figures as Marshall McLuhan, the Canadian media-critic, and Roland Barthes, the French linguist, both attempted to use the descriptive tools of the anthropologist to discuss fashion—the wearing of clothes— as a form of popular expression. "Pop fashion" came tumbling after, leaving in its wake the failed influence of haute couture and the dozen or so couturiers like Mainbocher who continued to design for a small group of private clients.

Surprisingly enough, Mainbocher and Coco Chanel (who reopened

MAINBOCHER IN RETROSPECT

As seen in Harper's Bazaar, July 1967.

1933. Bustled and bowed, flowered prints.

1937. The Duchess of Windsor in lamé plaid.

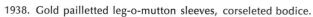

1935. Uneven hemline with giant trailing sash.

1938. The puff-sleeved long black dinner dress.

1938. Gold pailletted leg-o-mutton sleeves, corseleted bodice.

1941. Mrs. John C. Wilson and the famous evening cardigan.

1942. Mainbocher's uniform for the Waves.

1949. The casual dinner skirt with over-blouse.

1950. Herringbone dinner-suit lined in white mink.

1947. The apron dress, silver and crystal embroidery.

1944. Transparent black dinner dress with leg-o-mutton sleeves.

1954. The long jacketed suit with oversized collar.

1951. Cotton petticoat cracked open at neck and skirt.

1953. Tweed suit, cropped jacket.

1956. The paradox of tweed and gingham.

1962. The high-waisted bias crepe.

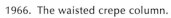

1966. The waisted crepe column.

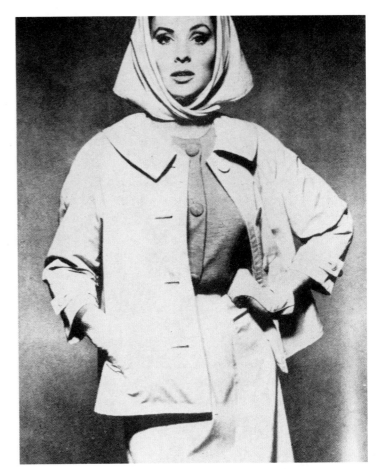

1960. The mink-lined shawl.

1960. Miss Suzy Parker, rainsuit with matching kerchief.

1965. Mrs. Natalie Cushing in a sweater costume.

1966. The cowled evening gown.

her salon in 1953) remained to epitomize the great chic of the thirties. Both had recognized the importance of the easy, casual sporting look and a certain inevitability in the use of fabric, allowing the design to proceed from the material itself. However, Chanel, an extraordinary inventor of a look and life-style that admirably fitted the emancipated women who emerged after World War I, was essentially romantic. Her suits were souvenirs of a moment that she lived to perpetuate. (Is this not the unconscious reason why her clothes play such an important part in Alain Resnais' *Last Year at Marienbad,* a film in which the heroine is caught between the present and a past redolent of the soignée world of the *entre-guerres* kept woman?)

Mainbocher's work, however, was a reaction against the romantic experimentation of the twenties. As an editor, he had been impervious to the avant-garde that delighted Chanel. At one point, she supported the Ballet Russe; Mainbocher preferred the opera in Munich. She piled period on period in the décor of her Paris apartment—ginger suede couches, blazing crystal chandeliers, bronze deer, mirrored stairs. Mainbocher stuck to flat white, brown and his "cool" but elaborate silver chairs from the court of Ludwig of Bavaria. Coco Chanel was delighted by artists, courted by poets. Mainbocher, even as an editor, lived a startlingly insulated life; he was more interested in the patrons of art rather than the artist. He visited the studio of Matisse long after Matisse had been made famous by a pair of rich American collectors. This was a matter of taste, a question of temperament, perhaps, but crucial enough, characteristic enough to explain Mainbocher's role in shaping and defining the style of the thirties, his most influential period.

Before 1925 (the year of the famous exhibition of Art Deco in Paris and coincidentally Mainbocher's first year as the editor of French *Vogue*) the "decorative arts" (a clumsy term that separates "craft" from the fine arts) had little consequence. Photography destroyed this impermanence. Such photographers as Edward Steichen, George Hoyningen-Huené, Cecil Beaton, and Horst used the camera to express an almost perfect sense of beauty. The films of Greta Garbo and Marlene Dietrich expressed a staggering experience of the feminine. There was in these heroines a fatality, an independence from the triviality of the tea dances and cocktail parties of the period that has glamour and sophistication. It is the "rightness" of Iris March in Michael Arlen's novel *The Green Hat* that was evocative of this extraordinary period. And there is, of course, that one almost religiously venerated object that summons up the whole epoch—the silver goddess with flowing, bias-cut draperies atop the grille of the Rolls-Royce (to which Mainbocher's dresses were often compared as expensive status symbols).

Photography gave fashion a new existence, an emphasis on material and form that once had been almost exclusively the province of painting, sculpture, and architecture. Mainbocher as an editor was one of the first to push "fashion" from this expanded viewpoint. As a designer, he carefully worked to embody his "ideas" with great clarity and simplicity, seeking always to identify his dresses with the women who wore them.

Mainbocher's expertise might have remained confined to the rather small world of Parisian couture if one of his customers had not moved into the limelight and history. Wallis Simpson's wedding dress was the most photographed, most copied, most talked about high fashion dress ever made. After it, Mainbocher, although he continued to work within his own very restricted definition of "fashion," had become a celebrity. The "elegance," the "simplicity," the "classicism" of his dresses became watchwords. His work for the next three decades were elaborations on themes he had introduced in the thirties.

Mainbocher has said that he saw his work in terms of musical development, a restatement of themes, closely related. Nowhere is this unity more remarkably evident than in the house drawings done for him by his friend Douglas Pollard, interrupted in the late fifties and early sixties because of Pollard's failing eyesight, and then resumed after a successful operation. The drawings are carefully, beautifully executed, the proportions constant, the silhouette static. But above the changing dresses, suits, coats, there is the same head: the same mouth, careful, red; the pearls; and the hair, a sort of Mayfair bob curled up at ends; the style one might have seen in London or Paris until the middle sixties.

Charles James, another important innovator of the thirties, who made dresses like sculpture to stand on their own, attacked Mainbocher for having taste but no creative power. Mainbocher replied, "Mr. James is madly in love with cut. Anyone who eliminates as much cut as is possible *would* seem familiar to him." *Cut* was anathema to Mainbocher, only drape would suit the fabric and the client.

For Mainbocher, there was nothing new in fashion. He possessed an extreme self-consciousness about his work that caused him to return again and again to his sources. Because of the length of his career and his sureness about his own accomplishment, he often repeated himself and glorified in the women who wore his dresses for twenty or thirty years and returned to have them copied. By day, severe spectator sports dresses or the little black dress. In the evening his ideal was Victorian, the opulence of Empress Eugénie, a parody perhaps of the *ancien régime*. But he found a closer, more intimate expression of that ideal in the paintings of Sargent, which often provided him with ideas.

When Cecil Beaton opened his highly idiosyncratic exhibition of twentieth-century fashion at the Victoria and Albert Museum in London in 1971, Beaton included only a few pieces by Mainbocher. Mainbocher's reputation had reached its nadir; against the con-

temporary tide of costume and tribal gear, his work seemed restrained, unimaginative. Whatever this shift in taste may mean, Mainbocher's achievement is undiminished, a highly realized statement of a stylish stylistic period.

In spite of his classical stance, Mainbocher's innovations as he describes them include: the short evening dress; the famous beaded evening sweaters; bare-armed blouses for suits; the costume-dyed furs (black mink and black sealskin); novel uses for batiste, voile, organdy, piqué, linen, embroidered muslin; the waistcinch; man-tailored dinner suits; bows instead of hats; the principle of the simple dress with lots of tie-ons (shirt-like aprons, changeable jackets); the sari evening dress; the "bump" shoulder (a sort of modified leg-o'-mutton sleeve) on suits and coats; the evening version of the "tennis dress" (a white evening dress with "V" neck and stole); the revival of crinolines; the rain suit.

For Mainbocher himself, there was yet another explanation for his work, a polarity that he identified in terms of his French and German ancestors; the significance of his name linking his European and American pasts. Against the restraint of his style, he posed the theatricality of the opera and the exuberance of the rococo, the aristocratic and highly elaborate fantasies of the eighteenth century. This was the moment in art to which he returned over and over—illogical, decorative, and gay. If he could remark with mock solemnity of his mother's pioneer blood and her birth beside a covered wagon on Indian territory, "It enabled her to survive Biarritz," Mainbocher was indulging his own American version of the baroque—simplicity elaborated beyond recognition in an infinite regress of mirrors and memories.

THE SHAPE

The emergence of Courrèges marked an end to the genteel couture. While Mainbocher had also used hard tailoring to different effect, he innately understood the power of the shape and, in his seventies, returned brilliantly to an almost radical simplicity, playing on his skill with fabric to carry off these white dresses, 1964. The afternoon dress, *below*, is of linen with a gently flaring skirt. The white crepe dinner dress, *right*, is Mainbocher at the top of his form, relying once more on the bias-cut to drape the body brilliantly.

Bob Richardson
Harper's Bazaar, 1964

Alix Jeffry

10

MAINBOCHER'S THEATRE

Hirschfeld

Mainbocher, *left,* in a planning session for *Tiny Alice,* 1964, with the director Alan Schneider and Sir John Gielgud and Irene Worth, the play's stars.

In Paris, Mainbocher had been drawn to the most flamboyant forms of the French music-hall and in 1932 he had done costumes for three acts in a revue, *Les Fleurs des Pois.* In spite of his obsession with the opera, Mainbocher was never drawn to do custumes as such. He despised the atmosphere of Poiret's orientalism and knockoffs of the Ballet Russe and excluded such eclecticism from his work. An avid theatregoer from his youth, Mainbocher was an unembarrassed fan.

He did not design costumes. He dressed actresses. His greatest concern was their working comfort. Their appearance was secondary —after all, wearing a Mainbocher took care of that. For Mary Martin, he installed shell-pink silk linings—a touch the audience had no chance of sharing. For Libby Holman's rare nightclub and concert appearances, he designed a sort of bodyshirt that would not ride up during performances. (The outfit, *above,* is from *Blues, Ballads and Sin-Songs,* 1954).

A mark of status, a dress by Mainbocher on-stage was an added assurance to the star, as actress after actress confessed to women's page editors. Mainbocher's confidence in his judgment of the stage was so great that he seemed to work only for hits, but in reality he worked only for friends. He did the dresses for Tallulah Bankhead's legendary tour of *Private Lives* during the Southern swing of which she would interrupt the famous sofa love scene by pulling a Confederate flag from her bosom and roaring to the audience, about her leading man, "Get this damn Yankee out of here."

Mainbocher also forms part of a footnote to the highly successful Garson Kanin production of *Born Yesterday,* 1945. Mainbocher designed the dresses for the tryouts with Jean Arthur who subsequently dropped out to be replaced by Judy Holliday. Mainbocher apparently did not care for the replacement and Judy Holliday marched into stardom—*not* wearing Mainbocher.

Blithe Spirit, 1941: Clifton Webb and Leonora Corbett, *above*, acted in the Noel Coward comedy with Peggy Wood. Leonora Corbett, the British actress, was one of Mainbocher's favorite performers although she was little seen on the Broadway stage. Her blonde good looks and worldly, witty style were an exuberant foil for his restrained dresses. The revival was produced by John C. Wilson, the husband of Princess Paley who worked as Mainbocher's chief saleswoman.

One Touch of Venus, 1943: Mary Martin gave one of the most memorable performances of the forties in this musical. "My Heart Belongs to Daddy" stopped the show. But Mainbocher's carefully thought out gowns gave her the particular luster of glamour. Mainbocher's transformation of Martin, including using a ribbon to play up her long, thin throat, is a well-known show biz story. His surprising use of pink, a theatrical strategy he would return to again and again, did the trick.

Call Me Madam, 1950: Ethel Merman, as party-giver and political big spender Perle Mesta, made quite a hit of this Luxembourg romp. While part of the charm of the musical was Merman's loud-voiced romantic shenanigans, Mainbocher's elaborate wardrobe for the star, complete with diplomatic sashes, took the edge off the middle-aged role and gave Merman a finish she had seldom had before.

Collection of the New York Public Library

Wonderful Town, 1953: Rosalind Russell in this musical adaptation of *My Sister Eileen* was virtually a one-woman Mainbocher fashion show. Russell, a stage-and-movie clotheshorse, switched from one expensive dress to the next with obvious relish. "I am eternally grateful," she wired the designer from the Winter Garden on opening night, "for your great help in creating my Ruth."

The Great Sebastians, 1956: Lynn Fontanne and Alfred Lunt, the American theatre's greatest husband-and-wife team, played a couple of down-and-out sleight-of-hand con-men caught in the Soviet take-over of Czechoslovakia in 1948. In one of their last appearances, the pair moved out into the audience to play some of their mind-reading tricks. Fontanne's gowns, showy and rich, were not particularly appropriate for the character but they made Fontanne's exit a blaze of glory.

206

The Sound of Music, 1955: Mary Martin capped her career in Rodgers and Hammerstein musicals with this long-running hit. Playing a nun who turns singer, Martin was dressed plainly except for her wedding. Pulling out all the stops, Mainbocher out-did himself with the dress—echoing the traditional coif and habit—but carrying the romance of his famous wedding dresses to an ultimate spectacular realization. Widely photographed, the cover of *Life,* the dress became one of the most-remembered theatrical costume designs of the century.

Tiny Alice, 1964: Irene Worth and John Geilgud gave powerful performances in this murky Edward Albee play—overladen with imagery and philosophical senten-tiousness. Worth played the richest woman in the world and her choice of Main-bocher to dress her was an obvious one. The scene, *above,* is a confrontation be-tween Worth, wearing a black lace negligee, and her priest, a moment as close to opera as Mainbocher was to get.

207

Mainbocher's Sources

Mainbocher had a disciplined and critical eye. While he depended very little on the past or his contemporaries for direct inspiration, he did acknowledge certain forces at work in his design. Among these were the image of femininity embodied in the paintings of Boldini and Sargent; the revival of the eighteenth century by Winterhalter in his paintings of the Empress Eugénie; and the popular images of Charles Dana Gibson's "Gibson Girl." When Mainbocher showed the nipped-in waist in his 1938–1939 collections, many observers were reminded of the illustrations in *Little Women* and French fairy tales. However this nostalgia was premature in the Victorian revival, such as it was, and the New Look had to wait until after World War II. Perhaps the greatest and most pervasive influence on Mainbocher was Mme Vionnet; her use of the bias cut and draping were to be the underlying motif of all Mainbocher's design. In fact, the Hoyningen-Huené photograph of a Vionnet dress has profound echoes of Mainbocher's work of the fifties and sixties, when his return to simplicity was complete.

McCardell

BY SALLY KIRKLAND

CONTENTS

INTRODUCTION

Bill Cunningham

"Drop everything!" an agitated dress manufacturer shouted to his designer. "There's a girl up the street making a dress with no back, no front, no waistline, and my God, no bust darts!"

The year was 1938, the "street," New York's Seventh Avenue, and the unnerving dress was the instantly successful "Monastic," so named because of its robelike appearance before the wearer belted it in to make her own waistline. As for the "girl," that was 33-year-old sportswear designer Claire McCardell, a quiet, mild-mannered, good-looking blond who was simply making the first of many stylish waves destined to carry her right to the top of the fashion industry in the next decade.

Many think that Claire McCardell was the greatest fashion designer this country has yet produced. Certainly she was the most innovative, independent and indigenous of American designers. Norman Norell thought so. "She should have had that first Coty Award for American fashion back in 1943 instead of me," he said in 1972, adding that he would have been happy to accept it the following year when Claire did in fact receive it. "Don't forget," he went on, "Claire invented all those marvelous things strictly within the limits of mass production. I worked more in the *couture* tradition—expensive fabrics, hand stitching, exclusivity, all that—but Claire could take five dollars worth of common cotton calico and turn out a dress a smart woman could wear anywhere."

Claire had studied and respected the tools and traditions of French *haute couture* dressmaking, but by the mid-thirties she felt that those clothes were too structured, formal, and—if copied verbatim—too costly to buy and keep up for busy young women like herself. Along with Claire, they were moving fast into a sophisticated world where keeping house was just one activity among many—jobs, active sports, spur-of-the-moment travel, and city–country commuting. They wanted their clothes to move right along with them.

Using herself as a "continuous experiment," Claire began making things with the sportswear feeling of ease, naturalness, and youth—even for dress-up occasions. At first many of her ideas wound up back in her own closet after a brief sortie through the nonplussed showrooms of her employers; but Claire stayed with her credo. Then World War II threw American fashion on its own with a double dilemma—to design without the accustomed help of Paris and within the limits of fabric restrictions. From that time, Claire's look became "The American Look."

When *Vogue* magazine, in 1950, wanted to define the prevailing American look of the forties, they chose these McCardell jerseys and leotards, documented as "the frugal, spare-silhouetted American primitive look," photographed by Irving Penn in this astringent view.

1

THE APPRENTICESHIP

Fledgling fashion expert, Claire McCardell aged 5, *above*, confidently tilts her shoulder-wide hat at a rakish angle. Established designer McCardell at 38, *opposite*, wears a workmanlike suit for a Louise Dahl-Wolfe portrait upon the occasion of her winning the prestigious Coty Award.

Claire McCardell was born May 24, 1905, in Frederick, Maryland, a small town that has its own corner on Americana, with its crisply red and white Federalist buildings surrounding the historic old Court Square where Francis Scott Key practiced law and the legendary Barbara Frietchie waved her country's flag.

The McCardells (in Gaelic, "son of mighty valor") had lived in that part of Maryland since their early nineteenth-century arrival from County Antrim, Ireland. The first McCardells had settled comfortably on a large farm, complete with slaves, in Williamsport, some thirty miles from Frederick. Their sons and daughters, first-generation Americans, married into old Maryland colonial families. By the 1850s, when potato famine emigrés began to flood the Atlantic coast, the McCardells had given up Catholicism for Protestantism, and farming for commerce in the nearby town.

Claire's father, Adrian Leroy McCardell—like his father before him—was president of the Frederick County National Bank. In addition he was an elder and Sunday school superintendent in the Evangelical and Reformed Church, a 33rd Degree Mason, a state senator, and a member of the State Tax Commission. He was as reserved as he was busy, and Claire probably inherited her shyness from him.

Eleanor, her mother, was a southern belle from Jackson, Mississippi, who kept a portrait of General Robert E. Lee on her parlor wall until her death in 1968. Mrs. McCardell was spirited, gregarious, and alive to the larger world.

Clothes were an early fascination for Claire, reflecting an interest of all the McCardell women. (Sailing to New Orleans, her great grandmother had brought along three silk dresses, one so stiff and full that it stood on its own in the stateroom during the long voyage.) From her mother's discarded fashion magazines, Claire cut out her first sophisticated paper dolls. Mrs. McCardell encouraged this interest and made Claire think about a larger life of her own, even though few women of the time had big city careers—particularly daughters of small-town bank presidents. Hurrying home from school when Annie, the dressmaker, came, Claire would sit alongside her at the treadle-powered sewing machine, observing every step of the intricate construction.

There was also the world she shared with her three younger brothers. They learned early that she could look after herself in the neighborhood sports—baseball, sledding and skating—where the girls were outnumbered. She earned the nickname of "Kick" for her efforts. Reminded once of her tomboy days in Frederick, Claire said she must have subconsciously learned that "some clothes, pretty though they might be, just got in the way when one was climbing a tree, or leading the pack in a game like 'Run, Sheep, Run!'" Clothes, she thought, should look pretty without "getting in the way."

By the time she was in high school, Claire was making most of her own dresses, some based on the sketches she made at the National Theatre in nearby Washington, D.C. Annie the dressmaker thought that many of these creations were too flimsily sewn, but Claire insisted "they achieved a certain effect." High school lessons made little dent on her, except geometry, which she used later in her designs. Graph paper checks later became one of her trademarks, turning up in her dress fabrics, personal stationery, and even in the packaging for a projected perfume.

To please her father, Claire gave higher education a try at Hood, a liberal arts college for women in Frederick. About chemistry, she remembers chiefly the lesson that "acid can burn the human skin; the blisters on my hand were proof." After two years, the professors, her father and Claire agreed to call off her college education. Moreover, she persuaded her parents—her father especially needed reassurance —to let her study fashion design in Manhattan at the prestigious Parsons School of Design, then called the New York School of Fine and Applied Arts.

Along with other out-of-town girls at Parsons, then located on Broadway at Eightieth Street, Claire lived at the Three Arts Club on West Eighty-Fifth Street. Her roommate Mildred Boykin, later also a well-known sportswear designer under the name of Mildred Orrick, was a soft-spoken Virginian with a solicitous mother who supervised the girls' settling in.

Claire came to Parsons expecting to sew, but she was soon disappointed. The initial emphasis was on art, not dressmaking. Mildred Boykin remembered her surprise when they drew their first supplies— gum erasers, drawing and charcoal pencils, rather than cutting shears and muslin. Claire gritted her teeth through the hours of life class, the museum research, and the field trips to sketch such New York scenes

As a school girl, Claire wears a conventional Peter Pan collar and prim hairdo for yearbook picture, *left*. The portrait below by an artist friend, Chester Slack, done while she was a Parsons student in New York, shows a more sophisticated and timeless view of Claire.

as the old Childs cafeteria and the Central Park Zoo. On the other hand, she found that fashion illustration or just plain sketching other people's designs—most notably the French—was one direct way to learn fashion. After all, something was bound to be gained from her studies in color, form and anatomy by the time she had graduated to cutting and draping clothes on the human figure.

Claire meanwhile had come across a surer way of learning about clothes. The wealthy patrons of the Three Arts Club would pass along their old dresses to the residence to be used in amateur theatricals or to be sold for as little as five dollars to the students. Many had Paris labels, and Claire learned something from every dress she took apart —either as costumes for some performance or to fit on herself. "There was a scramble to grab off the best Chanels and Patous from the discarded finery," Mildred Boykin recalled. "They were real bargains and scarcely worn. When we sat in a box at the opera we were most elegantly attired, even though we went there and back on the subway. People *did* ride the subway in evening clothes in those days."

Members of the board of the Three Arts Club would lend their opera boxes for the evening. Theatres would send unsold tickets to the club a few hours before curtain time to "paper" the house. (Claire saved her programs and by the end of the 1925–26 season, she had accumulated over fifty.) Sunday teas at the club attracted such celebrities as Lucrezia Bori, Jane Cowl, and Ruth Gordon (an ex-club member). "We were overcome with the proximity of the great but somehow managed not to rattle the teacups," Mildred remembers.

At a time when Paris was considered the source of fashion, Parsons School was of course totally French-oriented. Most of Parsons' instructors were French. There was a branch in Paris, on the sixteenth-century Place des Vosges, a magnificent square of residences built for the nobles of Henry IV's court. For Claire and her generation, Paris was the city of life and light, a mecca for expatriate artists and writers. In 1926, Claire and Mildred made the pilgrimage, spending their second Parsons year in study at the Place des Vosges. With a third Parsons friend, French-born Joset Legouy (later Joset Walker), they shared Left Bank quarters. All three were to be in the vanguard of American sportswear design. The trio's good looks, contagious high spirits, and passion for clothes and places to wear them were very much a part of Paris in the twenties. "We danced all over Paris," Mildred recalled, "from the street dances on the outskirts to the public balls at the opera."

Van Day Truex, the artist-designer who was to be president of Parsons, was their special guide and instructor. He recalled the three as "a kicky bunch of girls, very popular with the French but quite a handful for me, a timid young man just a few years older than they."

Van Day Truex took his charges off to the Cluny Museum, a trove of medieval treasures, to study the colors in the famous tapestries. As

McCardell

an assignment, he told them to match the ochre in one of the hangings with any material at hand and he was delighted when the trio later produced a little pile of yellow dust that duplicated the tapestry's strong yellow perfectly. A poultry market had supplied the material.

Paris in the twenties was the pulse of fashion, the nexus of modern dress. Corsets had been dropped, hair cropped, hems shortened. Coco Chanel was the fashion rebel with her use of sports fabrics such as jersey, dressed-up tweeds, easy, casual shapes and her amusing, frankly fake jewels. Mme Vionnet, Claire's idol, was revolutionizing modern dressmaking with the bias cut.

Four times a year, after the private clients and wholesale buyers had been taken care of, the Parsons students were invited to the salons to see the couture collections. When at the close of the season, the couture houses sold their sample dresses for as little as ten to fifteen dollars—coats and suits were somewhat more—Claire bought as many Vionnets as she could afford no matter what their condition. She would lovingly dissect them, much like the proverbial little boy with an alarm clock, and then put them back together. Mildred remembers,

> the mannequins of the late twenties were bosomless. So were we. It mattered little to us that some of the dresses we acquired were shopworn. We imagined our wardrobes quite superb from head to knee. From there down, not so good. The cost of silk stockings was prohibitive so we bought inferior quality. I even remember seeing cotton lisle with runs on some of the mannequins in the couture showings.

But years later Claire, writing about the transformation of women by fashion in the twenties, did not mention Vionnet or the Ballet Russe or the splendid mannequins with their cotton stockings. Rather:

> The big change came in the twenties. Novelists of the time talked about it. Ernest Hemingway describes Lady Brett in The Sun Also Rises: "She wore a slip-over jersey sweater and a tweed skirt, and her hair brushed back like a boy's. She started all that." The interesting fashion point is just where Brett wore this "look" she had started. On a brisk breezy day at the yacht club? No. On a golf course? No. In a country setting? Anything but. At the exact moment the narrator describes her, she is sitting at a bar in Paris. The time: 1926. Now notice the line: "She started all that."

Claire was already thinking about starting "all that" herself.

And in the spring of 1927, Claire caught a glimpse of the heady changes that lay ahead in her lifetime. One afternoon while drinking café au lait at the Dôme with Mildred, the two were swept off in a taxi by a friend from the Paris Herald to Le Bourget field, where Lindbergh was about to land after flying the Atlantic. Mildred recalled:

> Someone had spotted the plane in the dark sky. A shout went up. Everyone started running. An American sprinted ahead. He reached the plane first, grabbed Lindbergh, hugged him and screamed "Hello,

*St. Louis" and collapsed from the effort and the ecstasy of being first.
By that time, Claire and I had reached the plane. It escapes me why it
was so important for us to touch the plane but we did. Between us we had
lost the heel of a shoe, a hat, and our friend, in the wild screaming tornado.*

After the hubbub died down, the two started walking back to Paris but were rescued by Harry of Harry's Bar, who had fortuitously hired a taxi and brought along a supply of whiskey for the slow trip through the crowd.

Back at Parsons in New York for her third and final year, Claire's grades which had been mostly A's and B's suddenly turned up C's and D's, although the curriculum was now directed totally to fashion design, including a course in clothes construction. Clearly, Claire was finished with school.

After graduation, she took a small apartment in Murray Hill with Mildred Boykin and Mildred's mother. The job hunt began. Mildred almost immediately landed a job as a secretary-assistant to Natacha Rambova, the exotic stage and movie costume designer who had been married to Rudolph Valentino. But Claire was not so lucky. For two months she scouted all the likely places in search of work as a fashion illustrator or a behind-the-scenes sketcher. In answer to an ad in *Women's Wear Daily*, she tried out as a samplemaker on Seventh Avenue. A "one-day disaster" she later recalled. Finally, Claire settled for a job painting rosebuds on lampshades for a shop on Twenty-third Street at twenty dollars a week. Two months of rosebuds were followed by temporary modeling stints in Altman's French Room. Her salary: still twenty dollars a week.

At this point, Claire succumbed to a flat purse and a bad cold. She went home to Frederick to recover and possibly to forget the whole New York scene. In a couple of weeks, however, she was back in New York ready to try again—this time with the whole family's blessing and a small allowance.

Not long after, Gay Roddy, a fabric designer and friend from the Three Arts Club, did Claire the first of several big favors. Gay was determined that Claire would work in the garment industry and she persuaded Sol Pollack, a knitwear manufacturer, to hire her as an assistant designer at forty-five dollars a week.

Pollack remembered the young Claire with a shake of his head. "She was so shy, so gangly, and she walked sort of hunched over, like she thought she was too tall." (The famous McCardell slouch in embryo.)

But Claire's posture was not all that bothered Pollack. Claire's designs weren't going well. After a few months, Pollack let her go with a lecture delivered in the showroom. If she wanted to become a success, he told her, she should worry about clothes for other women rather than for herself. In the next booth was the buyer for Marshall Field, who overheard the confrontation and said, "Sol, you've just given that woman $100,000 worth of advice!"

Homeward bound on the *Leviathan* in 1927 with Mildred Orrick (at right), Claire wears her marked down Patou cape inspired by the gendarmes. "Joset thought it was dreadful," recalls Mildred. "She still talks about the red-lined cape flapping in the wind. But Claire and I thought it was absolutely super."

Mark Sha

2

THE MAKING OF A DESIGNER

The almost nightly galas, *above*, on her European trips caused clothes problems which Claire partially solved with jersey separates like the halter and culottes, *opposite*. They packed small and could be changed around, but when Claire showed them to store buyers in 1934, they shied away from them.

Claire McCardell left Sol Pollack's knitwear house with $100,000 worth of advice she was not about to take. But later she admitted that she deserved to get the sack. She had experience neither in knitwear production techniques nor in designing for the mass market.

Her school friend Gay Roddy once more came to the rescue, sending Claire to Robert Turk, a young designer just starting his own business. He took Claire on as assistant of all work, a job that included sketching, modeling, shopping for buttons and belts—any chore that came up. Turk's own business didn't quite make it and he went back to designing, this time for Townley Frocks. He took his young assistant along.

A year later, when the next fall collection was barely begun, Turk drowned in a sailing accident on Memorial Day weekend. There was no time to find and bring in another designer, so a grief-stricken Claire had to go on in the best thirties movie-musical tradition. And she did—with the help of an adoring chorus of sample hands. (One of them, Bessie Susterstic, who stayed with Claire during her entire career, remembers those days: "She was just a girl. She used to come to work in a tricot and skirt with her hair in a long braid down her back." That first McCardell collection may not have lit up the sky, but it did well enough to ensure Claire the post of designer at Townley for seven years, until the firm closed its doors in 1938.

The Townley letterhead showed a lady in a classic shirt dress, golf club swung high. For the garment industry the sportswear designation covered not only clothes for active sports but also for a new genre called "spectator sports." This category included patio pajamas, "sun backs" and dresses with jackets that looked suspiciously like street clothes. The Townley "sportswear" collections in Claire's day were largely devoted to such almost-town costumes.

Shaw

Claire loved "important" belts. When she couldn't find one dramatic enough, she designed it herself, as in this 1938 version of the gaucho's broad brass-studded leather cinch. She showed it with both evening culottes and a cotton shirt dress.

Louise Dahl-Wolfe
Harper's Bazaar, 1938

223

Seventh Avenue in the thirties was an uneasy amalgam of cheap labor, old world skills and the prospect of big money,* even in the midst of worldwide depression. Life on Seventh Avenue was far from the last word in gracious living. There was little aura of the art collecting, globe-trotting, hostessing designer of today. The atmosphere, in fact, was straight out of Jerome Weidman's novel *I Can Get It For You Wholesale*. However, there was a fringe benefit for most designers in established firms—the obligatory leisurely trips to Paris each year to buy models. "I did what everybody else did, copied Paris," Claire observed.

Claire often traveled with her friend Joset, and when they had finished their Paris scouting they often managed side trips to London, Venice, Salzburg or the south of France. In Paris they sometimes agreed on a joint purchase. "Two hundred dollars would get you a Schiaparelli," Joset remembered fondly, "and for that you could sketch up a storm." But the designer who enchanted Claire most was Alix, later Mme Grès. Alix's softly draped jersey—in wool as well as silk—influenced her, just as Vionnet's beautiful bias-cut dresses had in Claire's student days in the twenties.

In general, however, Claire got some of her best ideas from the travel itself, rather than the couture collections. She usually tried them out on herself first—"solving problems" as she called it. A style was beginning to evolve: functional, comfortable, unextravagant, but with dash and imagination. Some examples—after shivering on a moonlight cruise in a splendid but flimsy evening wrap, she made a long warm one in tweed with a hood. Icy ski weekends produced a snug wool hood. She later added one to wartime street suits. A long sweaterlike dinner dress was the result of country evenings in drafty farmhouses.

Tired of traveling with the burden of a steamer trunk (most people were still insisting on wardrobe trunks) and piles of suitcases, she made costumes in separate parts that could be packed in a small suitcase and switched around for variety and different degrees of formality. For instance, she made a low-backed halter top, a covered-up top, long and short skirts, a culotte. All were simply cut, made of black ribbed jersey with no trimming. With the right accessories, these separates rose to almost every occasion. But they were a puzzlement to many department stores. Admittedly, most stores were selling separate tweed jackets, sweaters and skirts in sportswear departments, but these day-or-night matching pieces of Claire's were something new. Where did they belong? And what if a shop were left with all size 12 tops and size 14 skirts? Claire had to wait for merchandising to catch up.

Claire's dress-up separates finally made it into the stores in 1941. *Vogue* showed these six pieces of wool jersey and rayon taffeta (three blouses, pants, short skirt and long skirt—here combined in three costumes) which cost altogether about $100 and could be combined in at least ten different ways for as many different occasions.

* In 1931 the women's and children's garment industry grossed over 1.3 billion dollars. By 1950 the gross had grown to 4.7 billion and in 1974 to more than 11.4 billion.

John Rawlings
Vogue, 1941

225 *McCardell*

(Claire's steamer trunk was but a memory in 1956 when I, *Life* fashion editor, saw dramatic proof of her ability to travel light but in considerable plenty. The photographer Mark Shaw and I were on assignment for the magazine in Austria when Claire joined us for a few days of her vacation. The day she arrived with one medium-sized suitcase and a duffle bag, a frantic cable came from *McCall's*. They were excerpting parts of Claire's book, *What Shall I Wear?*, and needed *immediately* a color photograph of Claire looking as if she were at work surrounded by a good part of her collection. Fortunately, Mark Shaw was highly acceptable to their art director and I was glad to give him the day off, but what about the rest of it? Even with the beds moved out, Claire's room in Vienna's elegant old Bristol Hotel didn't look much like 550 Seventh Avenue. The unflappable Claire organized a colorful corner with what appeared to be three dozen exciting outfits from those two suitcases. They didn't even need pressing!)

Aside from the separates, Claire introduced several other innovations which failed to charm buyers at first. The dirndl skirt was one. Like many other travelers to Austria in the mid-thirties, Claire had fallen for the gathered all-around cotton skirts worn by women and children. They were comfortable and young (the name means little girl), and she tried them out in city versions, but without success at first. "Two years later they were all over the place," wailed her boss at Townley, Henry Geiss, who was in a constant state of alarm over these maverick tendencies in his young designer: Why couldn't Claire just copy Paris or at the very least confine herself to established classics?

In spite of Mr. Geiss's gloom his business managed to stay afloat. Claire's salary was now $150 a week, enough for the rent on her own apartment in Murray Hill and the purchase of an old farmhouse in Frenchtown, New Jersey, near many of her friends in fashion and journalism—among them, designer Vera Maxwell, S. J. Perelman, *Newsweek*'s Ernest Lindley, playwright Jack Kirkland, Louise Dahl-Wolfe, Kay Silver, the fashion editor of *Mademoiselle* and her husband, architect George Sakier, and particularly close friends "Tony" Williams, president of MacDonald-Heath custom tailors, and his wife Peggy, the daughter of Best and Company's president, Philip LeBoutillier.

The leggy, blond Claire and her own distinctive way of dressing began to attract the attention of the fashion press. *Women's Wear Daily* reported her on the ski slopes of Stowe, Vermont, in a rough peasant cape she had bought at a farmer's market in France. And newsmen were there to photograph her when she returned from France wearing a reindeer coat, the first seen in America.

Not only was Claire adding a personal dimension to the accepted concept of sportswear, but she added something new to her show-

Andrew Wald

Claire's favorite model, Connie Wald, now one of Beverly Hills' best-dressed, still wears this 1956 McCardell linen and cotton evening outfit on special occasions. And in line to borrow it, when not in use, are friends Rosalind Russell and Audrey Hepburn.

room presentation. She chose a house model, Connie Polan (who later married Jerry Wald, the distinguished movie producer), who was the embodiment of her own unique look. Most house models were chosen not for their style or personality but because they had figures which were a perfect size, usually 12. It didn't matter that they were apt to be a grandmother, a retired chorus girl or the bookkeeper's sister. But Connie was no bookkeeper's sister. Her measurements were also Claire's: tall (5'7"), long of waist and limb, with a small high bust, tiny rib cage, small waistline but some hips and even a little tummy. Claire maintained that "tummies are beautiful, like Botticelli's Venus." *Harper's Bazaar* referred to her "stomachy" skirts as effective camouflage for a bulge.

Connie recalls that the first thing Claire did was to eliminate her bra and girdle. Next she gave Connie a hairdo like her own, pulled back in a little knot with short bangs and tendrils that she cut with the sample shears in her workroom. Then Claire taught her her own slouching lope of a walk—shoulders sloping, hands deep in the side pockets and hips thrust a bit forward. That stance is taken for granted now as *the* model's walk. Back then it was just the opposite of the usual mincing, wheeling model's walk. As a final Buck's County touch when the sun-back dresses and long patio culottes were shown, Connie strolled into the showroom barefoot.

Significantly, Claire's first commercial success, in 1938, came from an Algerian costume she had made for herself and did not think anyone else would like. She had worn it to a Beaux Arts Ball, liked its flowing lines, and had made a street length version in red wool, cut completely on the bias with no waistline—a tent until belted, when it did nice things for the figure in an easy-does-it sort of way. But no woman was likely to know that until she tried it on. It had no "hanger appeal." Claire put it away on her personal rack in the studio and went off on a holiday.

While she was gone, a buyer from Best and Company came looking for an "exclusive" to feature in an early fall advertisement. The regular Townley line had been well picked over. There were no "exclusives" left. In desperation the salesman wandered back to Claire's room and half-heartedly presented the shapeless dress hanging there.

The buyer ordered a hundred dresses—fifty in wool, fifty in faille. Best's advertising staff named it "The Monastic" and ran a full-page ad in *The New York Times* on a September Sunday. By Monday afternoon the buyer had phoned an order for two hundred more and from then on orders outstripped production.

Unfortunately, poor Mr. Geiss did not enjoy all the business generated at last by one of Claire's designs. Besides his production problems, he was vainly trying to stem the tide of "piracy": the Monastic had scored such a success and was so easy to make that

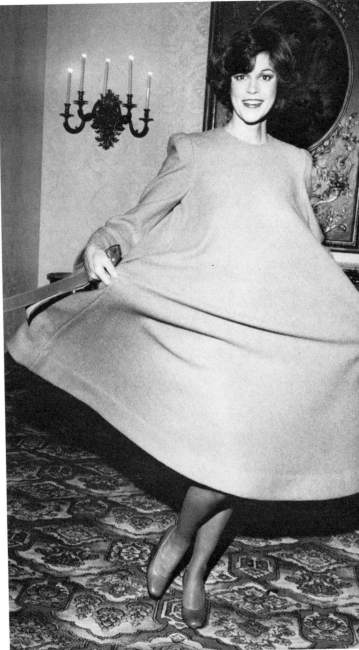

Bill Cunningham

228

Model Anne Coleman twirls in the 1938 monastic dress in 1974 retrospective fashion show. Its bias cut (on the diagonal instead of straight up and down) gives the fabric elasticity so that the voluminous tent shape (*opposite page*) clings softly without bulk when belted.

Above right. She is joined by another top model, Tasha, in a fifties McCardell which she found in a thrift shop and wears daily.

McCardell

Opposite. Claire's casual comfortable approach toward dress-up clothes began in the thirties with dresses like this easy fitting silk in a bright sporty plaid. *Right*. She wore it with the brass-buttoned red gabardine evening coat cut as simply as a shirtwaist dress.

Mark Shaw

cheap copies mushroomed overnight. The garment industry's trade organization, The Fashion Originator's Guild, did make an effort in those days to police its members and department stores, but each copy was treated as a separate case. "It was every day to the Guild, every day to the Guild," moaned Geiss. Finally, copying got completely out of control and the Monastic was declared an "open item." It could be made and bought anywhere for the devastating price of thirty dollars a dozen.

The copies didn't bother Claire. She continued the loose silhouette in her next collection, cruise wear. But it was too late for Geiss, who claimed to have lost all he had made on the first Monastic. Feeling he was on the verge of physical collapse, he closed his business. But the Monastic's enormous, unexpected success pointed to a far more casual, easy look for the American woman. And it was prime evidence of a new and independent American design talent.

The innovator, nevertheless, was out of a job. But not for long. Hattie Carnegie, whose wholesale and retail establishments were about the bluest chips in high fashion, had kept an interested eye on Claire's work during her ups and downs at Townley. She brought Claire and her whole Seventh Avenue task force in to design "Workshop Originals" and gave her *carte blanche*. Unfortunately, most of Hattie's customers didn't go along with this new wave. "They thought Claire's things 'too plain for the money,' " says Connie, adding with the arrogance of a perfect size 10, "Besides, those rich size 38s needed to be poured and stitched right into their clothes."

Norman Norell, who was also designing at Carnegie at the time, recalls that Miss Carnegie, who did not often care to be told she was wrong, took matters into her own hands. Ladies were apt to find they had ordered a Claire McCardell without knowing it. Diana Vreeland, then fashion editor at *Harper's Bazaar*, had brought in some French jersey in beige for a "little two-piece Chanel kind of uniform." She got a one-piece McCardell instead. Fortunately she liked it, asked to meet Claire, and grew to be one of her staunchest and most powerful admirers in the decade that followed.

Not Gertrude Lawrence, however. The English actress and musical comedy star was a stickler about her clothes for the stage, and she was not at all amused when Hattie chose a plain little McCardell number for her glamorous 1939 role in *Skylark*. Norell saved the day by whipping up a substitute that was plain—but beaded.

Shortly thereafter, Claire and Carnegie parted amicably. Claire had not lost sight of her main ambition—to make attractive and practical clothes for all American women, not just those who could afford Carnegie prices. For the rest of her career, she incorporated in her own work the custom details she had learned. A very smart cookie was Miss Carnegie and a girl could do a lot worse than spend a year and a half under her tutelage.

Bruyère

Frock of beige and brown, with yoke cape.

Harper's Bazaar, *1930*

A typical complicated Paris dress of the 1930s *above* by Bruyère contrasts with a simple wraparound evening dress (*right*) which Claire McCardell designed when she was on the staff of Hattie Carnegie. The price of both, however, was the same— high.

George Platt Lynes
Harper's Bazaar, 1939

233 McCardell

John Rawlings
Vogue, 1945

3

THE AMERICAN DECADE

Toni Frissell Collection—
Library of Congress
Harper's Bazaar, 1949

Claire McCardell was her own best model. Above, for *Harper's Bazaar,* she wore a pretty dotted swiss apron she designed to be made by the crafts shop of The Lighthouse for the Blind.
Opposite. And for *Vogue,* she designed and modeled a "future dress" in 1945. Made of sporty brown shantung, it was described as "merely two huge triangles that tie at the neck, front and back."

Part One: 1940–1945

We (designers) specialize in what we like best, in what we do best and in what satisfies us most deeply. For me it's America—it looks and feels like America. It's freedom, it's democracy, it's casualness, it's good health. Clothes can say all that.

Claire McCardell
What Shall I Wear?

In January 1940, Claire McCardell, still a designer at Hattie Carnegie, was one of an intrepid little band of fashion folk from the United States who attended the Paris couture shows—despite the war. They sailed on the U.S.S. *Washington,* its sides hung with illuminated American flags, to the neutral port of Genoa where they entrained for Paris, carrying emergency rations of food and drink. It was the last French collection any of them would see until 1946. It was the last one ever for Claire.

Two years later, America herself was in the war, but even earlier her fashion industry had begun to stand on its own young legs.

It was a wonderfully gutsy, fast-moving time in American fashion, particularly for Claire and her fellow sports designers. They welcomed the chance to design for American women without the elegant help of the French. Almost in celebration, they produced a genre of all-day-long, any-occasion clothes which were casual and easy fitting—like active sportswear, but elegant and imaginative enough to inspire American women to achieve a look of their own. That look was dubbed "The American Look," and at the end of World War II it took off around the world. Wartime conditions and shortages spurred them to home-grown ingenuity. In fact, they regarded the government fabric restrictions as a sort of sporting handicap and when late in the war they were offered an extra three-quarters of a yard if they pleaded design hardship, they turned it down.

In the fall of 1940, Claire's chance to design under her own name came from a most unexpected source. Henry Geiss of Monastic fame had recovered his health and acquired a new young partner, Adolph Klein and his old production man, Harry Friedman. The new Townley business was capitalized with $10,000 from each partner. One day, Geiss and Adolph Klein encountered Claire on the elevator in their building. The minute he introduced Klein to Claire, it was professional love at first sight. Claire was the kind of designer Klein had long wanted to work with.

A good-looking Brooklynite with charm, taste, and integrity, as well as the shrewdness necessary to survive in the garment trade, Adolph Klein had become a top salesman in several of the most successful wholesale houses while still in his twenties. When he and Geiss met, he was part owner of a medium-priced "misses dress" house named Morris and Strong. Despite his success, Klein was bored with the typical gambit of copying or "adapting" what the high-priced manufacturers did. He wanted his line to have some originality and excitement, design qualities that Claire had already proven.

But Geiss remembered the Monastic. He was also unnerved by gloomy judgments of Claire by other manufacturers on the Avenue, including her most recent house, Win-Sum, a low-priced manufacturer where she had spent a few disastrous months after Carnegie. "Better you should throw your money out the window" was the most optimistic prognosis. Finally the partners agreed to let the decision about Claire rest with a respected friend who ran a specialty shop in Boston.

The answer was slow in coming. If there were to be a spring collection, Claire McCardell would have to be signed to a contract at once. Geiss reluctantly gave in and Claire began. Years later, Mrs. Adolph (Lee) Klein confessed that the letter had actually arrived in time—not at Klein's office, but at his house—and that since it was so strongly negative, Klein had seen no reason to bother Geiss with it.

But Klein soon saw the side of Claire's designing that bothered Geiss so much. She wanted to drop the shoulder pads from her first collection. Introduced by Schiaparelli in Paris in the late thirties to give women a broader, slightly squared-off shoulder, and to make their hips look slimmer, shoulder pads had grown to grotesque proportions. Shoulders were being built *up* as well as out. Some designers, thinking two layers of pads would be doubly effective, were showing padded suits under padded overcoats so that the female shoulder seemed to start right under the ears. Claire wanted none of this.

Klein and Geiss protested that retailers would not buy padless dresses. Claire compromised. She tacked in pads so lightly that a

Asked by *Vogue* for a romantic but practical costume for young wartime brides (*opposite page*), Claire made this easy-shouldered, dirndl dress of soft wool to insure packability and warmth in unheated churches.
Below. Shoulder pads, stiff and angular, which Claire believed should be discarded. Most women, however, did not go along with padless clothes until the war's end.

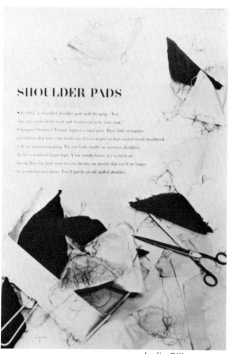

Leslie Gill
Harper's Bazaar, *1941*

Don Honeyman
Vogue, 1941

flick of the nail scissors would dislodge them. This was possible because she usually cut her sleeves in one piece with the bodice, a seam extending over the shoulder and down the arm. With pad out, the sleeve did not drop, as a sleeve set in separately at the shoulder was apt to do. Shoulder pads in place, her bosses let Claire do what she wanted.

Claire was a lucky girl the day Adolph Klein walked into her life. From the beginning, he proved to be her champion and confidant. He was determined to give her equal billing on the Townley label inside each dress, and to encourage stores to promote her and her name by joining in cooperative advertising. Since she was not a partner in the firm, Geiss feared that they might be building her up only to have another company hire her away. Klein didn't think so; her name went on the label after six months.* It now read:

CLAIRE McCARDELL CLOTHES
by Townley

The old-fashioned and limiting word "Frocks" had succumbed to the new Klein-McCardell thinking. Although there would still be plenty of dresses, "Claire McCardell Clothes" also came to mean evening separates, ski outfits, raincoats, and even a wedding dress that first year. Claire's ability to design across the board below the couture level had an enormous effect on moderate-priced designers who had been confined to rigid categories like coats, suits or evening dresses.

Claire and Adolph worked out a separation of powers. She did the designing with no interference; Adolph never came into the design room without permission. He saw that the clothes were produced and sold exactly as she had conceived them, or if this was impossible, she was told at once. "Claire gets no surprises in the finished garment," Adolph often said.

Actually, Klein was something of a manufacturing hero through his willingness to let his designer's revolutionary ideas reach the stores at all. The run-of-the-mill wholesaler really wanted no truck with innovative designs that were apt to be bought only in small quantities by a few experimental buyers, or worse still, might catch the eye of some fashion magazine editor who would ship them off to the Andes to be photographed.

"I can't tell you how I envied Claire," wailed Joset Walker. "The day after my first showing, 'Pops' (her boss, David Goodstein, a great manufacturer but not one to rock the fashion boat) would whisk all the most exciting things off the racks and hide them in his office closet. The only fun I had was when Diana Vreeland would sweep past all the button-up-the-front dresses in the showroom, go right to the office, and say, 'Where are the lemons?' "

* She became a partner in 1952.

The long American leg is glorified in Claire's first resort collection for the new Townley. This plaid silk playsuit with puffy bloomers was photographed at another American phenomenon, one of Frank Lloyd Wright's mountain-perched stone and redwood houses in Arizona.

Dahl-Wolfe
r's Bazaar, 1942

Klein was a remarkably independent manufacturer but he was also lucky to find a sympathetic buyer from a major department store in Marjorie Griswold, who had just joined Lord and Taylor. Marjorie was in fact a super version of the new American woman Claire and Adolph were trying to reach.

The daughter of a wealthy industrialist in Fort Clinton, Ohio, she too had shown an early independence. In 1924, a time when most midwestern families who could afford to thought it a big step to send their daughters "back East" to college, Marjorie at seventeen opted for Stanford University. Unlike Claire, however, she was not headed for the fashion business from the very first. It was not until the year she had graduated, a Romance Language major, that she heard of and joined Macy's Training Squad. That same year, 1928, Claire was graduating from Parsons. One of Macy's stars, Marjorie Griswold rose rapidly in the next ten years to become merchandise manager of all fashion accessories. "It didn't seem all that rapid—especially the year I spent merchandising notions," said Marjorie. "We had a million-dollar volume in a department where the average sales check was fifty-three cents."

In 1938, Marjorie was only thirty-one and probably would have wound up running Macy's before her next birthday. Instead, she quit. She had married a young research chemist, Richard Grisdale, had had a baby son, and wanted to live a city-country life between Manhattan and Old Ardsley in Westchester County—with time enough for job, family and an occasional game of tennis.

The Macy job was not geared to this combination. "In today's dollars, it was like running a thirty- or forty-million-dollar business," says Marjorie; so she resigned and stayed home for a year and a half. In the fall of 1940, Lord and Taylor lured her back to work by promising her a chance to do more creative merchandising—and that in a five-day week at a time when everyone worked six. "She wound up doing as much work in five days as the average buyer did in eight," said Melvin Dawley, retired Chairman of the Board. "Marjorie Griswold was a real visionary," said Katie Murphy, once Marjorie's assistant, later vice-president and fashion director of Bloomingdale's. "When everyone was worrying about what was going to sell next month, she could look ahead to what new young designers should be brought along even if it took a year or two."

Among the young designer discoveries Marjorie "brought along" in her years at Lord and Taylor were Emilio Pucci, Rudi Gernreich, Lilly Pulitzer and Rosemarie Reid; but the first and most striking was Claire McCardell.

One of Marjorie's first callers in the beginning weeks of her new job was Adolph Klein. "He said he had something new and exciting. Of course they all said that, but this time I really sat up when the first dress came out!" It was just a simple little rayon print, white seagulls

The American Look, *right,* in a World War II McCardell tweed suit: spare, rugged, functional, prophetic. The fitted hood folds down into a turtle neck when not worn up against the wind. Matching tweed gloves and all-one-color legs and feet add to the streamlined Flash Gordon effect. As shown in the *Bazaar* in 1944, with the illustrations on this page, proclaiming "a new aspect of fashion in the American grain. They have their roots in our own history. These clothes are related to the frugal modesty and dignity of the dresses worn by pioneer women . . . to the outlandish dash of our Wild West heroes, to the stitched and riveted sharpness of our American overalls . . . and to the almost abstract garb—the tunics and tights and hoods—of our great escape figures of the comics: Superman, Flash Gordon, the Phantom."

Louise Dahl-Wolfe
Harper's Bazaar, 1944

on navy—but collarless, zipped up the back, and although shown with a belt it did not have a "cut waistline." To Marjorie, sated with "hanger dresses" stiff with fake pocket flaps, big buttons with no buttonholes, pre-tied and sewn bows at neck or bosom, it was almost revolutionary in its expensive simplicity.

Marjorie bought McCardells that day and soon after persuaded Dorothy Shaver, Lord and Taylor's forceful vice-president, to give Claire McCardell the full "Name Designer" treatment. Lord and Taylor, where the phrase "American Look" was coined in 1945, was the most exciting store in the country during this period. The merchandising world watched its window fronts, the full-page ads daringly devoted to a single dress. "They did things with such heart and passion," said Diana Vreeland, "I used to call Marjorie five times a week."

"The McCardells weren't that easy to sell at first," according to Marjorie Griswold. "They were considered very radical then and it took a very sophisticated young woman to understand them." Of course there were markdowns along the way, but the markdowns often resulted in more business in the end. Women took limp-looking bargain-priced McCardells home in a what-have-we-got-to-lose spirit, discovered they could wear and enjoy them, and returned with their friends to buy more at full price.

By the late forties, Townley had grown to be the single biggest ready-to-wear account in the store and Claire's unstructured, undecorated, uninhibited clothes were no longer considered controversial.

Claire's most productive period, during which the McCardell–American Look jelled, was during the 1940s. Understandably, its fans are apt to get a bit testy when "the Typical '40s Look" is revived by young designers (including St. Laurent) who have done their research by watching World War II movies on the "Late, Late Show." *Their* '40s girls have padded shoulders, padded bras, and high, high heels. Claire's girls were padless, braless, and heel-less. *Their* girls are tightly encased in sexy rhinestone-trimmed satins for big dates; Claire's casual jersey dress-up clothes were more subtly sexy. And *their* girls wear their hair in a fuzzy pompadour à la Grable, whereas Claire's girls resembled Lauren Bacall, in a freshly washed, smooth pageboy bob. Claire's look has lasted through the years looking marvelous, as has Bacall herself, while the Grable look winds up as occasional fun in a faddy, campy way that goes back to the archives after a season or two.

In general, the typical McCardell girl looked comfortable in her clothes because she *was* comfortable. She always had deep side pockets, even in evening dresses, which encouraged a sort of nonchalant Astaire-like stance. Her dresses were both easy-fitting and easy-to-fit because of their uncut or adjustable waistlines, their sleeves cut in one with the bodice, or with dropped shoulders and

Norman Norell admired Claire's ability to turn "$5 worth of common cotton calico into a dress a smart woman could wear anywhere." *Harper's Bazaar* agreed, recommended *(opposite)* this one for a "hot city, a cool country morning or supper on any terrace in the world . . . with leather sandals or black satin slippers and diamonds."

Louise Dahl-
Harper's Baza

Claire's famous "baby dress" (*opposite*) also resembles the high-busted shifts worn, sans underwear, by the grown-up ladies of Napoleon's Empire. She made it first in wool jersey as a dress-up substitute for spangled satins, then followed with versions in fabrics as far apart as cotton calico and silk chiffon.

deep armholes. There was almost always a bit of bias cut somewhere to show off the figure if it was good or lend a little help when it was less than perfect. There were also certain recurring details—McCardellisms—which an artist friend once aptly remarked were as readily identifiable as the watermelons in a Tomayo painting.

Double Stitching (sometimes called top or blue-jean stitching).

Claire used it first as a reinforcement for seams on her heavy cottons, like the workmen's clothes she admired for their "honest" look. Soon she was calling attention to it in various ways—by using contrasting colored thread and by the architectual look of outlining the important seams; top-stitching fabrics as elegant as silk twill or cotton voile.

Little Brass Hooks and Other "Hardware" Closings.

At a time when many designers were fastening dresses with concealed zippers or dozens of hard-to-find tiny snaps and hooks, Claire preferred the functional appearance of metal fastenings in clear view. She used rivets, grommets, and dime-sized brass snaps like those on a child's windbreaker. But her absolute favorites were the small, sturdy gilt hooks and eyes shaped like those on men's fishing boots. They were ornamental as well as practical, and she put them on everything from bathing suits to evening dresses. Fastening a snug bodice beneath a low-cut neckline in a sort of Nell Gwynn effect, they were surprisingly sexy, "as if inviting a man to unhook them," said an editor who found them all the more provocative because of their naively utilitarian appearance.

"Spaghetti" or Shoestring Ties.

Most characteristic of all were the thin bias cords for which Claire seemed to find a zillion uses. Usually the ties were tacked just below the bust to give a woman a choice of waistlines, a principle tenet in Claire's code of fit. They could be wrapped high in her favorite Empire line or could crisscross down to a natural waistline, like the classic Greek fillets. She used them for halter necklines, high and low, front and back; she further accented bare skin by tying a bolero with them in back like a too-small hospital gown or winding them around bare midriffs.

At first, the spaghetti strings were a bafflement to even the most knowledgeable. Henry Callahan, later vice-president in charge of display at Saks Fifth Avenue, was then at Lord and Taylor. He remembers, "I would be working on the windows along about midnight, and there falling off a hanger would be six yards of bias-cut fabric with several feet of strings dripping from it. But it was usually Claire's and it always looked wonderful once I got the courage to put it on a figure."

A slender, high-waisted coat was shown here (*above*) with a muff and Claire's favorite chignon cap of fur for metropolitan daytime wear. But like most McCardell coats it was versatile, could go over her baby dress for evening or a sweater and skirt for work.

Louise Dahl-Wolfe
Harper's Bazaar, 1944

Unlike most American wartime suits, Claire's were never strictly man-tailored, but neither were they fussy. A 1944 brown tweed, *above*, is typically dropped shouldered and easy skirted but the top stitching and the pockets are like those on frontier pants.

But the fact that most McCardells had certain recognizable characteristics did not make them uniforms or commonplace. There were usually some more surprises. In addition to four yearly collections, someone was always asking Claire for something new to perk up a store window, launch a new fabric, or whet the interest of a jaded fashion photographer. She made all of it seem so easy, as if she had a filing cabinet crammed with ideas ready to spill out on demand.

"You never know where these dames get their inspiration," Adolph Klein once said. "It could come from a crack in the wall." Claire almost agreed. "Each new collection starts with the idea of comfort, need, fun. I am influenced by anything, everything, the ballet I just saw, an old engraving, what fabrics are doing. A T-square lying on my husband's drawing board sent me to my yellow pad . . . a squared-off jacket, half one color, half another, was the result."

Like most designers Claire was stimulated by the theatre, travel, museums, old costume books, and whatever passed for a flea market wherever she happened to be. Unlike many, however, she almost never copied anything whole or designed with a "theme."

She loved the high-waisted, slim-skirted dresses of the Empire and Regency eras, but she was apt to put their voluptuous necklines and tiny off-shoulder sleeves into a dress made of simple cotton calico. Then to even things up she would do a version of the prim, high-wrapped bodices and full skirts worn by nineteenth-century New England women in the most diaphanous cotton voile or nylon chiffon she could find.

Polaire Weissman, former curator of the Metropolitan Museum's Costume Institute, used to call the section with clothes from 1810 to 1830 "McCardell Corner." She remembers that several of the museum's children's clothes gave Claire ideas for grownups. The collarless neck and drawstring back of a little girl's party outfit turned up in one of Claire's best coats. A Dutch boy's full fold-over trousers were the inspiration for an excellent wrapped-front skirt. An elegant Edwardian lace-trimmed diaper cover metamorphosed into one of Claire's famous jersey bathing suits of the 1940s.

The railroad workers' double-stitched and riveted work clothes had led to specific McCardellisms. Also the workaday bandanna kerchief became one of Claire's favorite soft necklines when she stitched its triangular shape to the back of her dresses and knotted it in front. The right-angled pocket flaps of the cowhand's frontier pants turned up in the skirt of a wool street suit and the pants themselves were reproduced for girls in pink denim.

Some of her best-selling shirtwaist dresses were apt to show traces of the big-sleeved, wasp-waisted ladies in the Charles Dana Gibson drawings she collected. Others had the pleated bosoms and tab collars of contemporary custom-made English dress shirts.

Claire said that after her number-one inspiration, the American

A wintertime bicycling outfit (*opposite*) reminded some of a Superman comic strip, but its streamlined, hooded sweater, matching stockings, and trim knickers were ideal for cold weather sports. The belt bag was from Claire's contemporaries, the Phelps, whose polished saddle leather accessories were fashion landmarks. "Humans should be as well dressed as horses," they said.

woman, came the fabric she would use and what it could "do." In her knowing and uninhibited hands, many humble materials wound up "doing" things they had never done before.

Claire's choice of fabric was as down to earth as she was, but in unorthodox and often trend-setting ways: wool jersey or cotton for a cocktail dress, tweed or camel's hair for an evening wrap, mattress ticking for a town suit, nightgown nylon tricot for a dinner dress.

Cotton had played a major role in American history during a war and a panic or two, but it was far from a star in ladies' fashions of the twenties and thirties. It had been seen only in classic shirtwaist dresses, active sportswear and in a sort of octogenarian type of printed voile dress Marjorie Griswold associated with "little old ladies rocking on their porches all day long."

She recalls with glee a Lord and Taylor windowfront of Claire's blowy little printed voiles with her sexiest halter necks and bias-wrapped midriffs. The mannequins were seated demurely in boardinghouse rockers, but right there all resemblance to little old ladies ended.

Claire designed clothes for any place and any time of day out of cotton and the humbler their origins the better. In her first collection for the new Townley, Claire showed an evening dress that she called the "Kitchen Dinner Dress." Like so many of her best ideas, it came from a need in her own life. Claire liked cooking, and she wanted something practical to wear while stirring sauces in the kitchen, yet pretty enough to join the guests in the living room. The solution: long-skirted washable dresses, often in her favorite bold plaids and stripes, sometimes with a full apron to match.

Since the bold patterns were generally not available in the cotton goods market for women's clothes, Claire went afield to the children's and men's sports shirt market. Soon, she was a sort of heroine to the manufacturers of cotton textiles. William Lord, the retired president of Galey and Lord, remembers how she would arrive in his showroom pulling little scraps from her handbag—seersucker from a child's overall, textured white piqué from an English evening waistcoat, and chambray from a schoolgirl's uniform. They all wound up in high fashion and stayed there.

She encouraged the New England cotton mills to revive their prim little nineteenth-century calico patterns. Those calicos were symbolic. They had crossed the continent with the pioneers. Even the scraps had been saved and cherished in patchwork quilts. Claire's adventurous scissors cut the calicos into evening dresses and coat-and-dress ensembles.

According to Hope Skillman, the president of Skilmill, a top firm specializing in textured cottons, Claire had an eye for the inherent possibilities of a fabric even when at first it seemed a disappointment. In the early forties, when dyes and bleaches like the famous "Lucky

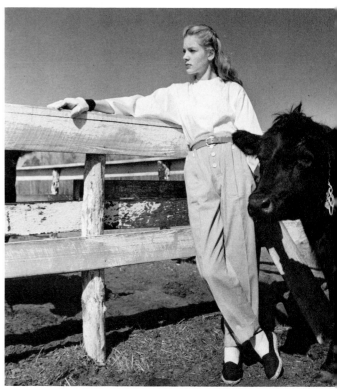

Louise Dahl-Wolfe
Harper's Bazaar, 1943

Young Lauren Bacall, lanky yet graceful even in pre-movie star days, models two outfits suited for life on the home front in 1943. *Above,* she "farms" in a wide-sleeved cotton shirt, mattress ticking pants cut full. *At right,* for a darning session and the war news, she wears a light-weight one-piece jump-suit like a mechanic's overall.

Louise Dahl-Wolfe
Harper's Bazaar, *1943*

Strike green'' had gone off to war, Skilmill's white was far from spank-
ing. But Claire liked the creamy, slightly mellowed color they offered
and in time that off-white became a staple in its own right as ''bone.''

When she spotted a cotton georgette, a weave new to this country,
she ordered an enormous yardage but did not ask for an exclusive
as would have been customary on Seventh Avenue. All she cared
about, the surprised manufacturer found, was that the georgette came

in twenty-three colors. Her designs took care of the rest.

Designer Donald Brooks believes that if Claire had been challenged to use only one material in making a complete and varied collection for any season, even summer, she would have chosen wool jersey.

Unlike cotton, wool jersey had had high fashion acceptance during Claire's Paris days. But in common with cotton, it was reasonably priced and available in quantity. Claire used jersey in ways Paris had never dreamed of—from her bias-cut bathing suits to full-fledged evening-on-the-town outfits. Rather than use cheaper versions of luxurious satins and brocades, Claire preferred to "switch to make wool jersey an evening fashion in its own right."

The switch to jersey was one of her most successful ploys, lifting her kind of inexpensive dresses into a class of their own. Women who could afford higher prices often preferred the fluid lines, packability and versatility of Claire's jerseys. They could "take" any accessory from pigskin belts to diamond clips.

Many think that Claire's faithful use of jersey as a year-round, clock-round fabric had a lot to do with the total acceptance of knitted clothes by women everywhere in the decades since.

Jane Kift, who was fabric editor of *Vogue* during the forties, said she always called Claire first for her reactions to new fibers and weaves—partly because where Claire led others soon followed, but mainly because she was receptive to new ideas from the textile industry.

Among these were the test-tube fabrics which were having a rough time winning high fashion acceptance after the war. In spite of intense promotional effort, including dozens of four-color ads and lavish fashion shows, most top designers found man-mades unappealing. "Drip-dry" quickly became a term of fashion opprobrium, no matter how many Dupont salesmen were pushed into swimming pools to demonstrate the virtues of their nylon and/or dacron shirts. But Claire was intrigued with these "miracle" fibers. Instead of treating them as practical but unglamorous substitutes for natural yarns, she went all out to give them fashion acceptance and prestige. For reasons known best to the mill, the first nylons available to dress manufacturers in the late forties were heavy, dark-colored fabrics. At the same time, lovely filmy chiffon-like weaves in light colors were going to the lingerie manufacturers. Claire used them for evening dresses. One was cut almost as simply as a nightgown with little spaghetti strings to make a waistline, but its colors—beige with a small figured print in orange—were very un-boudoir.

Claire's thinking about the man-made fabrics was not confined to the finished product. One day she was seen playing a game of cat's cradle with a flesh-colored elastic tube. It had been used as a chest bandage in World War II and Claire saw its possibilities for a strapless top which would fit anyone and stay up without bones.

Maria Martel

When nylon reappeared after the war, Claire made this filmy evening dress (*above*) of the lightweight variety used elsewhere mainly for nightgowns. The six-inch hem was a custom-made touch. *At right,* Vogue reported cloth-covered ballet slippers as wartime dancing gear.

Fashion Innovations

Claire would have been the last to claim too many firsts. She said so many elements entered into most successful new fashions that the order of origin was debatable. Even the Monastic dress was 2000 years old in principle. Nevertheless, many milestones of social as well as fashion history could be ticked off in Townley's little showroom during those first few years of World War II. The most memorable:

The Diaper Bathing Suit (1942).

In its first and simplest form, the diaper bathing suit was a length of checked cotton, the top bias cut, which hung from the neck in front, went between the legs and came around to tie at the waist in front leaving the back completely bare above the waist. When wet it kept its figure-hugging shape and since it was just a skimpy piece of unlined cotton it dried on the way back to the beach umbrella. Claire had made it as an alternative to the full-skirted cotton "dress-maker" suits which looked perky while dry but droopy when wet.

Even more than droopy cotton bathing suits, Claire disapproved of the West Coast bathing uniform, shiny Lastex in fluorescent colors with the over-inflated bosom common to Hollywood starlets riveted right in. In the next few years, using her beloved wool jersey, she turned out some of the most memorable bathing suits of our time. Many incorporated the diaper wrap, all were unlined and unpadded, usually bias cut somewhere for fit. Their tops varied from the barest of halters to one with long sleeves and a brass-hooked bodice.

Most were made in sober black, gray, or sand-colored jersey but they looked far sexier in their no-nonsense, unselfconscious way than the starlet's bright Lastex. Although Townley had never made bathing suits and these would have to sell for as much as McCardell's dresses, Adolph was game, and thousands were sold to some of the world's chicest women. (Pauline Trigère boasts that she wore her beige jersey McCardell for ten years.)

Ballet Slippers (1944).

The shoe industry was mobilized even before the garment industry to provide footwear for the military. Shoes had been strictly rationed, but soft, flimsy playshoes and ballet slippers remained "free." Claire had always liked the look of feet flat on the ground. The shortage gave her an idea. For her "shoeless" collections, she covered ballet slippers in fabrics to match her dresses or used them in the original soft kid in bright colors as a contrast. It became a fad—to Claire's and the chiropodist's consternation. "I only meant them for home or the country club, not the subway," she said. Eventually Capezio, the ballet shoemaker, found itself in the shoe business with sturdier soles and modest heels, but still keeping the comfort of the soft top.

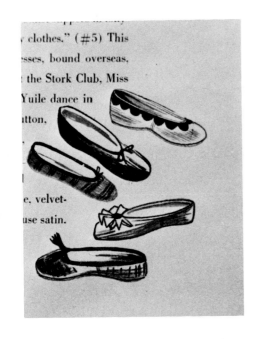

clothes." (#5) This
sses, bound overseas,
the Stork Club, Miss
Yuile dance in
tton,

e. velvet-
use satin.

gue, 1944

The Popover (1942).

One of Claire's most famous, versatile and enduring designs, the Popover, had its origin in the humble housedress. Made at *Harper's Bazaar*'s request to fit the requirements of wartime ladies whose servants had gone off to the defense plants, the Popover first appeared in the November 1943 issue above a headline, "I'm Doing My Work."

Mrs. Michael Phipps, the wife of the polo player, was photographed in a doorway of her enormous Long Island house wearing a wrap-around blue denim coverall dress. It had wide rolled-up sleeves, sturdily stitched dropped shoulders, and a quilted pocket "big enough," according to the caption, "for matches, cigarettes, the morning mail and the duster." A matching potholder and a quilted mitt hung from the waistband by bright red tapes. Adolph Klein had made a special deal with labor, since this was considered a "utility garment," and the Popover cost a mere $6.95. And *Harper's Bazaar* published a page of household hints: "Carbon tetrachloride—any drugstore—melts the wax right out of candlestick sockets" or "In making beds, tuck the sheets in head and foot first, then mitre the corners as you tuck in the sides."

Lord and Taylor persuaded Adolph Klein to up his original fabric order of 10,000 yards of denim to 75,000 yards, an enormous investment. And it was a group of Lord and Taylorites who gave the garment its name. (Lunching at the Hotel Algonquin, they had spotted the house specialty—a hollow muffin that pops over the tin when baked.)

Klein ordered the extra denim but only after a sleepless night. He begged Claire to think up something else in denim in case there weren't that many snappy dressers among housewives. Claire obliged with a suit and coat. But Klein need not have worried. Within a year Townley had used a quarter of a million yards of the denim for 75,000 Popovers. Moreover, the denim suit and coat sold well too and launched that doughty fabric on a glamorous career that has continued ever since. The Popover was made and remade in many other fabrics and, at the regular prices of the Townley line, became a staple in every McCardell collection from 1943 on. It was almost always wrapped around, but sometimes it crossed over in the back instead of the front, or was sashed instead of buttoned. By the fifties, the stores were advertising the Popover as the answer for every occasion from the beach to an evening out.

Leotards.

Among the most discussed and least successful fashions of 1943 were Claire's leotards.

Claire freely admits that the idea of using dancers' leotards as accompaniment to everyday clothes had come from Mildred Orrick originally. Mildred had submitted some sketches to *Harper's Bazaar*

Archives of Lord & Taylor

The first denim Popover, *right*, worn by Mrs. Michael Phipps, was intended only for wear in and around the house and garden but its trim lines took it out and around until eventually it turned up in many different fabrics as a beach coat, house coat—even as an evening wrap *above*.

Louise Dahl-Wolfe
Harper's Bazaar, 1945

Two milestone bathing suits of the 1940s
are neutral in color, smashing in impact.
At left, a grey jersey halter is wrapped
high around the neck in front, anchored to
diaper trunks below a completely bare
back. *Above,* a slim knit in beige has one
detachable shoulder strap set on the diagonal.

Louise Dàhl-Wolfe
Harper's Bazaar, 1948

but had temporarily retired by the time the magazine wanted to merchandise them. Claire, asked to produce some ideas of her own, adapted the tight fitting body suit for college girls in heatless dormitories and classrooms. She made them in wool jersey under wraparound tweed jumpers. *Life* magazine's editors were stunned, and put them right on the cover as a change from that week's war news. "Strange Looking Garments for Winter Wardrobes" ran the caption. "These funny tights are called leotards, named after the 19th century acrobat. The word appears in Webster's unabridged dictionary but not in the Oxford English."

To most buyers the "strange looking garments" had an even stranger price structure. The tweed jumpers retailed for a moderate twenty dollars but the leotards would have to cost more than twice as much; and since they had feet in them a new sizing problem was presented. But Lord and Taylor and Neiman-Marcus along with I. Magnin on the West Coast bought and advertised the whole notion, keeping it alive long enough for someone to figure out how to produce tights economically. One of this century's most entrenched modes of dressing is built on the "body suit," a direct descendant of the leotard.

Winter Playclothes.

Claire felt the need for winterized versions of the active playclothes she had worn in warm weather. She reasoned that women wanted to go right on bicycling and walking in the woods and in the winter might substitute badminton or bowling for outdoor tennis and swimming. Her models spun out of the dressing room in plaid wool shorts, striped knickers, hooded overblouses, legs in gaily colored tights and Robin Hood booties. Some outfits had many layers that could be put off and on as the wearer warmed up or cooled off. A short wool skirt unwrapped to show knee-length wool socks.

En bloc, the models looked like men from Mars or little Hamlets. There were nervous giggles from the first viewers, and *Vogue* later cautioned wearers to add bright lipstick to assert their gender. Those winter playclothes, however, were to become some of Claire's most influential designs.

"No matter how far out, even outrageous, some of Claire's styles might seem to us at first, they almost always filled some need and ultimately became classics," said Mel Dawley of Lord and Taylor.

The American fashion press played a major role in seeing that Claire's way-out or seemingly outrageous designs became established classics; she had a phenomenal coverage almost from the beginning. The fact that she herself photographed beautifully didn't hurt, but from the very first, the fashion press understood what Claire was driving at. Except for a few die-hard Francophiles among the older editors, the girls on the magazines didn't regard Claire's iconoclastic

This beautiful linen sheath, photographed at William Randolph Hearst's estate, San Simeon, was from Claire's last collection. Skillfully cut on the bias to effortlessly fit almost any figure. Its only "trim," the narrow white cord around the halter.

258

The first leotards, or as *LIFE* put it, "funny tights" (*above*) were of wool jersey and too expensive to be popular. The following year Claire dyed wool or lisle stockings to match her sweater tops to give the same all-of-a-piece look (*at right*).

A classic metal T-square lying on her architect husband's drawing board was the inspiration for Claire's squared-off beach coat, *opposite*. But its bold color combination, new to Western world fashion, was first seen by her in a Japanese child's kimono.

A trio of unusual black wool bathing suits includes Claire's 1942 jersey one-piece diaper suit, *opposite*, wrapped bare to the waist in back, high on the thigh in front; a ribbed knit, *above left*, like a female dancer's leotard; and, *at right*, a jersey with a top like a McCardell dress with deep cut sleeves, gilt hooks and eyes, cord belt.

Louise Dahl-Wolfe
Harper's Bazaar, *1953*

John Rawlings
Vogue, *1953*

McCardell

Louise Dahl-Wolfe
Harper's Bazaar, 1944

Contrasting top-stitching outlines the structural details of these bare midriff outfits from the mid-forties resort collections. The covered top (*opposite*) is rather surprisingly of wool jersey while the halter (*above*) is of a more usual cotton fabric.

McCardell

265

Vogue's John Rawlings photographed two McCardell favorites of the forties. *Left,* the diaper wrap resembled an oriental panung, in a playsuit worn by Sono Osato, the Japanese-American dancer then appearing in "One Touch of Venus." *Below,* spaghetti strings criss-cross repeatedly to form a halter back on a beach dress.

rd dinner dress

103

John Rawlings
Vogue, 1945

credo as just a *faute de mieux* kind of substitute for Paris news. Rather, they thought it was an important American fashion statement —fresh, relevant, exciting—one which would inevitably have been made, sooner or later, with or without Paris.

In tandem, the young reporters and Claire tackled the agreeable problem of getting the message across to the readers. Young, lithe models with natural healthy-looking skin and straight, shiny hair slouched across pages formerly occupied by worldly beauties carefully made up and statically posed. But the pictures were not snapshots; they had a new kind of planned beauty. Louise Dahl-Wolfe's girls on the Arizona desert made one think of Georgia O'Keefe; Penn's winter playclothes series was a stylized, intellectual exercise in glorifying the sharp integrity of American workmen's clothes.

For her part, Claire understood and respected the press; she knew that there had to be a certain amount of fantasy, fun and a feeling for what might happen tomorrow in the fashions they showed. She also knew enough about photography and the variable moods of managing editors to realize that a young editor's idea might not always work out; but backed by the indomitable Adolph Klein, she was always willing to give it a try. This was a refreshing change. Even before the editors got their notebooks out, most firms made it clear that they were only interested in showing them proven sellers. (Often these were the least photogenic.) Moreover, the loan of a precious sample for more than a half day was expected to yield at the very least a cover or inside color page. The effect was so inhibiting that the editor was tempted to go right back to Townley, where she was understood and where she liked the clothes anyway.

The young fashion editors of the forties were among Claire's most satisfied and stylish customers. Their lives on and off the job were very much like her own, and her solutions to the problems of dressing worked for them too. Importantly, since most of them were underpaid in a business where they were supposed to be well turned out at all times, the no-price look and versatility of their inexpensive McCardell saved many a day and night. Among the most decorative McCardell fans was young Barbara Cushing, then a junior editor at *Vogue,* and now Mrs. William Paley, considered one of the best-dressed women in the world.

The early forties marked several important developments in reporting American fashion. In 1942 the New York Dress Institute inaugurated semiannual showings in New York for the country's newspaperwomen. Claire's personal clothes philosophy and her kind of designing made good copy for them. As for the high fashion magazines, they tired of showing warmed-over Balenciagas and classic suits and began featuring low-priced original American designs like Claire's. At the same time a vigorous new group of militantly "young"

267

magazines like *Mademoiselle, Charm, Seventeen* and *Glamour* came into their own. "Claire was *our* Carnegie and Norell," said a former *Charm* editor. She added that even though her magazine had been low in the fashion hierarchy when she first visited Townley, she was given the same treatment as an important member of the *Vogue* masthead. In those fledgling years of reporting American fashion, Claire was not just another good story, she was our colleague and our friend.

A solid wall of press clippings displayed in Adolph Klein's Townley office forms a background for Claire wearing one of her quiet little "bread and butter" dresses.

4

THE AMERICAN LOOK TAKES ON A NEW LOOK

Martin inside keeps jacket skintight

Five-inch pleated cuffs inside waist

Small pads slope the shoulders

THE INSIDE

Whalebone and grosgrain waistband

Padding above tight waist

Harper's Bazaar, 1947

The intricate interiors of Dior's "New Look" costumes (*above*) contrast with a 1947 McCardell unlined cotton dress (*opposite*). Both have a defined waist, very full skirt attached to a bias cut bodice. Sleek sandals and a Phelps belt bag complete Claire's "American Look."

se Dahl-Wolfe
er's Bazaar, 1947

In the spring of 1946, Claire, Marjorie Griswold and I (then a fashion editor at *Vogue*) were lunching at the Baroque Restaurant on East Fifty-third Street—years before the days of *Women's Wear Daily's* "in" restaurants X, Y, Z, and O. The wartime restrictions on fabric had been lifted in May—too late to affect the fall collections. When Claire said that by the following spring she thought women were going to want very full and much longer skirts, Marjorie and I disagreed. We thought American women would want to change gradually, not outmode their wardrobes overnight. After all, having gotten used to zipping around in practical short skirts, why would they want to haul all that useless yardage along while getting in and out of cars, and so on? Claire didn't argue with us. She simply went back to her workroom and whipped up a group of spring dresses with full circle skirts, a good ten or twelve inches below the knee. They were charming and, fortunately for our reputations, Marjorie had planned McCardell windows for Lord and Taylor and I had a McCardell color spread for *Vogue* on the presses when M. Dior unloosed That Collection in February and everyone sang the Marseillaise and said that France was saved. It was not that McCardell had scooped Dior or vice versa. Clearly, they were individually thinking along the same lines—that with the return of plenty, women would want to break out of their limited wartime fashion mold and get into something markedly different. Dior's corsetted and buckram-lined, long-skirted costumes had much of the mannered elegance of the Belle Epoque. Claire's were much simpler. In movement, they reminded one of a Martha Graham dancer, lightly graceful with her feet flat on the ground.

Claire didn't just drop the skirts indiscriminately. She worked out a new proportion so that the unaccustomed length and fullness was set off by a snug bias bodice and a tiny waist. It was a young and

feminine silhouette often made more so with shawl collars or little capes and occasionally a softly flounced petticoat.

I also remember another lunch about this time. Adolph, Claire and I were at a kosher delicatessen, and as we walked back up Seventh Avenue toward the showroom, we tangled with dozens of pushcarts packed with little McCardell facsimiles for the Junior market. All the McCardellisms were there in miniature: the double-stitching, the denim, the spaghetti ties and brass hooks, and the rage of the moment—circle skirts. Adolph started counting the knock-offs out loud and when he skipped ahead to "one thousand and three, one thousand and four . . .," Claire, who had resisted the Junior market, shrugged and gave in: "Okay, you win." The next season, Townley manufactured a Junior line of its own—lower-priced and higher-waisted. It made money well enough, but after a few years Claire persuaded Mr. Klein to give it up. She didn't mind the juniors copying her, but she hated copying herself. (Paradoxically, it was Claire's idea to make some little McCardells for the size 3 to 6x group; these were not successful largely because of their high prices.)

By now, of course, Claire was allowed to do whatever she felt like doing. Fortunately for Klein and Geiss, she always felt like making a last-minute check for "bread and butter" dresses on the line and if they were in short supply, she would "do up a few." These included her famous shirtwaist dresses with their sneaky little bias tops which sold in the hundreds of thousands and, almost as popular, her classic pleated designs.

It was inevitable that Claire would like pleats, particularly in motion. She had owned several of the famous Fortunys of the twenties and thirties, the Venetian knife-pleated silk sheath that chic women kept rolled up in a small circular box like a corsage. When accordion pleats of a more or less permanent variety were possible after the war, Claire made her own versions. The one almost everyone owned—although nobody seemed to mind—was pure McCardell; in beige wool jersey, of course. It was finely pleated from its little tab collar to the mid-calf hem. A spaghetti cord was stitched high under the bust with several feet of loose ends to wrap around one's natural waist. Claire made a bare-topped long version in a red silk damask for herself. A coterie of editors got a lot of mileage out of their day-length versions—it was a great favorite with men—and only gave it up to the moths or the thrift shop when the hard-edged Courrèges kind of dress came along fifteen years later.

Claire's attitude toward coats was considered rather heretical in her own time. She didn't believe that a coat should be a solemnly chosen, major yearly purchase to wear over almost everything. She designed her coats as softly and with as much variety as her dresses, and urged people to gradually collect several so that there was always one in the closet to go with any dress or mood.

Her camel's hair coats were very successful and far removed from the standard boxy, wide-shouldered polo coats of the time. One was collarless, with a slightly high-waisted drawstring back; another buttonless and very full until tightly sashed. And there was the long camel's hair coat over an Empire-waisted silk foulard evening dress..

Her coats were all lengths, from hip to ankle, and came in every shape, from slender Empire to a full swinging tent. Some had enormous collars which could be pulled right over the head, some had none. Some used her signature double stitching as well as her hardware fastenings. She often lined them in an offbeat gay fabric; once she even lined a cotton denim coat in a bright wool plaid.

"There is a genuine McCardell if I ever saw one," exclaimed a lady at a Vermont ski resort bar pointing out a fellow guest in a long, striped jersey sweater dress. "And in it is the genuine Miss McCardell herself," said the man beside her, an athletic doctor who remembers Claire as a much-admired member of the floating fraternity of ski enthusiasts in the 1940s and 1950s.

Time magazine called Claire her own best model at fifty, and in many respects she was. She stayed slim and blond all her life, and kept a light year-round tan. (She was not above helping the tan along with a bit of orange rouge on her forehead, to look like a ski burn.) In the game "Categories," Claire's color would have been butterscotch. She had blue-green eyes that crinkled nicely when she smiled, which was often, and a tilted-up nose which probably should have been on a smaller girl, but was amusing and friendly looking on her stately five-foot-seven-inch form.

Claire had always had a weakness for "hatty" hats and used to wear scaled-down Queen Mary toques from John-Fredericks but she looked better when she plopped an untrimmed man's panama on her head like a Thomas Hardy heroine. Her hair was always long but she "did" it herself in countless ways according to mood and occasion. They might call for a fat braid down her back for skiing or Madame Recamier ringlets for a full-dress evening in one of her high-waisted outfits. Most of the time she wore it pulled back in a chignon which she often tied up in fabric to match her dress.

There were some important contradictions in Claire, just as there were in her clothes. She had a frugal streak. It was not stinginess—she was very generous with her friends—but rather the old frontier virtue of wasting not and making do. She hated to throw anything potentially useful away. In her own wardrobe she saved all her dresses, hats, belts and scarves.

But Claire had her luxuries, too: real cashmere ski underwear from Abercrombie's; elbow-length pigskin gloves bought by the dozen (even in Claire's time they cost about twenty dollars apiece); Hermès notebooks; lots of Joy perfume. Along with the mangy furs she loved,

Claire wore this pleated sheath, *opposite,* for her award ceremony with President Truman (page 291). An unbroken length of pleats is split and criss-crossed in a broad halter neck front and back, belted in with a wide sash. Everyone seemed to have the day version, *below,* which also hung free from the shoulders. A cord anchored around the bust wraps around and around the waist.

Maria Martel

Maria Martel

Louise Dahl-Wolfe
Harper's Bazaar, 1947

Louise Dahl-Wolfe
Harper's Bazaar, 1947

Classic sportswear gets the McCardell touch: snug-waisted tennis rig (*above left*) has deep-cut armholes for a free swing. That belt bag is only for the clubhouse. *At right, above,* a corduroy jerkin and pleated skirt are worn with a jersey shirt for golf. *Opposite,* Claire wears a cotton ski windbreaker. She skiied for twenty years, but as she admitted, "I never got very good at it . . . I just liked it."

"A revolutionary outfit . . . yet a classic the day it was born" is the way *Harper's Bazaar* described this wool jersey sleeveless top and long shorts for bicycling to a beach picnic or a game of badminton. Claire liked wool jersey the year round.

she also had mink, but used as a lining, and a leopard jacket (before the Wildlife Fund) fastened with the same metal clips as her ski parkas.

"Fashion can take a little kidding, even thrives on it," Claire said. She loved to tease Adolph Klein by wearing her fright-fur coat—the great-grandmother of today's fun furs—to Voisin for lunch with mink-coated buyers. But if Adolph looked too upset the coat had a precautionary cloth lining that could be turned to the outside.

Some things, like cooking, came easily to Claire. Others, like skiing, never did, but not for lack of effort. Hope Bryce (Mrs. Otto Preminger), one of Claire's models in the fifties, tells of seeing her doggedly practicing on the beginners' slope long after everyone else was drinking glüg in front of the fire.

In spite of attendance at a Dale Carnegie course (where she got "the red pencil" for the most improvement in a single session) Claire never got over her shyness. This reticence brought out the protective quality in men, particularly Europeans; but she was also perfectly capable of getting along on her own. At a time when most Americans couldn't cope in Europe without a Cook's tour or a savvy concierge, she breezed everywhere by herself at a moment's notice. Adolph Klein, no slouch himself at coping,* always said that Claire had taught him a thing or two about organization.

In the late forties a typical work day for the calm Miss McCardell might include designing for the new junior-sized division along with the regular line at Townley; a public appearance at a store or charity fashion show; a meeting of the Fashion Group of which she was an officer; and a teaching-critic session at the Parsons School or a visit to the Metropolitan Museum's Costume Institute, where she was an advisor. Then home at five-thirty or six o'clock, where as Mrs. Irving Harris, she ran an eleven-room New York apartment and two country houses for her husband and two teen-aged step-children.

Claire and Texan Irving Harris had met on a boat to Europe just before the war and married in the spring of 1943. A big good-looking man, rather in the style of Senator Barry Goldwater (and just as conservative politically), Harris was a consulting architect in New York. His much publicized, stormy first marriage had been to a Spreckels sugar heiress who died before he met Claire, leaving him with two young children, ample trust funds and a lifelong aversion to notoriety of any sort.

Although Claire was getting more famous by the minute in the forties, Irving managed to ignore the whole thing. He never met Adolph Klein (who was a good and lifelong friend of the whole McCardell family in Frederick, Maryland).

* In addition to serving as President of the New York Couture Group, an association of top wholesalers, Klein also at one time or another was business consultant to many major firms including Mollie Parnis and Norman Norell.

ise Dahl-Wolfe
per's Bazaar, 1949

279

Cotton tweed (*above*) in a characteristic check used for a trim halter and skirt for poolside lounging. *Opposite*, sheer dotted swiss, untypically rose-patterned, makes a petticoated dress an ante-bellum heroine might have worn except for the spaghetti strings, pure twentieth century McCardell.

Louise Dahl-Wolfe
Harper's Bazaar, *1950*

Two ways to show off a tan: a crisp white bolero (*opposite*) is cut to show bare shoulders and a bit of midriff above a swinging skirt. *Below,* oversized check broadcloth halter dress, its bare middle section crossed with bands of fabric.

John Rawlings
Vogue, 1946

It was typical of their marriage that if Irving wanted to sail, Claire crewed; but since he didn't think much of skiing, she went alone or with a friend. When, as often happened, someone would congratulate him or want to interview him on Claire's accomplishments, his response was one of unabashed ignorance. Whatever his wife did, and he understood that she did it very well, he would say, it was entirely her own achievement and her own affair; whatever he had to say on the subject could not conceivably be of interest to anyone.

Claire seemed content to let Irving's life-style set the tone of their home life to a considerable degree. Their New York apartment was pretty solidly establishment-English and rather masculine in feeling; dark wood furniture, lots of heavy gleaming silver, a wood-paneled library with hunting prints and Plutarch's *Lives* on the shelf. The exception was Claire's own bedroom, which had gay red painted walls, and white for the woodwork, fireplace and organdy curtains. A fine collection of Heideloff nineteenth-century English costume prints and some colorful little Japanese figures dressed in silk and framed in shadow boxes were grouped neatly on the walls. This symmetry was somewhat marred by piles of *Vogues* and *Harper's Bazaars* that teetered in every corner. She had only one closet here but kept a lot of her extensive wardrobe of separates and accessories in an enormous ten-drawered English fruitwood bureau, a sort of simultaneous high-and-wide-boy.

Neither of the two country houses was in the least grand but their uses differed widely. Fishers Island, New York, where they had bought a "cottage" in 1948, was an archetypical Eastern summer resort, loaded with Duponts and a Whitney or two. It was deceptively quiet and "simple" during the week, only to erupt into one party after another on the weekend. The Harrises' brown shingle New England shore-type house was unpretentious but roomy, and the family, their cook, and a couple of guests were there most summer weekends.

The leading ladies of Fishers Island immediately elected Claire to the committee to redecorate the "Big Club" and her ideas on fabric, colors and patterns received rapt attention. On the beach, however, the same ladies shied away from the McCardell bathing suits. Much too racy. They stuck to their full-skirted printed cottons.

The Harrises had also kept Claire's little white farmhouse at Frenchtown, where they spent many quiet weekends alone with no telephone. Claire did all the cooking and housework and a little painting in the time left over—mostly still-lifes of fruit or flowers, rather surprisingly prosaic. She was a superb cook, however, with a marvelous kitchen dominated by gleaming white ironstone and a bistro slate announcing what lucky guests would be eating from the iron pot bubbling in the fireplace.

Socially, their New York life was rather conservative and, again, seemingly dominated by Irving, although Claire was popular with his

Mark Shaw

Ex-McCardell model, Gillis MacGil, in a soft plaid wool at-home outfit—like a man's robe except that McCardell sashed it high for a tiny waist. *Right*, Turkey red calico street costume, coat lined in bright wool for body and warmth.

Oversized graph paper checks, a McCardell trademark, were used for a trim linen shorts outfit, *opposite*, worn in a Moucharabieh in Hammamet, Tunisia. The modern dance-like trio *(overleaf)* were photographed on the California desert.

Louise Dahl-Wolfe
Harper's Bazaar, *1950*
and overleaf, 1948

friends. There were subscription dances on the St. Regis Roof where Lester Lanin played, and the various functions of the Comedy Club, Irving's amateur theatrical group. They went to the theatre a lot, too, usually for black-tie benefits. Some McCardell fans feared that all this waltzing around the St. Regis Roof might rub off on Claire in the wrong way, that her dress-up clothes might lose that casual un-mannered quality she had fought so hard to put over. She had even produced a full-skirted dress in taffeta. But not to worry. A far cry from the crinolined strapless ballgowns of the time, it was *soft* taffeta, in an off-beat color—Hershey-bar brown; and its bare-backed halter top was cut like a pure McCardell shirt in front, fastening right up to a bow-tied wing collar with brass studs. Avid party-going actresses like Arlene Francis and Maggie Hayes (Mrs. Herbert Bayard Swope, Jr.) wore it for years, and a version in white-embossed piqué shone among the Fishers Island Saturday custom-mades.

In Brazil in 1946 on a location trip, photographer Louise Dahl-Wolfe, *center*, with *Bazaar* fashion editor Babs Simpson, and models all in Claire's cotton evening dresses.

Mark Shaw

Louise Dahl-Wolfe often said she couldn't take a bad picture of a Claire McCardell outfit and she proves the point in her portrait of a long-legged American girl in a very short beach robe. The fabric, soft wool jersey; the accessories, polished leather.

Louise Dahl-Wolfe

5

THE HONORS AND AWARDS

Paul Schmeck
The Washington Star

In 1950, President Truman presented the National Women's Press Club achievement award to Claire McCardell, *far right,* and five other outstanding women, including Olivia deHaviland, *center.* She is the only fashion designer so honored but the kudos did little to enlarge her Seventh Avenue cubby-hole, *left opposite,* where *LOOK* photographed her in 1953.

A glance at Claire's hefty scrapbook for the 1950s would have given the impression that she did little but trip around the country from dais to dais, podium to podium, making in-store "appearances" and picking up more honors and awards. Indeed, this was almost the case. However, Claire felt the traveling was worth it, to meet the women who admired and wore her clothes. (Not that they always wore them well. The sight of a woman with a rose pinned to the hem of her McCardell almost ruined a trip to New Orleans.) And the fast, comfortable planes got her around the country and back to the drawing board in time for each new season.

In the main, the fifties McCardell shapes were variations of those she had developed in the prolific 1940s. Playclothes were still bare, functional but zingy, like her bathing suit which resembled a beach ball until belted. Dresses were free-flowing with Empire waists; wraparounds like the Popover; or bias-bodiced shirtwaist dresses, usually with full skirts. When the fashion silhouette slimmed down and straightened everywhere, Claire produced one of the best chemise dresses. It was cut completely on the bias with no waist, usually in jersey. Even the side pockets were moved in to the hip-bones and its spare skinny lines gave it the name "string bean."

Her coats continued to come in all sizes and shapes but her suits usually combined simple cardigans with straight skirts, or short jackets with high-waisted skirts, either slim or quite full. She felt that short jackets were kind to hippy women because they eliminated two layers of cloth.

No matter what the silhouette, the most noticeable thing about a McCardell in the 1950s was apt to be its color. Claire had fallen in love with color and used it in great gobs of orange, or purple which she thought "fun to take out of the grandmother class," or in unexpected but sure-handed combinations: shocking pink and orange for a canvas beach coat; olive green and turquoise for a wool jersey travel outfit; melon and mauve in a cotton georgette halter evening dress. And at a time when all street suits seemed to be gray flannel, Claire's were shocking pink, red-and-black tweed—or a brass-buttoned red wool jacket and black skirt might be combined with an emerald green foulard blouse.

Her extrasensory pipeline was working well and the colorful McCardells became as much a part of the American scene as a Rothko abstraction, a Saarinen chair or a Philip Johnson house. In many ways, Claire's clothes had earned a place of their own in the world of art. A model in a jersey McCardell bathing suit on a Cape Cod beach was thrilled to have George Balanchine introduce himself. He wanted to say that she looked like a dancer in it.

Louise Dahl-Wolfe
Harper's Bazaar, 1953

A skinny chemise Claire called the "Stringbean" (*left*) could be worn with a cummerbund or hang plumb straight. *Opposite,* the calico bubble swim suit could be wrapped with matching sash for the water or cinched with a leather belt on land.

292

Maria Martel

Louise Dahl-Wolfe
Harper's Bazaar, 1953

When Claire made the space-dotted poncho for Avedon's 1954 cover (*above*) and the wavy striped party chemise for Dahl-Wolfe's picture in Spain, *opposite,* she might have been unconsciously joining the Op and hard-edged art movement, although it didn't come along until the 1960s.

In the mid-forties, the Museum of Modern Art had mounted a much discussed show built around Bernard Rudofsky's provocative title, "Are Clothes Modern?" Alongside an illustration of one of Claire's dresses, a caption made the point that "True inventiveness in design is practically restricted to playclothes, a category of dress, which, in time, may become the starting point for the creating of a genuine contemporary apparel." Three of Claire McCardell's simplest, most basic designs were shown side by side with fashions from the past and the most simple primitive garments.

A few of Claire's things, cut from geometric shapes, might have qualified for "hard-edge" art. There was a circle, four feet in circumference, made of powder-blue fleece. When a third of the circle was folded over on itself, it made a waist-length, double-tiered cape reminiscent of a highwayman's cloak. Claire showed it over a slim black evening dress. There were her cotton squares and rectangles in stripes and polka dots, which were slit in the middle and slipped over the head poncho-fashion to make effective and practical beach coats.

In 1953, the boundaries between her designs and art blurred even more when a major West Coast gallery gave an exhibition of McCardell clothes, 1933 to 1953. *Look* magazine speculated that this was "probably the first one-man show of dress designs exhibited just like any other works of art." The sponsor, Beverly Hills art dealer Frank Perls, had spotted his first Claire McCardell dress on a gallery-goer in New York, after his return from World War II. To him it seemed "the eternal dress straight from the Acropolis . . . all clean cut, nothing made up . . . nothing stuck on." Only then had he discovered that the dress was inexpensive *and* designed by an American woman.

For the West Coast exhibition, the clothes were shown on wire forms hung from an eighteen-foot ceiling, like Calder mobiles. On the back of the poster that showed one of Claire's sketches superimposed on giant graph paper, Stanley Marcus of Neiman-Marcus wrote:

> *Claire McCardell, as much as any designer I've ever known, designs as she pleases. She is the master of the line, never the slave of the sequin. . . . one of the few truly creative designers this country has produced, borrowing nothing from other designers.*

The day after the searchlighted, Hollywood-style opening, Greta Garbo arrived with her seamstress and asked for permission to copy a 1934 halter-back culotte that had been sent out from the Metropolitan Museum's collection. "It was the only thing I 'sold' from the show," Mr. Perls said, "But then look who 'bought' it!"

By the mid-fifties, the McCardell message had reached Europe—although the French, in particular Dior and Balenciaga, were making headlines with the sort of carefully fitted and expensively constructed clothes that Claire still felt were unsuited to the American sportswoman. On the casual side of the ledger, however, there was the comeback of the softly comfortable Chanel suit and the spirited

aristocratic sports clothes of the postwar Italians, led by Marchese Emilio Pucci. Coincidentally, Pucci thought Claire the best American designer. He always asked to see the McCardells on his trips to America—not to copy, but rather to salute her as a peer. Claire was surprised to find her message appreciated in Europe because she assumed it was dominated once again by the French. But the extent of her European reputation became apparent to her on a trip made with the author in 1955. Although she had been going to Europe two or three times a year since the war, it was usually to ski (by this time she knew every slope in Austria) or to visit London with her husband, who had friends and business interests there.

This time I had shanghaied her off to the south of France for a big *Life* story on a fabric first—McCardell clothes in cotton printed with the works of famous artists: Picasso, Léger, Miró, and Chagall. Essential to the story was the permission of each artist to let us photograph a model wearing a McCardell outfit displaying his print in his studio, with him alongside. Ostensibly, all the artists were waiting to see the clothes. Actually, they were waiting for Picasso's decision. We were all waiting for Picasso. We had assembled a rather formidable task force of photographer, editor, assistants for each, models from Paris and Rome, and Claire, who had even brought needle and thread. But our daily calls to Picasso at his villa La Californie in Cannes drew only "maybes." Then the Riviera grapevine said that our model Bettina, tops in Europe at the time (not only as a model but as a friend to all the exciting people, later especially to Aly Khan) might speed things up if she liked the clothes herself.

The inspiration for Jacques Fath and later Givenchy, Bettina must have had some couture-nurtured reservations when she saw the cotton prints rolled up in Claire's suitcase. But once she put the first one on she was off on a McCardell jam session, trying sashes high or low, knotting scarves on the head and neck. Everything fit and looked smashing—*épatante* as Bettina said. Claire silently beamed. I think it was the first time she realized that her American Look was really international. Not so coincidentally, we were welcomed within a day or two for a full afternoon with Picasso.

To her delight, Claire's reputation caught up with her again as we stopped over in London on our way home. Claire had for years admired James Laver, the world's best-known fashion historian, and had read and reread all his books. After shyly asking a mutual friend to arrange a meeting with him, she was astonished to learn that she was top on his "Must-Meet" list for a projected first trip to the United States. They had a terrific time over tea discussing his famous theory of the "erogenous zones." His were ankles that year, and she nominated bare backs and thighs.

Nineteen fifty-six was the year of the written word for Claire—a *Time* magazine cover story in May, and in November her own book,

Not many fashion designers make the cover of *TIME*. Following Claire McCardell's cover, there have been only Dior and Gernreich.

The scene: Picasso's studio in 1955 with famed French model, Bettina, modeling McCardell jersey pants and shirt of the artist's print. Picasso, reminded of a fencer's costume, produced the sword for a prop. Derby unexplained.

Mark Shaw
Life, 1955

Claire's bathing suits were usually cut like her favorite dresses and in the same fabrics and colors. *Opposite,* a draped wool jersey is photographed alongside a Tunisian Moucharabieh.

What Shall I Wear? was published to favorable reviews. Claire was only the third fashion designer to make the cover of *Time* (after Elsa Schiaparelli and Sophie Gimbel), and her work was treated seriously in its relationship to the American scene. The writer, Osborn Elliott, now editor and chairman of the board of *Newsweek,* observed that Claire and her American Look had updated Thorstein Veblen's 1898 theory of leisure; elegant dress could still be "the insignia of leisure," but "a leisure of action—barbecue parties in the back yard, motor trips, weekend golf and waterskiing."

Above, a triangular poncho with perfectly mitred stripes, photographed over a brief suit in the Canary Islands. Off figure it would look at home on a modern art gallery wall.

Louise Dahl-Wolfe
Harper's Bazaar, 1956

Claire designed briefly for the 3-to-6x set as well as for their mothers. *Below,* two miniature McCardell play outfits incorporate her favorite bold stripes and plaids in a halter-backed sundress and bloomer bathing suit. *Right.* Claire ties a high waist on movie actress Tuesday Weld, then a child model, in a 1950 Fashion Group show.

Christa

In *What Shall I Wear?* Claire didn't take fashion or herself too seriously. She did make a strong case for fashion being fun and affordable for women who used common sense in buying clothes for the lives they led. The fashion dimension, to her, lay in developing skills and imagination so that women could wear clothes and "make them their own." "The first step up the fashion ladder in Miss McCardell's opinion, is mastering the art of tying a bow," said *Women's Wear Daily*.

At times Claire sounded much like her southern belle forebears, then the period's greatest fashion individualists. Sensible shoes she wrote, were in order for following a man in a golf tournament, but "if you have a taxi lover in your home, be sure you have plenty of spindly heels to give him an excuse to take a taxi." Uncharacteristic spindly heels not withstanding, one of the strongest parts of Claire's book is that on accessories, and while she gives many examples of her own favorites, she also advocates independent thinking on the part of the reader—a full decade before "do your own thing" became part of the fashion parlance.

"My how we laughed when we made this one," said Bessie Sustersic, Claire's sample room head throughout her career. Bessie and her staff of four did all the original cutting and draping from Claire's little matchstick sketches. So they were not surprised when what looked like a shapeless jersey tube with a funnel for a collar and flippers for sleeves turned into the lissome cocktail dress at right.

Claire had worked out her own accessories from the early 1940s on. She called them "props," in the sense of scene-changers for a simple basic dress. At a time when most mass dress producers didn't want to distract a buyer's attention from their product above the neck or below the hem, she also pioneered in the "Total Look," a phrase coined later for top-to-toe dressing. This included caps or hoods for the head, fabric-covered soft shoes to match costumes, colored jersey stocking-tights she called "leg sweaters" and a few gags like Abominable Snowman fur after-ski slippers twenty inches long.

By the mid-fifties Mr. Klein, who had cheerfully but unprofitably produced most of Claire's peripheral ideas in his dress-oriented factory, had the inspiration to license them out to specialty manufacturers on a fee basis. In today's world, when every self- (and money-) respecting dress designer has added franchised sheets, towels, automobile interiors and office furnishings to his fashion repertory, it seems like a very small beginning. But a beginning it was. The Klein-McCardell team was leading the way toward proliferation of design. *Life* magazine devoted a color spread to the "busiest drawing board in town" showing Claire surrounded by her jewelry, sweaters, raincoats, head- and footgear (the latter by Capezio, not on a fee basis but for old times' sake) and that season's most amusing yet sensible accessory "Sun-Specs," tinted "granny glasses" which just protected the eyeball, minimizing the owlish white look around the eyes caused by more conventional sunglasses.

The Klein–McCardell team had many more plans for new enterprises which were cut short by Claire's untimely death of cancer in 1958. Had they materialized, there would have been a McCardell perfume and, coming full circle, a set of McCardell-dressed paper dolls.

Claire McCardell in granny glasses . . . shortening a model's outfit on location in the South of France while photographer, editor, and staff were nervously "waiting for Picasso" for our* big LIFE fashion story. * Author—Sally Kirkland, fashion editor of *LIFE*.

6

THE LEGACY

Young actress Tracy Brooks Swope wore her mother's 1949 taffeta halter-necked evening dress (*opposite*) in the 1972 McCardell retrospective show put on by New York's Fashion Institute of Technology. Another forties hit, *above*, was a top-stitched linen mini-skirted golf outfit.

By any yardstick, it was the smash fashion collection of the season.

Newsweek, June 5

There were cheers inside the auditorium as the clothes appeared on the stage and the fervor grew as the show went on, proving the basic concept: These are styles that can be worn today.

The New York Times, May 24

After seeing Paris and London, street fashion, prêt-à-porter and boutique fare, you might as well have stayed in Los Angeles for the Fashion Group's . . . affair.

Fashion Week (National Newspaper of Retailing) November 13

These reviews of Claire McCardell's clothes were not written at the height of her fame in the late 1940s, but in 1972, fourteen years after her death. They were occasioned by two big retrospective shows entirely devoted to McCardell designs shown on live models, the first at the Fashion Institute of Technology in New York, the second at the Los Angeles County Museum, with commentary by Rudi Gernreich, a leading McCardell disciple.

Claire would have been pleased but not entirely surprised at the favorable reaction to her clothes in the seventies. While she was without conceit, she had a profound sense of the importance of her fashion pioneering. "Good fashion somehow earns the right to survive," she said, and not only did she produce plenty of good fashions in her lifetime; she also had an instinctive feel for designs which, with occasional modification, were good enough to last through two generations at least. When the Metropolitan Museum embarked on a major updating of its costume collection in the 1940s to include American designers in depth, Claire's own closet was a valuable resource, beginning with the first jersey separates she made in 1934. The ninety-nine-piece McCardell collection which now extends through 1957 is heavily visited by students, established designers and retailers alike. Bloomingdale's executives came forty strong in 1970. Katie Murphy, vice-president and fashion coordinator for the store, described the visit:

> Partly I wanted to show them that almost nothing is really new in fashion, which was teasing. But on the positive side, since we were going into this soft, closer-to-the-body kind of thing, I thought they might as well see it done right—plus the work of a designer who really made a statement. The museum was terribly helpful, everything was hung on racks by dresses, suits, coats, active sports clothes. In a matter of minutes all of the females were trying things on and threatening to walk out into the streets of 1970 even though some of the things went back to the thirties.

A black tie $125-a-ticket capacity crowd turned out for the show. Students lined up three deep to cheer the fashion notables arriving. As *The New York Times* noted, "it had all the earmarks of a Hollywood premiere 'way back when." *Left to right* (*below*). Claire's banker brother Adrian Leroy McCardell, Jr., and his wife, Phyllis, wearing her sister-in-law's 1950s evening shirt dress. Lord & Taylor's former buyer, Marjorie Griswold in a McCardell cotton georgette, and designer Bill Blass who brought his assistants to "show them what McCardell was all about." *Opposite*. Commentator Nancy White, former Editor of *Harper's Bazaar*, and model in a 1955 bold striped raincoat, cut like a student's gown.

Bill Cunningham

308

Some favorites among the 90 pieces shown dating from the late thirties through the mid-fifties were: (a) Claire's spare-cut sleeveless dress and brass-encrusted belt; (b) her archetypical shirtwaist dress with dropped shoulders, wide push-up sleeves, its fabric fine men's shirting; (c) evening wool jerseys, including the 1946 "baby dress," adored by the models of 1972.

Bill Cunningham

a

310

b

c

311

 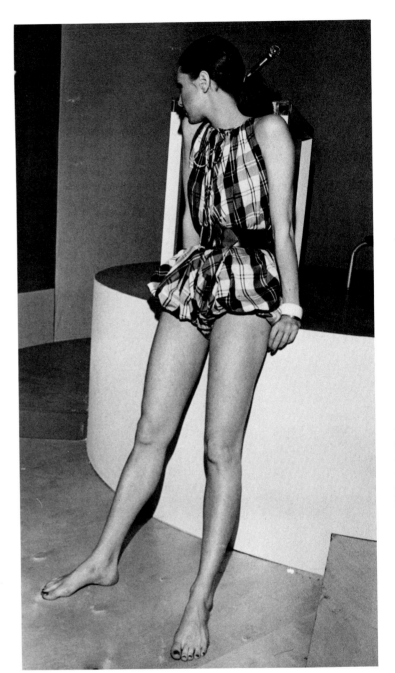

a   b

c   d

Bill Cunningham

The audience thought this bias cut jersey
hooded sweater and grey flannel culottes
(a) the epitome of the thoroughbred sportswear look. They also liked the plaid denim
(b) worn with a vintage Phelps belt, and
the classic black leotards (c) topped with a
white cotton version of a Mexican peasant's
jacket, and (d) a summer version of the
Swope family's taffeta halter dress in heavy
white pique.

One reason so many of her designs never date is because Claire "stayed loose" in the sense of not trying too hard to be *au courant*. As Diana Vreeland put it, "She knew and respected the human body and its proportions, totally, totally, TOTALLY," and although she designed to show off its best points she almost never used an artificial device to enhance it. When broad shoulders seemed desirable to the women of the early forties, to make their hips look slim, Claire could get the effect by the cut of the sleeve. When the doll-waisted New Look came along in the late forties, she made her version with snug, bias bodices that contrasted with full circle skirts independent of corselettes and crinolines. A 1947 full-skirted cotton McCardell could hold its own among the Halstons of today, whereas most Diors of the same year would look anachronistic.

But more important than any specific style of Claire's is the legacy she left in her philosophy of "honest" casual clothes, clothes that make a woman feel comfortable, pretty and "right" around the clock. Confirming this credo was Calvin Klein, winner of the 1974 Coty Return Award, who was cited as designing for today's young generation who want a casual look in clothes even in the evening. An even more striking convert was Marc Bohan, who in previewing his Spring 1975 couture collection for the house of Dior said he planned to have several dresses which would be *sans heure*. Claire would have been delighted with this concept since it was one she had pioneered.
I also think she would have enjoyed coming along with me to the Met's Costume Institute during Christmas week in 1974. I had asked to check a McCardell date or two for this book. Stella Blum, the curator, said that would be easy—most of Claire's milestones were out of the bins. The staff had had so many appointments to show them during the past few weeks they had decided to leave them on accessible racks.

As I passed one of the consulting rooms, a trendy young designer was having her first look at the McCardell Monastic and I could have sworn that I heard her say "Drop everything! . . . There's a dress with no back, no front, no waistline . . ."

A 1956 spring and summer evening outfit for almost any occasion and in almost any year. The coat and dress bodice are made of a linen-like cotton and rayon mixture, the dress skirt is of McCardell's always favorite cotton calico.

The monastic silhouette as Claire did it in the early fifties.

314

NORELL

BY BERNADINE MORRIS

CONTENTS

NORELL

The New York Times

Norman Norell when he stormed Seventh Avenue in 1940, a conservative dresser in checked suit and knitted tie.

The arrogant world of the Paris *haute couture,* for years the center of the fashion universe, is changing. Where a reverent congregation once assembled in hushed silence to witness the unveiling of a sleeve or a seam that would eventually change the shape of clothing everywhere, press photographers now roam the runways. They instantly disperse to newspapers around the world visual proof of the most bizarre creations.

The couturiers themselves are less concerned with evolving a seam or a sleeve than they are with their expanding ready-to-wear operations, their franchises for furs and undergarments, and their retail shops.

The few hundred private clients who care passionately how their clothes are made, who are willing to stand for endless fittings to be sure they adhere to their bodies, are no longer able to support the couture houses. Many of the women who could afford the price have defected. It's so much easier, and possibly more amusing, to buy things ready-made.

But in the 1920s and the 1930s, the glory was still rising. Wealthy women from the four corners of the earth converged on the couture salons to collect the badge of social eminence, a Paris wardrobe. The finest handwork, the most fabled fabrics, and the most elegant designs were assembled for them.

In 1928, a delicate young man with intense brown eyes sat absorbing everything. He was accompanying a formidable woman who knew all there was to know about clothes and was eager to impart her information to the slender, intense youth.

Later he was to say, "I learned everything I knew from her."

It was only a small exaggeration. The young man was Norman Norell, fledgling fashion designer. The woman was Hattie Carnegie, imperious despite her four-foot-ten-inch frame. Head of one of the most prestigious fashion operations in the world, she had a custom operation, a retail store, a wholesale enterprise which distributed her merchandise to stores throughout the country.

To feed her multiple operations, she went to Paris twice a year and bought prodigiously in all of the custom salons. Later, after helping to select the clothes, her designer, Norman Norell, would translate them into American terms. Twice a year, he would examine hundreds of designs, pulling them apart to see how they were made. He learned what to accept and what to reject, but most of all he learned how to recognize and appreciate quality. This he would never unlearn, never compromise.

"If you buy something, buy the best you can afford," he told people all his life. "If you can't afford expensive furniture, buy wicker, but the best wicker made. Buy just a few things, not a lot of junk."

Sometimes, as he saw the prices of the clothes he made rise to astronomical heights, he was apologetic about this predilection of his for the best of everything. He would spend fifteen or twenty dollars a yard for an organdy interfacing that would never be seen, even on the inside of a jacket, but it would give the shape he wanted.

"It's terrible," he would say, "but it's the way I am, and it's too late for me to change."

When he first began those voyages to Paris with the indomitable Miss Carnegie, Norell was just twenty-eight years old, though he looked even younger, as he continued to do through most of his life.

Years later, he remembered his first encounter with Miss Carnegie.

"She wore a beige velvet coat with a lynx collar, a beige cloche hat, and diamonds, and I was terrified," he recalled. "She asked me, 'Do you make pretty clothes?' and I mumbled something, so she gave me a trial."

He must have passed the test, for he stayed twelve years, concentrating mostly on the wholesale operation. With Miss Carnegie's help, he not only developed his taste in clothing but in home furnishings and antiques. Though they were never close friends—Norell was always a private person—they did go to auctions in Paris and New York together.

For the most part, he labored silently in the background, though he became known to the insiders in the fashion business and to some glamorous clients with whom he worked: Constance Bennett, Paulette Goddard, Lilyan Tashman, Pola Negri, Gertrude Lawrence. From his earliest childhood, Norell was stagestruck. He always said he spent more time in theatre than in school.

It was over a dress that Gertrude Lawrence wore in *Lady in the Dark* on Broadway that he had his final clash with Miss Carnegie. His employer objected that a royal blue sequined number Miss Lawrence wore was too elaborate. After the show opened, she wanted to reproduce it in a more demure version for her private customers. Norell stuck to his guns. He thought the dress was theatrically effective and he refused to change it. He left Miss Carnegie and decided to go into business for himself.

The time, 1940, was propitious. The guns of war had silenced the elegant messages from the couture salons in Paris. France was occupied by the Germans and though some struggled on, many of the couture houses had closed. In any case, Paris was no place for American buyers.

This isolation from the couture was to continue for five more years, but nobody knew that in 1940. For the United States, the war would not begin until the Japanese bombed Pearl Harbor on December 7, 1941. Of course, the Paris couture would rise again from the ashes with the brilliance of Christian Dior's New Look in 1947, but the fashion world would have changed by then, as it was to change again in the nineteen-sixties.

What happened in the 1940s, however, was that the American fashion business came into its own. Cut off from its traditional source of inspiration, it began to develop its own styles, its own designers.

Fashion built its own panoply of stars: Gilbert Adrian and Omar Kiam emerged from the movies; Nettie Rosenstein and Pauline Trigère made elegant ready-to-wear clothes. Claire McCardell, Claire Potter and Bonnie Cashin developed sportswear, a new category of clothes that Paris had never given much importance to and the tailor, Ben Zuckerman, developed coat- and suit-making into a high art.

A bit of a dandy in the 1920s, he wears white suit and carries a walking stick, *above;* in a boater and sailor overblouse, he cavorts with his mother and a friend in Venice, *right.*

John Rawlings
Vogue, 1944

322

Evening glamour: Norell could manage an exotic look in evening clothes during World War II by draping them discreetly, as in pegged-skirt style, *left,* or by embellishing them with sequins, *right.* Sequins were not considered essential to the war effort and their use was not restricted.

George Platt Lynes
Vogue, 1942

But the strongest luminary of all was Norman Norell. His first whole-sale collection in 1941 transplanted the couture mystique of the Paris salons to the showrooms of Seventh Avenue, the headquarters of the fashion business in New York.

It was one of those opportune moments: the right man in the right place at the right time.

Anthony Traina, a manufacturer who was as indomitable in his way as Miss Carnegie was in hers, needed a designer. He heard Norell was at liberty.

"Mr. Traina called and asked me to join him," Norell was to recall. "He offered me a larger salary if my name were not used, a smaller amount if it were."

He chose the smaller sum and Traina-Norell was born. For years, women spoke of the "Trainas" with the same reverence they gave to their "Chanels" or their "Balenciagas." It wasn't until 1960, when Traina retired after suffering a stroke, that the name Norell appeared alone in plain block letters on the label of the most prestigious clothes in the world.

In 1941, Traina was known as a manufacturer of expensive clothes for mature women who usually wore large sizes. Norell was an unknown quantity, a man behind the scenes at Carnegie. When they joined forces, there was a fashion explosion.

There were many reasons for the success of that first collection, but perhaps the chief one was that it gave Americans the opportunity to overcome their deep sense of inferiority to Paris. In terms of technical progress, the American fashion industry was already the most advanced in the world. It had pioneered the concept of ready-to-wear clothes which would fit almost everybody. In France and Italy at that time, the "little dressmaker" still flourished. Even women of modest means had their clothes made to order, or made them themselves.

But in America, this wasn't necessary. Ready-made clothes of good quality and a certain chic were widely available at reasonable prices. Technically, the garment industry which dated back to the turn of the century had made great strides in producing inexpensive clothing. But creatively, and especially as compared to Paris, it was lagging.

Merchants in the higher price brackets, such as Miss Carnegie, made their pilgrimages to Europe where they found styles to copy or adapt. A "good" Paris style could yield a collar for one dress, a sleeve for another, a pocket idea for a third.

Manufacturers in the price bracket just below them copied the styles they produced, which were in turn copied by producers one step down the line. To a large extent, the clothes available for the American shop girl and secretary were watered-down versions of what had appeared in the Paris salons.

In a more general way, the length of hemlines, the shape of the clothes, the colors of the fabrics and the fabrics themselves all took

Wartime elegance: despite restrictions on the amount of fabric that could be used, Norell contributed an elegant daytime look during World War II. His shirtdresses then had wide shoulders and narrow skirts that just covered knees.

Eric/43

John Rawlings
Vogue, 1943

Two Norell themes, developed in the early 1940s, which he never dropped: shirt and skirt look, *left,* glamourized with matching umbrella, and sweater look, here with striped overblouse matched to suit lining of wool jersey.

John Rawlings
Vogue, 1944

NORELL

John Rawlings
Vogue, 1944

Some enduring Norell looks of the late 1940s: *left*, the jersey overblouse and skirt; *right*, the Empire-waistline gray flannel evening dress, here with furred jacket; *far right*, the very simple black dress.

John Rawlings
Vogue, 1944

John Rawlings
Vogue, 1948

John Rawlings
Vogue, 1950

The fifties: Norell a pace-setter with his "little overcoat," *left,* and his wasp-waisted dress with tiny fly-away bolero, both worn over butterfly-bow silk blouses.

John Rawlings
Vogue, 1951

their cue from Paris. The only rival source of inspiration was the movies. The white-collared dress Ginger Rogers wore in *Kitty Foyle* spurred as a rash of imitations. But this was a far cry from originality.

So when Traina-Norell presented clothes with panache as well as technical skill, the hosannahs were swift.

And the clothes? Beautifully made, creatively designed and quite expensive for their day. Dresses started at $85, a suit sold for $159 (including the blouse). "We made one day dress for $169 but nobody bought it because it was too expensive," said Norell many years later, remembering that first collection. He also remembered fondly a cashmere evening dress covered with spangles that went for $110—and sold quite nicely.

Norell didn't just show a line of dresses or coats, as most of the other houses on Seventh Avenue did at that time. He showed a collection, in the French manner, that covered most of a woman's fashion needs —in fact, the fashion needs of many women. There was the pink satin short evening dress ("short" meaning "ankle length") modeled by Rita Hayworth in *Harper's Bazaar*. There was the black silk sheath with its "wickedly slashed skirt" and pink sequined sleeves advertised by Marshall Field of Chicago for $235, and the silk jersey dress with wide midriff and draped skirt, advertised at $135 by Bonwit Teller.

Skinny long evening dresses in wool were topped with chunky hip-length capes spattered with sequins and lined with a quilted fabric for warmth. There was also an elongated sweater, stretched to dress length and ribbed, that was a precursor of all the sweater fashions to come in the years ahead, both from Norell and from every other fashion designer in the world, including those in the Paris couture.

What Norman Norell had accomplished in that first collection was to give American fashion—producers and wearers alike—a freedom from dependence on foreign sources of inspiration. The American industry felt it could set its own directions, it own styles. Women didn't feel the necessity for a French label to confirm their taste and their status.

It didn't happen overnight and there were to be innumerable setbacks, the most recent being the Midi fiasco of 1970. But Norman Norell had at last shown it was possible to create artistically in the ready-to-wear medium. He was also to perfect the technical skills required in clothes making. And he did it in ready-to-wear, not custom-made clothes. He was thus the bridge between the tradition of couture and the future of ready-to-wear.

"American style: sharp and clean" the *Bazaar* caption read, "a parlormaid's collar and cuffs of snowy organdy on a fitted jersey top, a snowy skirt, a streak of patent and a red, red rose." Sure-fire fashion by Norell—then "Traina-Norell."

Below. The embodiment of the neat, precisely shaped, beautifully accessorized look
of the early fifties . . . at the hands of
Norell, master tailor.

...ell cuts away his usual black jersey top
...are minimum and fashions a flamboyant
...t of fuchsia taffeta for one of the most
...king fandangos of the 1950s.

NORELL

Other views of the early fifties: evening dress, slashed into ribbons, *left;* bouffant white satin skirt mated with gray flannel fitted jacket, collared in satin, *right.*

Harper's Bazaar, *1950*

Rene Bouché
Vogue, 1956

The later fifties, a little frivolous: tiered and flounced chemise, echoing Norell's favorite 1920s, *left;* low-waisted dress with hip-belt and flared skirt, *right,* also twenties in feeling.

Rene Bouché
Vogue, 1956

Lillian Bassman
Harper's Bazaar, *1956*

Tube top and flounced skirt of 1956, *left,* in starched white pique and in crisp black silk, *right. Far right:* an early version of the trouser suit, the same year, with overdress to wear at home.

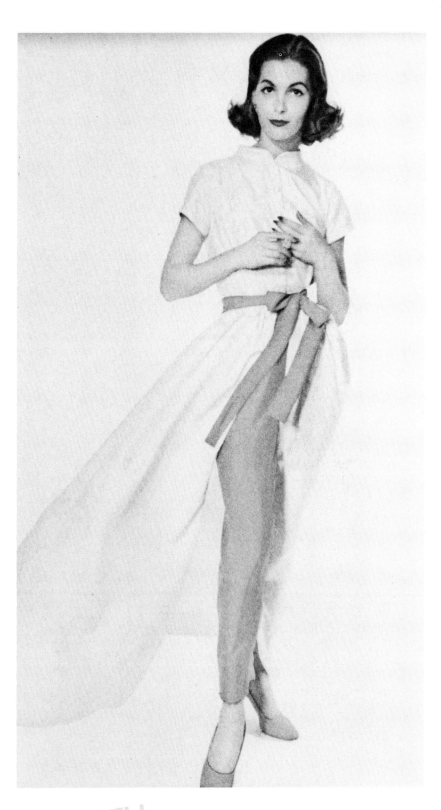

341

NORELL

2

HOW HE WORKED

Norman Norell at work at his desk at 550 Seventh Avenue, *left. Above,* mannequin parades a design while assistants await his reaction.

Hattie Carnegie was a perfectionist.

"She was hipped on shoulders and sleeves," Jo Hughes recalled. Now a super-saleswoman at Bergdorf Goodman, Miss Hughes was Carnegie's girl Friday in the late 1930s, in charge of her advertising and publicity.

> She had a fantastic eye. She would say, "Norell, that shoulder is one-quarter of one inch off, that button is one-tenth of one inch off; you know how I like my jackets down in the back."

> Once during the night before an opening she had him take a sleeve out seven times. They would rip those things apart so much, I never knew how they would get them together in time.

> She had terrible fits of temper, but I never heard him raise his voice and I could never understand how he remained so calm.

Carnegie was famous for her perfectly balanced suits with their perfectly cut shoulders. As her designer, Norell ripped out sleeves; as he adjusted buttons, he learned what made them perfect; he absorbed her taste, her eye for detail. But he never developed her temper. "He never raised his voice," said Denise Linden, thirty years after he ripped the sleeve out seven times for Miss Carnegie. "He'd always say, 'Would you please?' or 'Do you mind?' or 'What do you think?' and everybody would knock themselves out for him because he was so kind to us. I never saw him angry at his work."

In his last few years, Denise was Norell's head model and chief organizer. (Norell's models were always known by their first names.) "He was terribly orderly," she said. "He kept the whole collection in his head. He knew exactly what each girl would wear, which outfits would go together, though sometimes we wouldn't see them together until the day of the show. At the end, we would each have the same number of styles to show, though we could never figure out how he kept track of it."

343

There was little ripping and pinning at any time at Norman Norell, although occasionally a style would be discarded. "If he didn't like it, he would throw it out. Either it worked or it didn't work: he knew right away. Sometimes he would start three or four coats and not use any of them because he would get off on another theme. But there wasn't any chaos or hysterics ever," Denise recalled.

The preparation for a collection would begin as often as not in the New York Public Library, where Norell would stack old fashion magazines in front of him on the reading table and pore over the illustrations. Denise feels that he probably already had an idea in his mind, and was considering different ways of executing it.

A few months before the collection was to be shown, he would go to Europe to select his fabrics. At his prices, with his position, he knew he couldn't use the same fabrics that appeared in the other collections on Seventh Avenue. That's why his showings were a month or two after everyone else's: not so much because he feared being copied but because his fabrics arrived so late. Very often, his materials would turn up in the couture collections of Paris and Rome for the same season; in the case of his rustling silk taffeta plaids, a few years ago, his designs were more attractive than anything done in the same fabric in Europe.

Occasionally, he'd put some ideas in work before he left for Europe, having them made up in muslin or in any fabric he had in the house.

Often what he found in Europe would give him the theme for a part of the collection. The crunchy alpacas in natural shades of beige and gray provided the clue for the casual coats and suits of his last collection, for fall 1972. In the previous collection for spring, it was an awning-striped woolen, in bright green, red or black with white. He used it in combination with solid colors for the separates look that was coming in so strong at the time. Denise, who was with him on his last trips, recalls:

> He was a very fast buyer. He innately knew what was right for him, and he'd quickly make two piles of the samples he was shown: one for the things he wanted, one for the things he discarded.
>
> He loved sharp, crisp fabrics because he liked to tailor clothes. Claude Staron, the fabric man, was a good friend of his and they used to work out prints together, but in the last few years, he wasn't big on prints.
>
> He was very fussy. He would never pick a printed dot—it had to be woven. He'd spend as much time picking out the lining as he did the fabric for the coat. He'd even pick out the buttons. And he was very knowledgeable. He could always tell the fiber content. And he knew instantly what he could do with it.

When the fabrics arrived from abroad, he'd get a swatch of everything he ordered and put them on a board. Then he'd get out his

Norell discusses technical problem with an employee. He understood production work as well as designing.

jersey swatches—he had ninety-nine colors to choose from—and if he couldn't find the shade he wanted, Racine would make it up for him. He would begin picking the jersey colors he wanted to go with the coat fabrics he had bought. (The dresses under the coats were usually jersey; sometimes he chose a shirt or sweater and skirt rather than a dress. The models never understood by what process he decided upon separates rather than a one-piece dress.)

With the fabrics before him, he would start turning out sketches—rough, working sketches, sometimes swatched or with a descriptive phrase or two. Norell used to say he never did learn to draw, but his associates knew perfectly well what those sketches meant. Muslins were rarely resorted to, except when something new was being tried, or when Norell ordered a couple of different collars made because he wasn't quite sure what he wanted.

For the most part, the fabric would be cut into directly. Coat and suit sketches went to Carmello Cardello, the head tailor, who had eight tailors working with him. George Oliva did the jersey styles, as had his father before him. Mrs. Hildegarde Dargatz took care of the dressy clothes and the pants.

As the clothes were completed, Norell would call in the girls who were to model them for their fittings. He could tell whether a shoulder was one-eighth of one inch off: it was his Carnegie training.

At the first fitting, Norell would decide on the details: whether he wanted a pocket straight or on the bias. At the second fitting, he would check the garment and take a length. That was usually all that was needed.

Often the girls wouldn't fit the coat and the dress that would be worn with it at the same time. They might not see the outfit together until the day of the show. But Norell knew: it was all in his head.

A few days before the show, usually a Saturday, he would start sketching again. On plain brown paper, mounted on a board, he would illustrate for each girl the clothes she would wear in the order she would wear them.

These sketches would be swatched and the accessories shown, so there could be no mistake. There was no problem with the line-up. Each girl knew who she would follow and what style she would wear. At the showing, "he would tie all the bows and hand us the jewelry," Denise remembers. "We would all work so hard for him."

After the show, duplicates had to be made so the clothes could be put into production. Whereas most designers leave it in the hands of a production man, Norell took care of this himself.

He made it seem easy, too. He had a cage or a torso to slip over the body of the girl who was doing the fittings and adjust her measurements to a perfect size eight. He'd check the duplicate, and if it was all right, the pattern graders would adjust it down for a size six, up for a size ten or twelve. "He didn't visualize women being size fourteen or sixteen," Denise recalled. "Those sizes were available, but they had to be specially ordered."

No buyer ever fooled around with a Norell style. They didn't ask for a different neckline or a different collar. The style was bought the way it was shown and usually in the color it was made. Norell's taste was trusted—as was his infinite attention to detail.

Norell collapses after a hard day on the job. He could never imagine doing anything else for a living except designing dresses. Sometimes he thought he might have liked being a doctor—he was always prescribing for his friends.

Leonard Kamsler

Derjinsky
Harper's Bazaar, 1961

ATTITUDES

Bert Stern
Vogue, 1965

Frivolity has its place at night. Norell rev-
elled in little madnesses such as this feath-
ered cape of 1961, *left*. He also liked simple
necklines and collars that followed the arc
of the neck meticulously, *above*.

"Arty talk about haute couture *gives me a swift pain," Norman Norell
told an interviewer for the* Saturday Evening Post *in 1962.*

*It's nothing but phony pretension to cover up ignorance or bad taste.
I went through that phase when I was a kid.*

*The first outfit I ever made was for my mother for a train trip we took
from Indianapolis to California in 1920. I tricked her out in a red chiffon dress down to the floor, a big straw hat with flowing black ribbons
and a lace-trimmed parasol. We were on that train for a full week
and nobody spoke to us. They thought we were Bessarabian gypsies.*

Norman Norell never did indulge in arty talk himself. Using earthy
language, speaking in a swift, slangy rhythm, he would, as he said,
"cut through the crap." Asked by another interviewer ten years later
what he thought most women did wrong in their dress, he responded:

*They don't do as many wrong things as they used to with their flow-
ered hats, their mink stoles and awful accessories. I would rather see
someone threadbare in something good than cheesy in the latest
fashion.*

*Being clean is the most important thing. I'm thinking of the young
people. I don't care how much hair they have, they should be clean.*

Neatness was an obsession with him. In 1958, he said, "I think they
(American women) look best when they are immaculately scrubbed
and exquisitely groomed. They always ought to wear white gloves and
pearls and own one good dress."

Another of his concerns was simplicity during the day, leaving hijinks for night. That's the way he designed his clothes. That's the way
he liked to see people look.

The backbone of his collections were the simple wool jersey
dresses that changed their shape only infinitesimally from season to
season. He made them in the twenties; he was still making

them in the last collection he worked on before he died, that for Resort, 1973.

If he had to pick a favorite period of fashion, he would invariably mention the nineteen-twenties. "Women are still wearing, and throughout this century will continue to wear, the changes that came about in the twenties," he said in 1960. He enumerated the changes: "Short hair; interesting make-up; red, red lips; the basic black dress (before the twenties, black was worn only for mourning); the color beige; fake jewelry; short skirts; plain pumps for daytime; nude stockings, and gloves that pull on easily."

Clothes, he pointed out, "became easy and comfortable for the first time. They were loose and sexy and a woman could relax, un-trammeled by rigid bones, stays and long skirts. What's more, she could go from morning to dinner without changing."

Norell was lucky that he began designing clothes in the 1920s, when dress shapes were fairly standard and the real challenge was where to put the decorations. In fact, when asked just before his death what he considered his major contribution to fashion, in a career that spanned five decades and part of a sixth, he went back to the twenties:

> When I started out, the idea was for a designer to come up with a new neckline on an old dress body. That seemed to be the first rule of designing. Well, I hated necklines. I always thought they made women look older. So I started making simple Peter Pan collars or no collars at all. Just a plain round neckline, no crap on it. It looked neater, cleaner, younger, the simple no-neckline dress. I do think it changed the look of clothes. Traina used to say to me later, "Thank God you never would do necklines."

The simple, high round neckline was a Norell trademark to the end.

The second contribution to fashion of which he was proud was the no-waistline dress, the chemise. This also was a discovery of the twenties, but one that lay dormant during the next decade when fashions were characterized by intricate cutting and seaming.

Norell returned to it in 1942. World War II was on and the United States government had introduced a restriction on the fashion industry known as Limitations Order L–85. What it limited was the amount of fabric that could be used in each garment. It placed restrictions on the depth of hemlines, the use of metal (as in zippers), even the use of linings made of wool. Norell didn't find these edicts stultifying. "We all made pretty good clothes during the war," he said later.

For himself, he was to find that the no-waistline dress required less fabric than the government restrictions permitted. "We used about half of what we could," he recalled. But that wasn't the main advantage. The simple shift he devised was the basis of "the clean, tailored look for daytime." He would vary it later, submerge it in belts, but the clean, tailored shift remained the bulwark of his dress collections.

Sometimes he would reminisce about the past, though he would

Sheath and flounce allure. Astonishingly, it's a knit appliqued with beige silk flowers embroidered in gold—hence the cling to the figure, the soft bounce of the flounce.

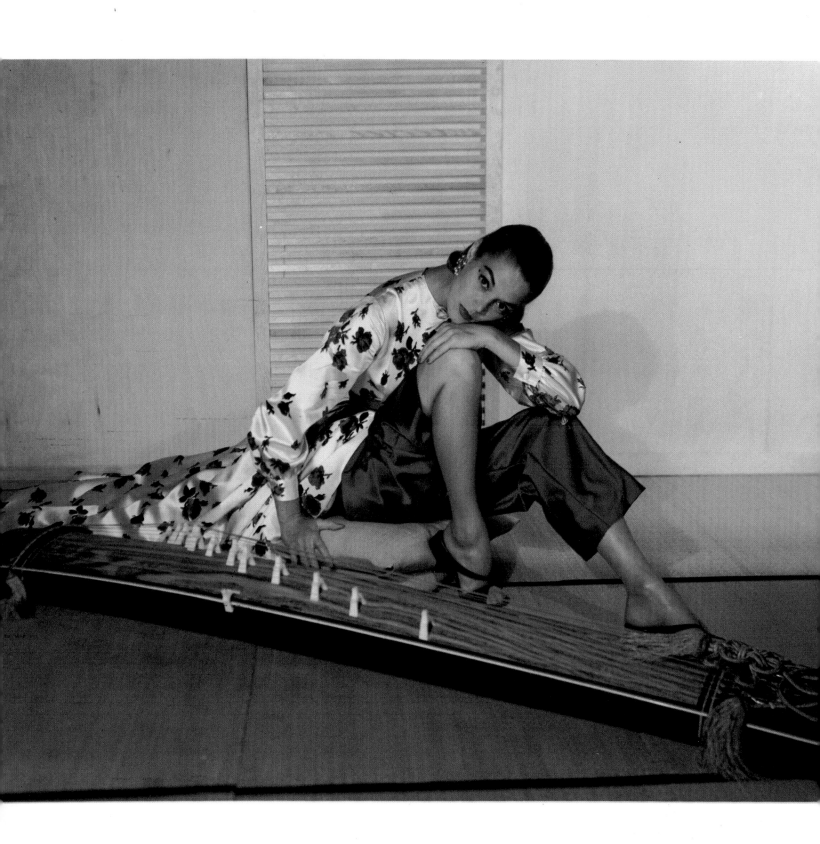

never cloud his view of the present. As a designer, Norell had his feet firmly on the ground, aware of changing life-styles, and aware that clothes should be subordinated to the needs of the people who wore them. "There are people who say that designers change fashion often to make women buy clothes," he once said. "I do not believe it. Fashion's function is to enhance the beauty of a woman. It must also serve her needs in a constantly changing world. Fashion follows very quickly on the heels of a new way of life. It changes constantly because women want it to."

He recalled that when he started out, there were many women who devoted their lives to their wardrobes.

> They went to the races every week—many fashions were launched at Longchamps in Paris. They dressed to go to the theatre. They took infinite pains: many had casts made of their hands so their gloves could fit perfectly. They kept dressmakers going. Everybody wanted to know what those women were buying. They needed so many things in 1920: they'd wear one outfit in the morning, change into something else in the afternoon, put on another dress for tea dancing and something else for dinner.

> Now if a woman makes two changes during the day, it's a lot. It's not necessarily a deterioration. It's putting things in their place. Of course, fashion is less important than it used to be. Women have other things to think about.

Thinking over the most influential designers of his lifetime, he mentioned Mme Grès ("because she has done her own designing forever,") Vionnet, Chanel, Balenciaga and Courrèges ("whether you like what he did or not, he changed fashion"). "I'm sure there are lots more people who made beautiful clothes, but that's not the point. The point is, who changed fashion."

Of American designers, he said, "I always thought Bonnie Cashin was good," and he gave high points to Galanos.

> For me, he is a great designer, but he is not terribly consistent. I think he's so intent sometimes on making elegant, unsnappy clothes because he doesn't want all those tootsies in Hollywood to wear them. I used to worry about that myself. I don't know whether he is aware of this fear, but I bet that's what it is.

As for Halston, Norell said he deserved credit because he launched a look. "Give him another five years, and we'll know."

How did he like women to look? "They can never be too simple during the day or too elaborate at night, as far as I'm concerned," he said, harkening back to an old theme. "American women still wear too much make-up during the day and too little at night, though they're getting better about it."

Norell always disliked fancy shoes, preferring plain pumps. "Sometimes the shoes in fashion are ugly, sometimes they're dangerous. I always want to tell women to just get a simple pair of shoes that fit."

Lounging pajamas photographed in the Modern Museum's newly erected—in 1954 —influential Japanese House. Satin coat flocked with velvet roses, ruby satin trousers, Norell pioneering.

But he hardly ever had the nerve to tell them. A man of legendary
modesty, he would try to hide out in the fitting rooms of the stores
to which he brought his collections. "I could never tell the women
how gorgeous they were, I just couldn't," he said adding that he was
afraid to suggest a particular dress to a woman, since she might buy it
because he said so and be miserable with it.

He also avoided mingling socially with his clients. "I never had the
time for that, I escaped it my whole life," he said. "I never did what
a designer is supposed to do."

Nor did he ever have an assistant to take some of the labor off his
shoulders. "At least you could get away after finishing a collection and
come back a little fresher for the next if you had help," he said, a
little wistfully. Norell couldn't get away because he supervised every-

Spangles were part of evening festivities in
most Norell collections. In the early 1960s,
he did jackets in the manner of Chanel.

Bert Stern
Vogue, 1965

thing—the making of the duplicate samples, the pattern making and the grading.

But the truth is, he didn't want to get away. His life was focused on his work. He went to his workrooms on the tenth floor of 550 Seventh Avenue every morning at ten, stopped for lunch with his models at Bill's across the street or Jack's Epicure a few blocks north, and left at five-thirty, six, sometimes seven o'clock. He'd eat at Schrafft's in his neighborhood, or perhaps Hamburger Heaven ("there's nothing between that and La Grenouille,") usually alone. Then he'd go home, read *The New York Times,* watch television and go to bed. "I never read books unless someone gives me one," he confided. The last book he read was Joan Blondell's *Center Door Fancy.* He loved it. It gave "a great picture of vaudeville—that was my time." Indianapolis, where he grew up, was "a big theatrical town—when I was eight, I started going to the theatre. Everybody told my parents they shouldn't keep me out so late, but I learned more than I did at school."

He never paid much attention to his own clothes, claiming, "I can't stand to have fittings at a tailor." Deprecatingly, he said, "When you get to be my age, all you can do is look clean and neat." He had a navy suit and a gray suit in winter-weight woolen and a navy suit and a gray one for summer. He also owned a navy blue blazer and a bunch of sweaters he bought in boys' departments.

His ties were always red ("it's easier—it doesn't matter which one you pick") and his shirts were striped in red, white and blue or were solid blue. "It simplifies things for me—I have no time for myself." It also simplified traveling. One suit packed, and he was ready to go.

Norell was not unhappy with his life. "I see so many people who hate to go to work in the morning. They hate what they do. I couldn't function if I dreaded it. I have fun at the fittings. The models are my friends. When I'm working on a collection, I think, 'Oh, God, I'm so frantic,' but when it is over, I'm left hanging like a chandelier. I miss it."

He couldn't imagine any other life for himself. "Designing has been good to me," he once said. "It's what I wanted to do. It never made me rich, but it gave me a comfortable living."

Jerome Ducrot
The New York Times

THE LIFE

Jerome Ducrot
The New York Times

Norell took care of his own fittings. *Left,* with one of his double-breasted tailored coats of the mid-sixties; *above,* adjusting one of his "little overcoats."

Norell had the greatest eye I'd ever known. It was uncanny. He saw things nobody else saw; he literally did. And not just in fashion. In art too. We saw a Renoir exhibit in Paris and he stopped by a painting of a woman and child in front of some pale mauve and orange flowers and he said, "How clever he was to let the light fall on the mauve flowers and the shadow on the orange ones." I've never forgotten.

He could be critical too, even of Michelangelo. We went to a Picasso exhibit at the Louvre, where we saw the civil war painting, you know, Guernica. It was dazzling. Afterwards, I said, "Let's go upstairs and look at some of the old things." He said, "No, after this nothing is going to look like anything." "Not even the Mona Lisa?" "No, not even that."

He was always very sure of what he was looking at and he had opinions. He admired Balenciaga enormously, but he would sometimes say at his collections, "He knows better than that—he shouldn't fool around with that sort of thing." He usually was talking about the soft things—Balenciaga was never very good with soft fabrics. When I said perhaps some customer had a need for that kind of style, he'd say, "Well, he shouldn't show it in the collection."

The speaker was Wilson Folmar, a longtime friend of Norell and himself a designer. They met on a boat to Paris, before World War II, when Norell was still at Hattie Carnegie and Folmar designed custom clothes for Jay Thorpe, across Fifty-Seventh Street. Later, when Folmar too moved to Seventh Avenue, he joined the luncheon group at Schrafft's on Forty-Third Street just east of Broadway, which Norell was to make as much a landmark for the garment center set as the Hotel Algonquin's Round Table had been for Dorothy Parker, James Thurber and company.

"We'd crowd around, six or seven of us at a table for four," said Robert Knox, a charter member of the Schrafft's group and for years the designer for Ben Gershel, a manufacturer of expensive coats and suits.

> First, there was just Norman and me. Then Wilson came, and the younger designers—Louis Clausen, Frank Adams. Traina ate there too. Occasionally, there'd be an outsider.

> Norman always ordered the same thing: scrambled eggs, bacon very crisp, vanilla ice cream, chocolate sauce—light on the ice cream, heavy on the chocolate. The waitresses never even asked him what he wanted.

What did Knox admire most about his friend's designs? "The perfection of his clothes. He continued to make the same things through the years, but he was constantly improving them, refining them, until he got them exactly right."

Mr. Knox remembered a young Norman Norell, more vivacious than the somewhat withdrawn, reclusive personality he became.

> When I first met him, he lived in a walk-up at 25 West 10th Street. It was very modern—the furnishings all came from Vienna. In the living room there was big, black patent leather furniture that nobody could sit on because you slipped all over. Then he moved to 59 West 12th Street, and it was still modern, but now all bleached wood and beige upholstery. Everything was beige and white.

> We'd have dinner at a place on 34th Street and Lexington Avenue run by two eccentric women who were friends of his. It was called the Waffle Shop. But at that time he was fond of good restaurants as well and sometimes we'd go to Larue's and drop into a few nightclubs.

> Then we'd go back to his apartment and sit up till two, three in the morning making sketches. He had a big, very modern desk and would sketch endlessly on these little white pads. He'd fill one after the other. We'd talk about clothes until we were exhausted. Halfway through the night, he'd put on a pot of coffee and then go back to his sketching. He continued that sketching until the day he died.

> He always knew he was good. He had a great facade of modesty, but he was also sure of himself. And he never stopped working, never. He lived his work, every minute. The young designers today have other things to do with their evenings besides sitting up making endless sketches.

In the 1930s, Mr. Knox believed Norell received about five hundred dollars a week from Carnegie, "but he spent it—he never saved a penny. He spent it on the theatre, restaurants, living."

The road to success was not too stormy. It began in Noblesville, Indiana, on April 20, 1900, when a son named Norman David was born to Harry and Nettie Levinson. His father operated the family's men's clothing store in one of those myriad midwestern towns "with the courthouse and the businesses all located around a square," recalled Norell.

His father decided to open a one-price men's hat store in Indianapolis, to which he traveled by trolley. "A cheap hat was a dollar and an expensive one was three dollars," Norell recalled, "so he decided to split the difference and have everything two dollars." The store prospered and soon added other men's furnishings. It's still there, Harry Levinson and Company, run by Norman's older brother, Frank, and Frank's three sons, Frank, Alan and Harry.

"We were all so proud of him—we'd get all the clippings," said the younger Frank. "Our wives understood what he was doing better than we did."

The nephews are all married today, with children of their own, but Alan remembers when he was seventeen years old and in the navy during World War II spending weekends at his uncle's apartment on Twelfth Street. "Uncle Norman was never there—he was always working in a hospital, changing bedpans and things like that."

When Norell decided that he wanted his models to wear panama hats when they showed his spring collection in 1972, his brother Frank was helpful. He provided the hats. They were men's styles, but nobody knew.

By the time Norman was five years old, the success of the hat shop seemed assured, and the family moved from Noblesville to Indianapolis. "I was the worst child that ever lived," he recalled late in life. "I had a horrible temper. I was spoiled and mean. I threw everything and yelled and kicked. I was always sick and they let me get away with murder. I was always so thin. I weighed forty-seven pounds when I was twelve. When I was nineteen, I came to New York and I didn't have anybody to yell at, so I just got over it."

He wanted to study fashion designing, but there weren't any courses. So he studied illustration at the Parsons School and lived in a room his father found for him on upper Broadway.

It was about this time that he changed his name. Levinson sounded too prosaic. "Nor for Norman, L for Levinson, with another L added for looks," he once explained. He never changed his name legally.

He switched to figure drawing and costume design at Pratt Institute, but he spent more time at the public library "because my room was so cold I went there to keep warm," and at the theatres "because I was always stagestruck."

When he was twenty-two, he became a costume designer at the Astoria studio of Paramount Pictures where he designed clothes for Gloria Swanson in *Zaza* and Rudolph Valentino in *The Sainted Devil*. When the studio closed, he worked for some musicals on Broadway and, for a time, joined the Brooks Costume Company, designing burlesque shows, vaudeville and nightclub reviews.

In 1924 he joined Charles Armour, a manufacturer of dresses in the $39 to $100 price range, then considered quite expensive. "I didn't know anything, but we had a fancy showroom and I was sent to Europe for the first time," he recalled. "I bought buttons and a lot of arty junk that must have been left over from Paul Poiret."

Both his theatre background and the wholesale experience were useful when he joined Hattie Carnegie in 1928, since she had a lot of theatrical clients. He made clothes for some of Hollywood's best-dressed actresses in the 1930s, among them Constance Bennett, Joan Crawford, and Rosalind Russell. At the height of the furor over "hot pants" in 1971, he remembered doing a spangled pair for Paulette Goddard in 1938. "She complained they wouldn't let her into restaurants in them."

Anthony Traina was making large-size dresses and his business was foundering in 1941 when he offered Norell a job. From then on, for the next thirty-one years, he towered above the rest of the American designers.

"Ben Zuckerman once told me," said Sydney Gittler, Ohrbach's legendary buyer, "the only designers he would deign to copy were Balenciaga and Norell. No one in America made clothes the way he did. They're the equal of the top couturiers in Paris."

The Paris designers approve of his work too. *"C'est très serieux, très classique,"* said Pierre Cardin. "His materials are very good and he's not fancy. He knows very much what he is doing and I respect him."

To innumerable women, Norell brought assurance and security. "He's made me feel well dressed over the years," said Mrs. Sidney Goodman of Minneapolis. "I wore an eleven-year-old Norell to the symphony and everyone assured me I looked marvelous."

The timelessness of Norells is a good part of their charm. Countless women have amortized the price of a Norell over a period of ten or more years and found, despite the high initial investment, that the dress was a good buy.

But the aesthetic appeal is strong too. Mrs. Mortimer Solomon of Purchase, New York, insists she collects Norells as other women collect paintings or jewels. Mrs. Charles Revson remembers her first Norell dress; her mother bought it for her when she was eighteen years old. It was black satin, low cut in front and with crossed straps in back. Today she has closetsful. "I don't mind wearing the same dress a few nights running," she says. "I don't go anywhere else, except for sports clothes. There's no point—everything I want I get right here."

In 1960, when Norell took over the business upon the illness and subsequent death of Anthony Traina, his theatrical sense came to the fore and he made a bit of a splash by introducing culottes or divided skirts for women to wear day and night. By the end of the decade, trousers were to be commonplace, but in 1960 even culottes were controversial.

Other than the culottes, the transition to Norman Norell from Traina-Norell went smoothly enough. Norell was enabled to buy the business with the aid of some silent partners, among them Prewitt

The popular Norell jersey dress, *below*, loosely belted and baring the knees in 1966; *right,* the Norell suit with short skirt, long jacket, and pussycat bow.

Bill Cunningham

Bill Cunningham

The go-go sixties: skirts way above the knees. *Right:* Norell with three short-skirted models, two in suits for the street; the short sequin-banded chemise for cocktails.

Evening games and grandeur in the late 1960s: fur-bordered tunic ensemble, *left;* dresses with built-in jewels, *right,* necklaces are sewn to bodice.

Bill Cunningham

365

Bill Cunningham

The end of the 1960s: simple jersey daytime dress, *above*; cape-collared coat, *right*;
belted mini-coat and navy dress with wide
white belt and scarf, *far right*.

Bill Cunningham

NORELL

367

Semmes, a Detroit businessman. In the end, he was in full control because of the successful introduction of his perfume in 1968. With the money from Revlon, which produced the fragrance, he was able to buy out his backers.

All great designers win their share of awards and Norell was no exception. He started with the first Coty American Fashion Critics Award in 1943, which has the same relation to the fashion business that the Oscar has to the movies. The ceremonies took place in the main hall of the Metropolitan Museum of Art, and New York's pugnacious little mayor Fiorello LaGuardia was there to do homage to Norell and the burgeoning fashion industry.

It would have been inconceivable for such an event to have taken place earlier, so low did the fashion people here rate their industry in terms of creativity. Paris was the fulcrum of the fashion world. But World War II was raging, and cut off from the font of creativity for three years, the American fashion industry had flourished. Besides, it had produced a Norell. Everyone was proud.

He was cited for the trends he had launched in the past year: his sequined cocktail dresses (sequins were not an essential material like metal, which had vanished from clothes, along with zippers), cloth coats lined with fur or studded with spangles, the economical-with-fabric chemise dress, and fur slacks for heatless homes.

The Coty Awards proved to be an institution as enduring as its first winner. It voted him a return award in 1951 and five years later, in 1956, elected him to the Coty Hall of Fame, its highest honor.

There were other awards as well—an honorary degree, Doctor of Fine Arts, presented by Pratt Institute in 1962 and, the following year, the International Fashion Award from the London *Sunday Times*. There was the party in his honor at the Metropolitan Museum of Art organized by the Council of Fashion Designers of America, of which he was president. It was held on the eve of the Metropolitan's exhibit, "The Art of Fashion," on October 24, 1967. A year later, there was a supper dance at Bonwit Teller just before his perfume was launched. At fifty dollars an ounce, it sold a million dollars' worth the first year and was the first successful perfume launched in America under a designer's name. He described it as "a new floral with green overtones—not the heavy, vampy, femme fatale-y kind of thing. It's pleasant and has a kick to it."

And all along, there were the color pages in *Life* magazine, the covers of *Vogue* and *Harper's Bazaar*. The black-tie openings of his collections twice a year were social events, with champagne flowing and the kingpins of the fashion business in attendance. The evening openings had started with the first Traina-Norell show in July, 1941. Though other designers had tried it, no one was able to get people to their showrooms at the end of the working day.

For almost thirty years, the night openings continued to give

Norell's Amster Yard Duplex. "I love to come home and shut the door." At home, Norell was happy to be surrounded by the enduring courtly elegance of past centuries. A magnificent Coromandel screen, antique crystal chandeliers, ancient Chinese porcelain, Aubussons. All changed for summer to Mexican cottons and sunflower silks.

Retrospective show at Metropolitan Museum of Art in 1972 recapitulated Norman Norell's career. It included candy-striped capelet dress of 1933, *left,* and bouffant petticoated dress from his post-New Look collection in 1948.

Heroine's clothes for the 1940s. Pin-striped grey jersey jumper swathed in misty Norwegian blue fox. Pearly perfection to the draped turban and striped gloves. Pure Norell.

Three moods for evening: tunic dress edged in feathers, *left*; taffeta dress, propped with petticoats, *below*; and hobble skirt paved in sequins, *right*.

Cunningham

cachet to the wholesale business, but when they outgrew their usefulness, Norell dropped them. Many people lived in the suburbs where train service at night was erratic. There was the fear of muggings for people who lived in town. So in 1969, he showed his collection at 5 P.M. Later, he was to move the time back to 3 P.M. The clothes, of course, were as effective in the afternoon as they were at night.

The final honor of his career was a retrospective showing of his work of fifty years at the Metropolitan Museum of Art on October 16, 1972. Norell was not to see it. After spending the previous day arranging the accessories and working on the sequences, he suffered a stroke on October 15. He never regained consciousness, and died ten days later at Lenox Hill Hospital.

Bobby Short played Noel Coward at the funeral service at the Unitarian Church of All Souls. Norell's models, his workers, his clients all came to pay their respects. The minister, Walter Donald Kring, read Psalm 121 and some poetry from Rabindranath Tagore. His physician, Dr. Kevin Cahill, gave a eulogy and Charles Revson called his departure a tragedy "to the fashion world and to the city where fashion is king." Mrs. John V. Lindsay mourned the loss of "two great men of this city"—Jackie Robinson's funeral was being held at the same time.

But the most touching comment was from Carmello Cardello, his head tailor.

"You didn't have to put a label on them; people recognized his clothes," he said.

Finale of Metropolitan Museum of Art show: a display of sequin mermaid dresses, many from the last Norell collection of fall, 1972.

NORELL

THE CLOTHES

Reprinted by permission from Women's Wear Daily, October 27, 1972. Copyright 1972, Fairchild Publications, Inc.

The Norell hallmarks, *above*—as sketched in *Women's Wear Daily. Opposite*, a smile from Norell after one of his showings. Until the late 1960s, Norell presented his collections at 9 P.M. and the audience wore black tie or evening dresses.

I Cunningham

My approach to design consists of a great deal of thinking and not much designing. I believe in thinking out what the next logical and natural trend in fashion will be. Once I have decided, the rest is easy. I simply take the most straightforward approach to it, without any extra, fancy trimmings. I don't like over-designed anything.

This statement of Norman Norell's in 1952 does more to explain his work than any elaborate detailed analysis. For him, as for any artist, the magic was in knowing what to leave off. Like Matisse, the older he got, the simpler his work appeared.

But fashion is not a painting to be hung on a wall and admired from a distance. A dress is to be worn and to be worn in a social context that constantly changes. So the trends that must be considered are not simply changes in the cut of a sleeve or an armhole but the more generalized ones of how people live, and how their clothes must respect the spirit of the day.

In this sense, Norell succeeded admirably. In addition to being recognizably Norells, his styles, over a sweep of half a century, reflect the spirit of the time in which they were made.

There are the recurrent themes, notably the chemise, hallmark of the 1920s when Norell was starting out, brought back in 1941 as a means of coping with fabric shortages, returning in 1951 as a relief from the taut-waisted, corseted shape that came in with Dior's New Look in 1947. Ten years later, at the instigation of Balenciaga, the chemise became the shape of the moment.

Norell made some of the most bizarre interpretations: balloon shapes that *Harper's Bazaar* dubbed the "armada" because they resembled a ship in full sail; the most extravagant tent dresses and smock coats; even hobble styles with a tight band at the hem, below the billows. Everyone was doing the chemise, and Norell knew his had to be noticed.

But when the flurry subsided, he knew he had hit on a good thing, and to the end of his life he made chemises. He made them in jersey and, when fashion decreed, he put a belt on them. But the waistline was unmarked in the basic dress—and it was, despite the ups and downs of hemlines, his most successful style for twenty years.

The sailor dress was another perennial. He remembered as a child being dressed in "Peter Thompsons," sailor suits in blue serge with white linen or duck collars—his portrait was painted in one of them. The little girls wore sailor dresses in the same fabrics. All his life, he was to make new versions of the sailor look for bigger girls. As early as 1933, he was pairing a navy blue jersey blazer with a white wool skirt and a striped pullover for the yachting look at Hattie Carnegie.

Into the 1950s and the 1960s, his sailor dresses were simple affairs with nautical symbols for day or great whirls of starched organdy at night. Behind all of them lay the memory of a small boy in the sailor suit he liked so well.

Many of his ideas, including those which seemed most radical, had their source in the myriad styles he bought in Paris for Hattie Carnegie in the 1930s. Pants? There were linen "plus fours" for the beach, along with shorts and slacks in 1933. The bathrobe coat? One appeared in 1934, in gold lamé, tailored like flannel, lined with velvet, and meant for teatime or informal dining at home. Sequin dresses? Carnegie advertised one in October, 1937. Sweater dresses? A hand-knitted sweater with a lamé collar topped a lamé skirt in 1938.

Ideas from the 1940s found their way into collections of the 1960s. In 1942, as a wartime measure, he sewed necklaces on the bodice of wool jersey dresses to give them some zip. In 1968, he embroidered Maltese crosses on the chest of crepe evening pants outfits. There wasn't any question of economizing, but women were becoming a bit nervous about wearing their good jewels out at night.

Throughout his life, the same ideas kept turning up, high-voltage looks such as fox or sable borders on evening clothes, calmer styles like tunics or waistcoats or jumpers. And styles that could be either high-voltage or calm, depending on how they were handled, such as the shirtwaist dress.

Hemlines went up and down, waistlines moved in or out, following the general movement of fashion and Norell's instinct to be one step ahead. The dolman sleeve had a little rage in 1972—Norell showed it before the European designers did. Separates were coming into fashion in 1971—Norell showed jersey "sweater jackets" as his version of the casual mood. In the same spring collection, he introduced plaid taffeta skirts with solid color shirts as a crisp, clean evening look. The identical plaids turned up in the European collections, but handled in a much less fresh manner. Sensing the return of the waistline in 1966, after the chemise had been the dominant fashion for most of the decade, he brought back belts and soon everybody else did too.

Norman Norell as a child in his "Peter Thompson" sailor suit. All his life, he used nautical details on the clothes he made.

Bill Cunningh

378

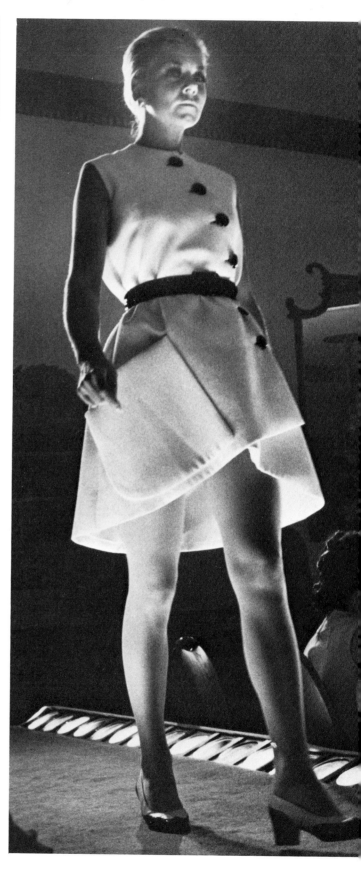

Nineteen-seventy was a year of contrasts. It opened with short, flippy styles like these, *starting left:* short evening dress with gored skirt, side-buttoned day dress, tunic suit, and tailored coat.

380

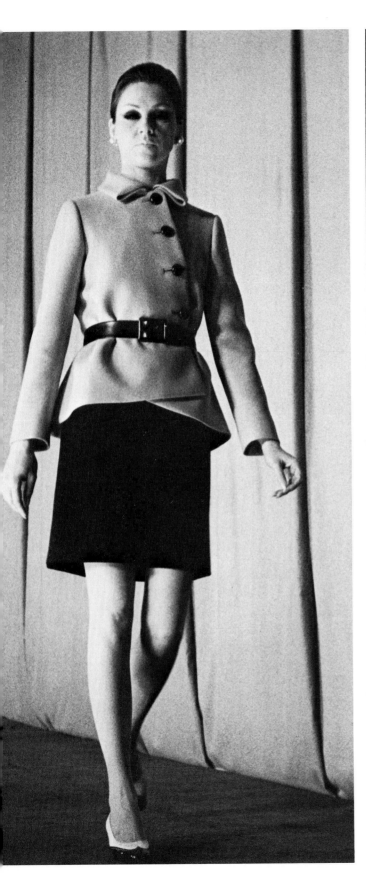

NORELL

By the fall, skirts plummeted, and Norell's coats reached near-ankle length, like the one at *left*; his suits acquired a new severe proportion, but the pussycat bow remained.

Bill Cunningham

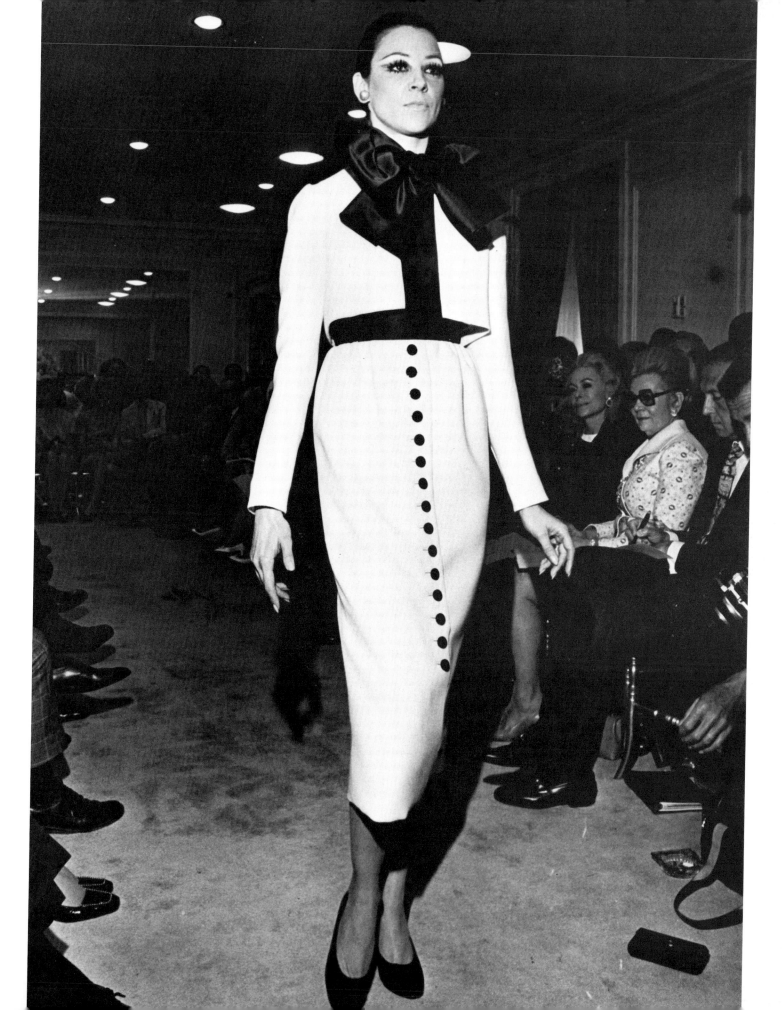

Bill Cunningham

In the early seventies, Norell's range included velvet dress with organdy collar and
bow, *left*, and sweater with sequin pants,
above. For evening, he tucked and pleated
silk, *right*, or spattered it with sequins, *far
right*.

Clothes were growing softer, more casual, as in this sashed coat, *left*.

In 1946, Norell's jersey town coat set style that has never dimmed. News in th grey, in the fabric, in the polished silv buttons, in the tailoring perfection.

Louise Dahl-W
Harper's Bazaa

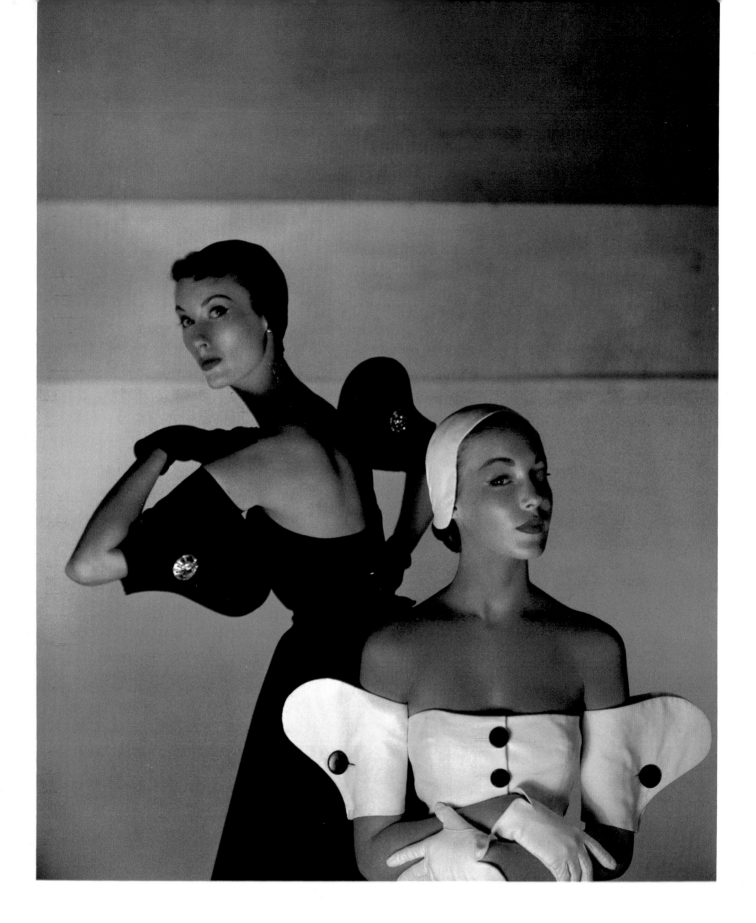

uise Dahl-Wolfe
rper's Bazaar, 1950

Bill Cunningham

Separates were coming into vogue, so Norell showed wrapped jacket with pants, *above.* The one-button suit, *left,* is from the same show.

twins, featured on a 1950 *Bazaar* cover
the newest accessory—the clip-on cuffs
flatter bare shoulders and give a new
adth just above the elbow. Cotton pique
red by Norell.

389

Bill Cunningham

By 1971, skirts were whirling and waistlines were belted again. Norell expressed the ultra feminine look in black, plaid taffeta, and his always-favored sequins.

391

The tailored suit was due for a revival, Norell reasoned in 1971, so he brought it back just before some European couturiers thought of doing so, too. It's shown at *left* with contrasting binding; *far right,* with pants. He also was shortening skirts and continuing sailor details.

Bill Cunningham

NORELL

393

Evening hijinks—with sequins. *Above*, shirt-waist of twinkling layered tulle. At *right*, rambunctious separates with balloon sleeves, enormous pussycat bow on blouse, and sequin pants.

The return of the deep dolman sleeve—interpreted in sequins. A fluid, serene dress, simple lines.

Unquestionably the most famous of all the pictures of Norell, here flanked with his mermaids paved in sequins—fashion pyrotechnique that was every chic woman's cachet (who had the figure and the price) and always and only Norell's signature.

Milton Greene

The next three pages: A capsule Norell Opening—a thousand and one nights entertainment . . . shown at breakneck speed in minutes . . . belying the thousand hours of preparation that lay behind. Brilliance and exaggeration . . . discipline and denial . . . surprise and recognition . . . shock and charm . . . affirming the virtuoso talents of Norell, undisputed master of a twentieth century art.

Bill Cunningham

And the dolman in soft white wool, characteristically high neck, typical black buttons, and wide draped belt.

The last and the best: Norell's final collection, all in beige, gray, and white. *Left to right:* shirtdress, short jacket and pants, overcoat and suit, and loose coat with four checked pockets, all on the bias.

Relaxed evening looks. This page, the bathrobe coats. *Right,* the little overcoat and the softly draped covered dress.

Bill Cunningham

Fashion, to Norell, wasn't a mad rush from one style to the next, rejecting today what had seemed marvelous yesterday. It was a logical progression, a search for perfection. And so his best styles endured. Women could pull them from their closets ten years after they were purchased and wear them to applause, with great delight.

This was as true of his understated jersey dresses, the basis of his daytime look, as it was of his spectacular sequin-studded styles, which made everyone who wore them glow like a mermaid. It was true of his coats, marvels of tailoring and balance, and of his suit jackets, which he had learned to shape under the exacting eye of Hattie Carnegie in the thirties. Thus can sanity sometimes be found at the heart of even such an ephemeral business as fashion.

Which doesn't mean that Norell overlooked the fun and games that are necessary to give that business a special glow. In 1968, when fashion was devoted to the most indiscreet exposures, Norell spoofed it by showing an evening outfit with such a widely bared middle, he popped an emerald in the mannequin's navel. He also showed a transparent black evening dress over a flesh-colored bra and pantie stockings. To his surprise, people bought it.

Toward the end, his radar was working perfectly. He anticipated the return of sportswear with his spring collection in 1969, which emphasized blazers, shirts and skirts. In the fall of 1971, he did the one-button tailored suit better than most designers in Europe. His spring collection for 1972 emphasized the dolman sleeve a little bit before anybody else thought of doing so.

His last collection, presented on August 2, 1972, at 3 P.M. showed Norell in top form. Having found a beautiful alpaca fabric in Italy, he used it in natural colors—gray, white and beige—for all of his daytime coats and suits, designed with maximum simplicity. And at night, there were his sequins, glowing with color. The collection reiterated his lifetime theme: simplicity for day, hijinks at night. There were no gratuitous seams or frills. Every style was pared down to its essentials.

"I hope I have dressed women more simply," Norell said, toward the end of his life. "If I have accomplished that, it would be enough to do."

He had outgrown his "arty" period, but he never outgrew his dedication to quality. "I realize it (quality) is not as important as it once was, but it means everything to me and I'm too old to change."

And so, in the end, that was his legacy: a constant striving for perfection, a refusal to settle for second best.

He tried to keep alive, in a world increasingly devoted to quantity and mass production, the product of skilled craftsmanship, the concept of perfectibility. This was far more important than any dress or coat design, no matter how surpassingly beautiful, and it provided a guideline for other designers during Norell's lifetime. It should continue to do so far into the future.

High voltage evening fashion: sequin siren dress sheltered by long fleece overcoat.

The last success. The last goodbye.

Bill Cunningham

TRIGÈRE

BY ELENI SAKES EPSTEIN

paulinetrigère

CONTENTS

TRIGÈRE THE DESIGNER

Pauline Trigère receiving the distinguished Silver Medal of the City of Paris at City Hall in Paris, June 22, 1972.

She had dressed in a white wool weskit and skirt with a matte jersey maillot blouse, perched her gold turtle pins at strategic areas, worn the see-through vinyl-and-patent pumps she had worked out with shoe designers Herbert and Beth Levine, and then debated with herself whether she had selected the right outfit. Hardly what you would expect of Pauline Trigère—but then this was a momentous day.

Pauline Trigère is a mercurial, emotional woman, quick to laugh and quick to cry. She did a little of both that Thursday, June 22, 1972, when she received the Silver Medal of the City of Paris. The noon ceremony, attended by friends and relatives at the Hôtel de Ville, was an emotional highlight in her life. It was very moving for Pauline to have Raymond Colibeau, the Deputy of the Ninth Arrondissement where she had lived in earlier years, make the presentation at City Hall. To the irrepressible Pauline, it was also an amusing irony.

Thirteen years before she had been named a three-time winner of the American Fashion Critics' Award, thus being elevated to the Coty Hall of Fame. In celebrating this rare honor she had addressed the Women's National Press Club at the Mayflower Hotel in Washington, D.C. The wife of the then French Ambassador, Madame Hervé Alphand, was of course invited to attend. However, she managed only the gesture of stopping by for sherry before the luncheon and the fashion show. Obviously, Pauline was not a "French" designer to the French, although born there.

Her parents, Cécile (Coriene) and Alexandre, arrived in Paris in 1905, fleeing Odessa as the Sino-Russian war loomed. The French dressmaking industry quickly absorbed Russian-Jewish emigrés whose portable skills were in their hands. In the country they had left behind they had worked at the only trades open to them, and tailoring was one of those skilled trades.

trigère

The family lived in a second floor walk-up one block from the Place Pigalle. Her father's workrooms were in front, the living quarters behind. The whole Trigère world was imbued with fit and fashion. The origin of Pauline's talent is easily traced. Her brother, Robert, recalls that their father was a skilled technician and wholesale clothing contractor. Their mother was a dressmaker. All had worked for the Russian aristocracy making military uniforms. It was this milieu with its emphasis on excellence in fit and quality that produced Trigère.

The summer she turned fifteen, Trigère was apprenticed to Martial et Armand, a famous tailoring establishment in the Place Vendôme where she worked after school. After only six weeks, the *chef d'atelier*, M. Arnold, declared there was very little he could teach his gifted pupil. She had shown an immediate grasp and mastery of the bias cut and other dressmaking techniques that most seamstresses could

barely absorb in a lifetime. Then she helped out in her father's coat and suit business, working to get money to buy silk stockings, perfume or theatre tickets. Soon she was in contact with numerous New York store buyers. Through her brother Robert, Pauline met the American designer, Adele Simpson, then a buyer for the firm of Ben Gershel where a Trigère uncle was also employed. Pauline and Adele immediately became friends and have remained so ever since. It was Adele who took Pauline to Jean Patou to see her first Paris couture collection. At the luncheon Adele gave afterwards at the Hôtel du Rhin for her Paris commissionaire and friends, impressionable Pauline came home to tell her frugal family that these strange, rich Americans did not eat every bit of the asparagus, but only the tips!

In 1937, as the possibility of another world war hung over Europe, the Trigère family set out for a new home in Chile via New York. Pauline had married Lazar Radley, a coat and suit maker who had also emigrated from Russia and been introduced to her father, who had found work for him. Radley met Pauline when she was a very young girl and waited for years to marry her. Trigère's father had died in 1932 of a stroke; the emigrating family consisted of Madame Trigère, Robert, the Radleys and their two small boys—Jean Pierre, two, and fourteen-month-old Philippe. Pauline had talked her husband into stopping in New York to see their relatives. On arrival she called Adele Simpson, who had been trying to persuade the family to come to the United States for years. Pauline found New York vibrant, exciting and challenging, and with Adele's urging Chile was quickly ruled out. Pauline went to work briefly at Ben Gershel's. Then to Hattie Carnegie's where she was an assistant to designer Travis Banton, who had already won fame in Hollywood. Trigère's Carnegie experience paralleled her earlier apprenticeship in Paris. Banton soon remarked to Lilly Daché, the well-known milliner, "there's a French girl working with me at Hattie Carnegie. She is very clever and very nice." Her career was on its way in America, only to be closed off by yet another war. When Pearl Harbor came, Carnegie pulled in the reins, anticipating fabric shortages and a curtailment of customers. There was a general closing down of workrooms. The bad news came a week before Christmas. Not wanting to spoil the holidays, she did not mention it to her family.

She had wanted a business of her own, and that dismissal slip proved to be the catalyst. Borrowing $1,500 and pawning her diamond brooch and diamond barrettes for $800, Pauline and her brother, Robert, went into business in January, 1942. Her first collection consisted of twelve dresses at an average wholesale price of $39.75. (Today the average wholesale is $159.) That first collection was an immediate success. Pauline will forever have a warm spot in her heart for a small Park Avenue shop called Polly's. Polly's gave her her first order—for eleven of her twelve dresses.

trigère

Trigère's business moved several times in the late forties; her first address was the old Hattie Carnegie loft on East Forty-Seventh Street, then to West Fifty-Seventh Street. The Big Final Move was to the sixteenth floor of 550 Seventh Avenue in the wholesale clothes mecca of the world. Today, the Trigère name in bold red script graces everything from business letterheads to labels stitched inside the coats, suits, and dresses shipped daily from 550 Seventh Avenue.

Here is the only showroom on Seventh Avenue with a stage. It was designed for sportswear designer Clare Potter by her husband, Sandy, some thirty-five years ago and remains essentially unchanged. Its off-white walls form an ideal background for the modern sculpture and contemporary paintings.

Here, Pauline's award-winning clothes are shown to buyers representing leading department and specialty stores throughout America and Europe. As each season's fashions are shown to press and buyers, Pauline delivers her witty, informative and often knife-edged conversational commentary. Here Pauline is "on stage."

This woman at the beginning of her career knew one thing. "I had to make a living to support my children." (Her marriage had ended in divorce). What she knew best was how to cut coats, suits, and dresses. Her son Philippe—now a Russian language expert and teacher of Russian Literature at New York University at Stony Brook—sums up this stage of his mother's career: "Necessity is the mother of a lot of creativity. If circumstances force you into a situation whereby you have to be independent, you become independent." And so it was.

Hirschfeld

Leaving the Executive Mansion after her first visit in 1962. Ever since she has referred to it enthusiastically as "My White House." "I felt the same emotion when I visited the President's house for the first time as I did when I revisited Versailles."

trigère

415

TRIGÈRE AT WORK

Emma Gene Hall

u de soie, the fabric with superb capa-
ty for drama. These and the one follow-
were designed by Pauline Trigère in
55. Stiff as paper taffeta yet soft enough
define the figure. Black, touched with a
ze of "Trigère's Diamonds."

Self-made, always seeking to learn something new, and possessed of
a demanding self-disciplined mind, Trigère believes she can accom-
plish almost anything. A $4,000,000 annual business is proof. Besides
her clothes, there are other Trigère treasures—her fabulous furs,
jewelry, perfume, and men's ties. She tried working with a men's shirt
manufacturer but decided they weren't reaching the right clientele.
The shirts were priced at $14 and $20; Pauline felt they should have
been designed for a different market at $25 and $50 per shirt. As she
ruefully said, there are two ways of franchising—"One is do it their
way, and the other I don't know."

   In 1963, discovering she didn't like the undergarments available to
women who would be wearing her clothes, she created a line for
Formfit Rogers. The Trigère bras and girdles with their little bias top
and a little bias bottom thereafter set the standard for the entire
undergarment industry. She designed demi-bras too, always trying
for lightness of construction, simplicity of design, and the absence of
rigidity. That lingerie exercise mastered, she went on to something
else.

   Her son, Philippe Radley, now operates the perfume business she
created after three years of testing hundreds of fragrance formulas.
Bottled in a contemporary crystal cube, Trigère's perfume follows a
successful tradition of famous designers naming perfumes after
themselves—Chanel, Lanvin, Lilly Daché, Adele Simpson, Norman
Norell, Anne Klein, and Nina Ricci. Until she created her own
fragrance she was addicted to Guerlain's musky classic, Shalimar, still
one of her favorites. "Most women are perfume collectors. If you
really want to know the fragrance a woman likes, the index is the one
she buys for herself, not what she is given," Trigère says.

   When she realized women were not traveling with their jewels for

trigère

fear of theft, she responded in 1970 by designing "Trigère's Diamonds." These are made of crystallized strontium titanate and, when cut like a diamond, their refraction of light and brilliance appears deceptively real. At $55 a carat, the barettes, pins, and diamond "drips" dangling from a neck-ring, originally designed for herself, fool and enchant the eye.

In all of these fashions, Trigère is an intellectual designer, the designer's designer. Her clothes are so well assembled—with a sense of the body and movement underneath, and such a strong sense of shape—that function is never sacrificed for chic. In essence, Trigère has provided made-to-order couture for the wholesale market—not an easy accomplishment.

Trigère is unusual in that her preconceptions are not inflexible. On occasion she has reversed her own fashion thinking. Formerly an outspoken critic of women wearing pants in the city, Pauline retreated by saying, "You never say 'never' in this business." She sensed, however, that something new was happening in the early seventies. Many women were turning away from pants suits, seeking an alternative. The time was right to reintroduce the bisected skirt. This culotte concept began with the premise of sweater and skirt looks worn so well by Mrs. William Paley, Mrs. Winston Guest and others. These are elegant women, secure in their taste, who can confidently wear a simple skirt, sweater, belt and beret in the daytime. But Pauline knew, too, that not many women possess that degree of finesse. Her popular solution that fall in 1971: bisected skirts that ranged from simple jerseys for day to knee-length velvet versions bordered in silver fox for gala occasions. "Why should women come to Trigère for pants when they can buy beautiful ones in a boutique for so much less?" she reasoned, only to insist in 1974 she had again changed her thinking and that pants were a must in practically every active woman's life. She began to include at least one pants outfit in every collection. Thus Trigère continues her tradition of evolutionary design; she does not discard ideas because she has used them before. But in evolution there must be an edge of newness or she is not satisfied.

To James Galanos, Trigère is a creator, a force with a certain sense of style few others possess, here or abroad. She is not a copyist but the individual designer the European couture produces. To Robert Riley, head of the Fashion Institute of Technology's Design Laboratory, Trigère represents an almost extinct species in the dress business of today because of her insistence on quality, excellence, and taste.

How does she work? She professes to work in a closed circuit with her fabrics and her models, trying to do the things she feels.

Her brother Robert Trigère, who left the firm in 1972, refers to the "magic role" fabric plays in her designing. It is her greatest ally,

419 *trigère*

virtually commanding her to do certain things when she cuts into a difficult plaid or any other of the quality fabrics she uses.

From the first collection, her clothes have been characterized by a total smoothness in tailoring and an elegant simplicity; the key is always her spectacular skill with scissors. Like Vionnet, Chanel and Balenciaga, Trigère cuts directly into the fabric without toile or paper pattern.

TRIGÈRE'S FABULOUS FURS

Whether dark mink as here, or Persian lamb or broadtail or fox, pelts are handled with no more inhibitions than if Pauline Trigère were handling fabric. And coats, capes, evening dresses, and even suits of fur occur with grace, sleekness, and enormous distinction.

SIGNATURE TOWN COATS

Each says "Trigère" without a label. *This page.* A single-button tuxedo that has sharp, spare lines, immaculate lapels, characteristic diamond insert, all in all, the precision cut of a tailoring family that made uniforms for Russian aristocracy. Spring 1974. *Opposite page.* Black fleece reversible to pink. Its great collar lies without a ripple to make this one of the most notable coats of the decade.

Left. Butter yellow tweed with bat slee ending in a squared armhole. The bias is actually a half circle which deeply ov laps, emphasizing the ascending hem. Lig bulky beauty of 1965.

The becoming fashion for a high-colo great coat with a close cap of fur has sa fied more than a generation of chic Ame cans. The stamp is assuredly Paul Trigère's.

Genevieve Na

Right. Very high-waisted town coat with smooth even flare and high wide lapels. A great favorite. The late sixties.

The quiet-as-a-dove side to Pauline Trigère's design talent. In 1945 she fashioned a molded yoked short coat with full sleeves, gentle neckline. Draped a chignon-covering soft hat and achieved a casualness sought thirty-five years later.

Louise Dahl-Wolfe
Harper's Bazaar, 1945

Checks and balances through the years. *Right*. The clear diamond-check straight coat with no button, belt or collar to distract, was featured in *Flair* magazine in the spring of 1950.
Opposite, left to right: Windowpane checks, a double-faced tweed squared over black or the reverse. Neat houndstooth coat with single button and high bodice. Houndstooth coat, with matching hat, has back panel that widens to hem. Fall 1968.

Maria Martel

Sculptured tulip coat that swirls in concentric lines without a bobble or pucker. Tour de force of tailoring.
Right: One of Trigère's graceful coats—close at the neck and shoulders with the lithe swing of a full cape. Imported burgundy and green plaid skilfully worked on the diagonal.

Left. This is the Caliph Coat which ranks as one of the most popular of Trigère's career. Its diagonal tweed makes the most of its bulkiness. Buttons and scarves to scale. Fall 1960.
Right. Big turf tweed coat with semi-fitted bodice, huge pockets, and a swashbuckling chin-chin collar. Excellent Trigère bravura 1969.

Is it a suit? A cape and skirt? A bolero and skirt? This is how Trigère often handled the suit look through the years. *Left*. In the sixties—clear check with its top half-way between cape and bolero. *Right*. In the fifties—capelet smooths the shoulders of its matching weskit. This, a beautiful caramel tweed.

Peter Fink

Trigère has always treated cotton with the respect and enthusiasm that she accords fabulous silks. The surface-texture of pique, whether ribbed or cloqué, is a fascinating design advantage to her. She cuts it away to formal nudity, gives it transparent accents or the shine and stiffness of patent. No wonder she won a National Cotton Award.

Gillis MacGil, *above*, modeling two Trigère hallmarks at once: the bare shoulder, the wide hem of fur. (When a customer asked Pauline Trigère what in the world she should wear over such a dress, she shrugged, "A limousine, of course.")

She terms it nonsense to think that she sets out in March fully knowing what she will show in June, for customers who will buy in September. She never knows exactly what she is going to do until the design inspiration hits her, until it becomes a "dictator."

She doesn't take long vacations because her work is her greatest enthusiasm, her most absorbing hobby. Much of her enjoyment consists of time spent with certain customers and certain buyers who trust her judgment. To sit and talk in the showrooms after a collection, to receive "feedback" from her work delights her. Jean-Pierre Radley, the firm's comptroller, analyzes his mother's whirlwind temperament: "She flies off very quickly, and her thoughts often outrun her ability to write, say, or do, so she'll jump ahead faster than other people might do. She can be very stubborn. Artists come in all sizes and shapes. Some are loud and raucous, others quiet and gentle." His mother is both.

Model Gillis MacGil, who heads the Mannequin Modeling Agency, remembers the years she worked with the volatile Trigère as being hectic and frantic, but never unkind. If there was shouting when collections neared presentation time, it was not meant to frighten people, Gillis believes. Pauline simply prefers not to have shrinking violets about. Instead she wants people with her own brand of strength, those who can stand up to her, who are assertive and intelligent. Because she respects these qualities, she demands more from the models than a pretty face and figure. "Trigère wants you to respond to her clothes. It's this same quality that allows her to respect her seamstress, a good shipping clerk, or the accessory button or belt man who visits her in the showroom."

In 1961, Trigère became the first high fashion designer on Seventh Avenue to employ a black model. Beverly Valdes answered an advertisement in *The New York Times* and was selected from forty applicants.

It was on Beverly that Pauline fitted her sable-bordered brocade Rajah silhouette with its small high-shaped A-line. When photographs and newspaper stories of Beverly Valdes were published throughout the world, they provoked pounds of hate mail—and tremendous acclaim. This was recalled by Betty Terry, herself black, who calls herself Pauline's "sounding board." It is an apt description; Betty Terry has worked for Trigère for twenty-two years. She recalls that Robert Trigère worried a great deal about the black model decision but stood fast, and that it proved to be a breakthrough in Seventh Avenue's high fashion industry.

The supportive cast that surrounds Pauline is all-important. She cannot function without it. Workers in the showroom, Margie Lefcourt and Linda Skladzien, band together to form the easy attentive ambiance in which she can create. Behind the "tough lady" role she plays, they say, is a very vulnerable woman.

trigère

Opposite page. Supplesse is the title Trigère gives to the supple wraparound theatre costume. Back narrows from shoulder to ankle. Fabric is golden puffs on charcoal with slit decolletage edged with self cord. Dolman sleeves, 1964. *This page.* Hand-loomed knitted sheath with yoke and sleeves of sparkling silver and crystal. Silver arrows. Example of the Trigère styling discipline that makes for great elegance, 1973. Lucie Porges sketch at left, the reality at right.

trigère

Three long black gowns whose drama is their chiselled decolletage. *Far left.* Lacquer organza with smooth two-leaves bodice. Unlined organza cape. *Left.* Characteristic Trigère wool gown. She showed this sheer tweed in October 1959 when she was named to the Hall of Fame of the Coty American Fashion Critics' Award, presented at the Metropolitan Museum of Art. The halter neckline curves into a point just above the waist. *Right.* When less is more: Cutaway shoulder gown of silk marocain. 1973.

Every evening dress must have its own escort: Trigère credo forever. As here, this black crepe sheath, *left,* with its beautifully shaped white satin shell.

Blonde lace—crisp and frothy. Ligh[t] feather skirt and beautifully molded [b]worn here by Mrs. Winston Guest.

Louise Dahl-Wolfe

The white faille evening dress is escorted by short boxy jacket and long open crisp collar frame, *right*.

Gold and white brocade evening ensemble in a photograph by Louise Dahl-Wolfe which captures the whole evening excitement of the mid-fifties—every detail of coiffure, jewels, gloves . . . all unabashed perfection. The beautiful aristocratic model, Mary Jane Russell.

Drawing
Lucie Porges

Handkerchief points, favorite device of the twenties and thirties, fascinate Trigère both as hemline and over-wrap silhouette. In organdy, chiffon, sheer wool, crepe, or satin, as here. *Left.* Beautiful green ombre Charmeuse tunic costume, perfection with pointed skirt. *Right.* Slim black crepe sheath, essence of the thirties. A boa, of course.

Charming dresses with an easy undeniable romantic flavor. *Left,* the mille fleurs silk surah evening skirt wraps over an exactly matching chiffon print dress. *Opposite.* "The first dress I ever made was plaid taffeta . . . pure silk, with three organdy collars, one edged in blue, one in red, one green." Pauline Trigère made it again thirty years later using her favorite tartan silk surah this time with *one* capelet. Both, 1971.

448

Lucie Porges

David Norman

PAISLEYS ARE FOREVER

Right. Their intertwining patterns, more beautiful than ever, enlarged to a giant size, their pomegranate Oriental silhouette often outlined in sparkling beads makes them more fabulous than ever. *Left*. A "diamond" studded hooded evening version, 1970.

Fantastic evening costumes that are them-selves theatre. Ostrich flies over the white organdy coat and skirt of a black chiffon conical dress, *right*. Concoction, summer 1966, *above*, eyelash sheath with plumes on chiffon.

Two extremes of cover and uncover. *Far right*, doublet up-to-the-ears in jeweled emerald and ruby flecked tweed escorts a satin gown with souffle hem. And, eleven years later, *far left*, bare-but-for-one fas-tener black crepe de chine evening pajamas encrusted with crystals.

trigère

453

Evening pajamas of deep blue and red crepe—very elegant, soft, and relaxed as the meandering design. Skirt-wide pants. Beneath the doublet a transparent blouse embroidered in a paralleling pattern of sparkle.

David Norman

Lucie Porges, who has been her assistant for some twenty-three years, would agree. Lucie arrived in New York in 1952 from Paris, where she had done illustrating and designing for numerous French magazines. In Paris a Trigère design, a simple jersey draped dress with a turban photographed on Lisa Fonssagrives, had caught her eye. She could not forget it. She had to see this person, Trigère, in New York. When numerous calls produced no appointment, Lucie boldly popped in at 550 Seventh Avenue with her drawings. By chance Pauline passed by just as the receptionist stopped Lucie, and in French asked her what she was doing there.

Pauline didn't need an illustrator but she did need an assistant. Taking Lucie at once to the fabric room, Pauline cut away some fabrics from their bolts, handed the pieces to Lucie and told her to design something from them and bring them back to her. Today Pauline and Lucie work as one.

If America is the marketplace for Trigère's talent, Europe is still the market basket for her material. A European working trip for Lucie and Trigère is usually scheduled to last two weeks. In that time they will look at everything—buttons, buckles, scarves, fabrics, trimmings, embroideries, many of which are expressly designed in anticipation of their visit. Split-second appointments are made with fabric people, but if a tempting gallery or a gift shop is sighted, both will simultaneously say, "Let's go in, this place looks fantastic." Once, on a working trip Pauline came across a beautiful set of tall faceted beer mugs, designed around 1890. She bought them for use as vases and sent them to friends as gifts, filled with flowers.

Having thus been sidetracked, the two will then proceed to the business appointment. They usually arrange two appointments in the morning and two in the afternoon, with a break for luncheon at a new spot Pauline has heard about or an old bistro favorite. There they will discuss the special properties of a fabric and how it fits into the plan for achieving a new design direction Pauline is seeking to project in the next year. In the fabric houses of Italy, France, and Switzerland, Trigère is listened to with keen interest because of the authority of her taste and the influence of her collections.

Nothing is too much trouble for European textile houses. They work out special coloring, exclusive fabrics, weaves and weights. Constant interaction with the designer is an important part of their design laboratory.

In Paris, Trigère and Lucie will visit Staron and Leleu. In Como, the heart of Italy's textile empire, they will select silks and buy scarves and buttons at Tatti's. In Switzerland they will call on the firms of Abraham and Brachbar. In Zurich, home of Gustav Zumsteg and the prestigious Abraham firm, they always dine, as do many world-famous fashion designers, at the Kronenhalle, a family-owned res-

trigère

Trigère knows that there is no more instant elegance than a ruff, cuff, muff, or hem for that matter, of fur. She chooses black, silver, or Norwegian blue fox with equal effectiveness. All of these fashions are from 1971 but the fur predilection began years before and continues.

taurant with Giacometti sculptures at the bar and walls filled with paintings by famous artists.

On their return to New York from one of these buying and inspirational visits to Europe, Pauline gave Lucie a small-scale dressmaker's mannequin, feeling that her assistant would be less hesitant to work with it than with a full-sized dress form. Now Lucie has learned to cut into fabric as Pauline does, without fear. She insists "No one can fit like Pauline. When Pauline puts her fingers on the fabric, puts a few pins in, suddenly a dress is there."

Inevitably, ten days before the end of designing a collection, Pauline becomes "impossible." This sudden tempestuous turn of mood used to upset Lucie, but today she understands that a true designer must insist on doing things a certain way. "You can't be sweet about it. People just don't listen. You have to be forceful." Lucie discovered this for herself the year Pauline had to leave two weeks before the completion of the line. Adding the finishing touches, Lucie remembers, she became just as nervous and impossible, just as eager to achieve the right and beautiful. "You see," she says, "I have this perfect example in front of me all the time."

trigère

457

TRIGÈRE ON THE ROAD

Opposite page. "Most women want clothes that proclaim they are women of cultivated taste . . . and every woman wants to add her personality to what she wears." In this instance the dress is a white and black tunic; pared down and perfectly tailored, self-sufficient handsomeness.
Above. The designer with three models ready for the road.

Salesmanship and a dramatic presence play a tremendous part in the success of a modern American fashion designer. It is away from Seventh Avenue that Trigère's *chutzpah* and hustle work best for her. The shows she enjoys doing most are those with great cachet, like a benefit held at Lincoln Center by Bergdorf Goodman for the New York City Opera Center of Music and Drama, or Saks Fifth Avenue's presentation at the Arizona Costume Institute Ball.

In this format Trigère often shows retrospective fashions dating back to 1943 along with the current collection. The costume wing at the Metropolitan Museum of Art, the Brooklyn Museum, and Robert Riley's Design Laboratory at the Fashion Institute of Technology, all have a difficult time collecting Trigères. No woman wants to give them up—even though donating them may mean a large tax deduction.

This illustrates a philosophical point of unique importance. Pauline Trigère believes that you can't keep changing yourself each season. The extraordinary timelessness of her fashions prompted *Life* magazine to feature a color spread in 1959 entitled "Trigère through the Years."

The Trigère customer may be in her twenties, thirties, forties, or older and can be a size 4 or a size 20. She is likely to be an affluent woman who trusts Pauline, the designer, totally. She is also a member of the Trigère Clothes Cult, often with an active retrospective collection in her own closet. (One customer wrote recently that she had four closets full of Trigères.) The woman who buys Trigère is going to listen to her and come back for more clothes, and more advice. Customers have bought as many as twenty-five Trigères at a time. To all she is a known quantity, a designer whose clothes are refined and beautifully made in the finest fabrics. At Martha's exclusive shop in Palm Beach, Trigère has totaled up orders of more than $100,000 in

Essence of Trigère. Taffeta dinner dress with its own navy blue wool cape-fichu, cut as geometrically as the taffeta plaid that lines it.

Richard Avedon
Harper's Bazaar, *1948*

Pauline's romp with a new-old design form The Evening Culotte. Playing here, actre Nancy Berg. Low fitted torso blouse ov full gathered culotte. Pajamas outnumbere evening dresses in that 1964 summer co lection.

just one promotional week. Customers often come in to the shop in tennis clothes just to have a look at her, to see in person the tortoise-rimmed, amber-tinted glasses that set off her sleek hairdo. Some women who have checked *Who's Who* and noted her birthdate drop by to marvel at the youthfulness of this woman who every morning "bathes her brain" by standing on her head doing yoga exercises.

Indeed, Pauline is her own best model and example of a chic-woman-in-a-Trigère. She is able to wear many different silhouettes and styles. She frequently proves her point by showing women who say "I could never wear a Trigère like you do. I'm not tall enough for a cape." She can show, by putting one on herself, that it is scale that is important, a matter of the right proportion. Trigère is 5'4". Once a customer in a fitting room said that she didn't see that the outfit "did anything" for her. Pauline shot her a quick cold glance. "What is it supposed to do, tickle?"

When an entire collection is put "on the road" it is packed in huge, bright red boxes that are easily spotted in an airport. All are recorded on a memo to the store and arrive complete with accessories, jewelry, hats and shoes. They go by station wagon to the airport, "babied" all the way.

Still, accidents happen. In 1956 the entire Trigère fall collection, meant for Louisville, was diverted to the Kansas City Municipal Air Terminal, lost, and located only because a cargo employee remembered seeing lots of big red boxes after he heard the news on the radio. Now, as often as possible, the collection, which may be valued as high as $300,000, goes along with Trigère as excess personal baggage.

When the samples arrive, they are picked up and checked in by the store in which Trigère will appear. Each costume carries its style number and retail price along with a swatch book from which women can select the various fabrics and colors they prefer. The next day or evening Trigère will personally fit the twelve models. Occasionally she takes two New York models with her. Following the show, she and a showroom assistant begin working directly with the customers and the salespeople. Ads by the store have preceded her; interviews, television shows for her visit are scheduled to coincide with major local events, such as an opening night performance or a charity ball.

Trigère prefers fashion audiences that contain men. It is more exciting for her. "I like men in the audience, men who can afford my clothes for their woman. They understand quality and relate to it. Clothes are meant to be shared—to be seen at theatre openings, art shows, the opera, a concert, at a ball." The latter are familiar to Pauline, who lives the life of the people she likes to dress.

As she insists that her collection be shown to perfection, it is equally important to her that she look the part of a successful dress designer. She has made every best-dressed list with her Trigère Plan,

he total town costume that the Trigère oman always expects. Plaid *en point* which ly the most skilled tailor can bring off.

TRIGÈRE'S OWN RETROSPECTIVE

Twelve fashions photographed here from her extensive collection dating back to 1943 which she sometimes shows with her newest designs. A brave idea since the generally accepted essence of fashion is change. Still the consensus is "I'd like to wear that right now." As you can see from this sample, it isn't because these clothes were considered "safe" that they survived so brilliantly as fashion for thirty years.

CITY WOOLS

David Norman

Fall 1968. Trigère teamed many of her wools such as this oatmeal tweed with thigh-high glove leather stocking boots.
Spruce green jersey with the smoothest shape due to the inserted belt, the mini dolman sleeve, and the general expertise of cut.
Coat dress with off-center buttoning detail . . . mitred diagonal striping . . . a sound investment in fashion with growth-value the essential factor.
Versatile sheer wool that is practically seasonless and practically seamless. Only one diagonal seam from shoulder to hem achieves the fit.

Lucie Porges

Lucie

"The Capuline," *opposite*, peignoir-like cape dress of heavy black crepe has the ripple and flow and the neat shoulder and neckline Trigère admires. *This page*. Wrist-length wool cape bordered with jet cabachon and passementerie.

Fink

Capes forever. Since almost her first collection, Pauline Trigère has produced capes . . . that swing, circle, cling . . . always have beautiful smooth shoulders and therefore "sit well." *Far left.* The big diamond cape and hem costume, 1974.   *left.* A double jersey goldenrod cape over a multi-design silk print, 1973. *Far right.* Beige wool rimmed, stitched cape and skirt over a printed maillot, 1970.

David Norman

Lucie Porges

471

The cape's the thing. Striding along, *opposite*, in a snug cape and dress of soft diagonal tweed with snood and spat-boots she is every inch the independent twentieth century lady. *Right*. Royal green and red tartan cape, very full, with matching tartan crochet-weave dress.

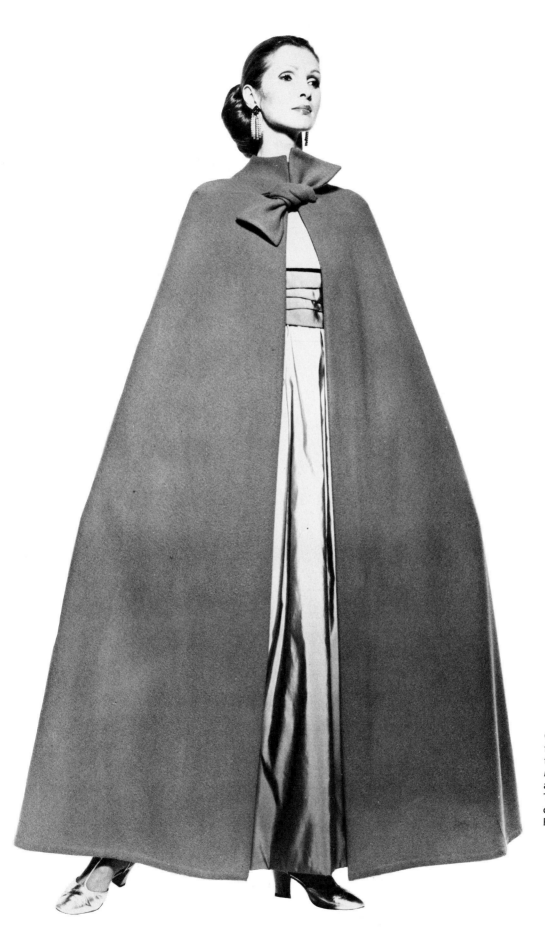

Capes . . . capes . . . capes. Long capes for evening. Blue woolen double-face cape to match its kingfisher blue ballgown. *Far right:* Blonde mist mohair cape weightless and glorious over any evening costume. The severe sketch of a great high-collared cape typical of the Trigère genre by Lucie Porges.

Sketch
Lucie Porges

Above, the Long Wool Evening Coat. Impressive, luxurious. Bittersweet triple yarn without a fastening showing. Deep fox cuffs.

Drawing: Lucie Porges

Twin examples of the Trigère penchant for long wool evening clothes. They have an unusual sense of come-what-may completeness that is almost medieval. Whether velvet or faille or tweed, whether furred or jeweled or befrogged, Trigère tailors these high-necked, long-sleeved dresses and their companion coats with a special discipline that makes them unsurpassed evening ensembles.

which involves building a wardrobe around a single color. Black, white, gunmetal, and red are her favorite choices, and a personal appearance wardrobe will have a coat; a dress or jumper; skirt, pants and weskit; a gown, and accessories for all. This cuts down on what she takes with her on the road. A checklist evolved over the years quickly yields the items she will need for a trip to Los Angeles, to Philadelphia, or Paris. It is complete even to notations for hair, face, nails, eyes and bath preparations, alarm clock, money converter, scissors, and stationery. Sometimes even her needlepoint is packed for a long journey. It is all a matter of taking herself and her designing seriously.

Fortunately she can also laugh at the occasional disaster. There was the case of Mrs. Ourisman's "break-away" dress, as Andrew Goodman called it. Mrs. Mandell Ourisman of Washington, D.C., who had bought the dress at Bergdorf Goodman, describes what happened:

> As I removed my coat, the rhinestones on the sleeve caught themselves in the chiffon and suddenly my left shoulder was bare. I tried to ignore it. My right sleeve then fancied the side of my dress and while I tugged gently, but in vain, the material of my right elbow dissolved. A general in full dress and decorations then greeted me. When we parted, I was wearing his Legion of Merit. Through dinner I was avoiding sequins in my salad and trying to disengage myself from the table cloth. The crowning blow fell at home after the Symphony Ball at 3 A.M. My sleeve caught the back of my embroidered sofa. Whereupon my husband said quietly but firmly, "Send that damned thing back with a letter recommending the dress be sold to the military. There is nothing that they have that could so effectively win a war for us."

Immediately thereafter came a credit from Bergdorf Goodman and a letter of amused apology from Trigère, signed in the bright red ink that is her trademark.

The Washington Star

477

Left, Trigère's "Plus Coat" of 1969. Its drama —its pure lineal quality and the surprise play-off of rose-ash double-facing taupe tweed.

Right. This claret velvet coat was photographed for *Harper's Bazaar* by Louise Dahl-Wolfe in the 1940s. Couldn't be better for the 1970s.

TRIGÈRE AT HOME

Left. Scenes from La Tortue, Pauline Trigère's country house, named for her favorite symbol, the turtle. *Above*, Pauline's turtles as a fashion print.

Her Park Avenue apartment and her country home in Westchester County are Trigère originals every bit as important to her as her designs. They possess the high drama that always surrounds her.

Pauline's passionate pursuits are travel, cooking, gardening, art, music, dancing and decorating. Although she doesn't cook much in the New York apartment, a Trigère-trained cook has her techniques down pat. Guests ramble about during a short cocktail hour admiring the porcelains and contemporary paintings, which include a Zao-Wou-ki, a Parisian artist she discovered years ago. It is Pauline's special kind of décor.

Cocktails are served in a small mirrored library lined with red felt. Everything—chairs, pictures, accessories—is small scale.

A dinner party guest list often includes New York's Senator and Mrs. Jacob Javits, retired movie mogul Joseph Levine, Leonard and Felicia Bernstein, the French Consul General and his wife, Andrew and Nana Goodman, the Stanley Marcuses, a writer, a painter, or a fashion expert like Jerry Solvei of Elizabeth Arden. A great part of her enjoyment lies in being an accepted part of the creative world of artists in every discipline, here and abroad.

Guests may dine in a candlelit foyer, in the living room, or, if there are only six, in the chandeliered kitchen—years ago Trigère ripped out a dinette to extend the kitchen area. The success of her dinner parties stems from having the same help for ten years, she says, crossing her fingers.

At La Tortue, her 133-year-old Pound Ridge country house, she entertains less formally. There her guests often pitch in and help while Pauline cooks many of the vegetables grown in her own garden.

This three-story extension of Pauline's perfectionism was named after three turtles she spotted sitting on a rock when she was country-

trigère

house hunting, several years before she actually purchased the property. She decided then to name the place La Tortue if she ever bought it. It is indicative of the power of that symbol that she occasionally receives mail addressed to "Madame Tortue."

The turtle, Chinese symbol of longevity and good luck, is her favorite symbol not only in jewelry, but also in many of her fabric prints and color schemes. Her tortoise-rimmed spectacles are a trademark, as caricaturist Hirshfeld recognized when he sketched her. Her 600-piece art collection depicts every species of turtle in existence, in every medium from gemstones to clay. There are turtle doorstops, paperweights, inkwells, dinner bells, garden ornaments, bibelots and boxes, acquired over the years as gifts from friends.

Fellow designer Bill Blass says, "She is at her best when entertaining in the country. She so obviously enjoys her life there. You can just see she adores her house and loves to cook for her friends. She is a great woman who has time for other things than her business."

Perhaps she loves La Tortue most because there she is surrounded by close friends—Jerry Silverman and Shannon Rodgers in Pound Ridge, and longtime friend Adele Simpson in Greenwich. They exchange recipes constantly and often visit on weekends. And together, the four were responsible for one of the most imaginative parties fashion writers have ever seen.

One lovely summer day in 1969, four busloads of fashion journalists attending Eleanor Lambert's fashion press week in New York were invited for a Sunday in the country. Pauline set her *al fresco* party on the three and one half acres she had helped landscape. A bed of tulips shaped like a giant bow with streamers across the sloping lawn was the first glimpse of Trigère magic that greeted her guests as they drove in to La Tortue. Her home being the first stop on this gastronomic house and garden tour, she served omelets, *pâté en terrine*, French bread and coffee cake. Next came Jerry Silverman's and Shannon Rodgers' pool party, enlivened by their four dogs who joined in for a swim. Fresh fruit arrived in Chinese porcelain bowls followed by sausages encased in pastry crust, and mini hot dogs and hamburgers. At Adele Simpson's stately home, Pauline came with the editors to sample a dessert table filled with cheesecake, lemon cake, fruit, strawberry pie and chocolate cake heavy with shaved chocolate and calories.

Time, taste, money and ingenuity have been put to good use at La Tortue, which has been shown in leading home decorating magazines. *Architectural Digest* featuring it in the March–April 1974 issue, described La Tortue as "a subtle blend of chic, originality and appropriateness." One sees this in the faience and barber shaving plate collection acquired over the years in many lands. This "tapestry of plates" as she calls it, decorates a wall in the dining room. Indeed, she is an intrepid antique collector. Among her prize finds are four black tables that once stood in the old Fulton Cafe in Brooklyn. When one of them was cleaned she discovered that it was Chinese teak inlaid with pink-and-gray marble and mother-of-pearl. Together, the four have been combined to form her country dining table.

Each room has charm and comfort; and each has some evidence of her imagination and a piquant element of surprise. In the guest room which is decorated with a Trigère signature print, two desks confront each other—a Louis XIII vis-à-vis a desk from an American country school. In the ample living room, with its curved fifteen-foot sofa, is a coffee table made from an old French game box once used for miniature bowling. Fireplace mantels, doors, desk, and game table date from the reign of Louis XV. The contemporary art and sculpture provide a dramatic contrast. There are Zao-Wou-ki and Matisse drawings, Consagra sculpture, and a mercury and oil painting by Ronald Mallory which revolves, creating fascinating forms as it moves.

No one laughs more at Pauline's spontaneous enthusiasm than Pauline herself. When she bought La Tortue, her mother gave her $1,000 "to fill the place up with some furniture." Instead Pauline ordered hemlock hedges planted. When Madame Trigère saw the line of trees she shook her head. "In Russia we cut down the trees, we don't spend money to plant them."

La Tortue is evidence of Trigère's ability to create beauty not only in clothes, but in the whole of her life.

trigère

Joseph Silverm
The Washingto

5

TRIGÈRE THE TEACHER

On these pages, Pauline Trigère demonstrating cutting and fitting, lecturing, judging, theorizing . . . in a design class at the Fashion Institute of Technology.

"Before Picasso began to make all those crazy noses, he knew how to draw a straight line. You can't begin to break rules unless you know them." Pauline is explaining to a class of twenty-three students at the New York Fashion Institute of Technology that even if they should win a prize it will not make them a designer; prizes alone are not a substitute for work and constant learning. A young man continues to press a garment while she is talking. "Would you like to listen to what I have to say?" she asks, demanding undivided attention. Then she explains that she might give them her time, a lot of it, but she cannot teach them to become designers. "If you feel you are going to be one and if you have it in you, it's going to come out one way or another."

What she is trying to get across to them is the peril of imitation—to have confidence in themselves. Teaching is a new Trigère dedication. She speaks easily; she has a lot to say. Yet, she is the first to admit that "it is difficult to express in words what I can do with my fingers."

The Fashion Institute of Technology was founded in 1944 in midtown Manhattan, to help develop the talent that will flow into the fashion industries. Many designers have come with sketches, models, and other props, to pass on their knowledge.

Trigère does not have props—she has herself, her scissors and a magnetic pin-holder strapped to her left wrist. She is wearing a striped silk maillot and a matching ascot. A golden turtle pin sits at the tip of her jacket collar. Before the deep, husky voice has let you know she's in the room her arrival has been musically announced by the jangling of the armload of gold bangles and amulets on chains around her neck. When Trigère cuts directly into fabric without a pattern it is always good for gasps, whether the audience is part of a Smithsonian Resident Associates lecture in Washington, D.C., on "The Designer as

trigère

a Creative Person," or her students at FIT. For this Critique Program, she will have come to the school at least four or five times during a semester.

Trigère was invited to FIT in 1973. With her apprentice background she had, of course, not gone to a formal design school herself. At first she found evaluating the work of the students difficult. It was like "correcting ten papers in ten different languages."

For her next session in 1974, she assigned her students the same design problem—take a classic silhouette (the princess) and interpret it individually. Her objective was to teach what she knew best:

Joseph Silverman
The Washington Star

cutting and draping, for she is acknowledged to be one of the finest fitters in the world. During critique sessions she had students go through all the procedures involved in the making of a dress in *couture* ready-to-wear.

The Design Studio Class at FIT is described by Professor Sica as a "specialization workshop modeled after the design room procedure of a couture house, where the designer and his or her assistants, sample hands, tailors and finishers, fulfill the designer's idea of an original fashion." Students thus learn the evolution of a design idea, from the first sketch or muslin to the actual garment shown to buyers.

To enlarge their experience, Trigère has invited them to visit her workrooms, to see her assistant Lucie Porges at work, watch corrections being made on a model, and see how fabric is selected by the designer. The class learns quickly from her that it is not enough for a dress to have model or eye appeal—"It has to hang right on the hanger." To prove her point, Trigère will spotlight her famous wool jersey dresses that fit so well. "They do not develop out of thin air. If I don't explain to my production man why I must have the fabric going in only one direction, the dresses will look like noodles on the rack."

Not everyone in the class takes criticism well, and so Trigère says, looking at their work, "O.K., prove to me why your idea is better." And she listens.

Then, going from one student's work to another, stopping to tell a student why her choice of linen was wrong for her dress though the sketch was excellent, Pauline finally shakes her head sympathetically, and in an aside to Professor Sica says, "It is difficult for one person to sketch, to cut, to stitch, to press, to drape. I can drape anything, but somebody else would have to press it. I cannot sketch. These kids are expected to do everything."

She leaves them with this message: "Designing is hard work. I never dreamed I would be a great designer. I work harder than I did twenty years ago."

trigère

TRIGÈRE, CELEBRITY

Trigère with Baroness Gillian Bayens

Opposite. Receiving the "Hall of Fame" Coty Award of American Fashion Critics, presented at the Metropolitan Museum of Art, 1959. Among her dozen other honors were the National Cotton Award (1949), the Neiman-Marcus Award (1950), the Best Dressed Hall of Fame Award (1973), and the Fashion Institute of Technology Designer Award (1973).

Pauline Trigère is a star. She casts and costumes herself and writes her own lines. She is sought, invited, entertained. She moves in the company of the most accomplished people of her time. She has a self-generating energy which helps produce the exciting life she lives.

"I created Trigère. At first it was a game. I am thoroughly enjoying it." This force that took her through a snowstorm to the swearing in of President John F. Kennedy, and later to his Inaugural Ball is the same drive that sent her to Israel, to which she has returned several times at the invitation of Ruth Dayan, to help with Maskit, a project which uses native craftsmanship in helping to build Israel's fashion industry.

Of course Trigère enjoys being a celebrity and having her name, birthdate, and face adorn a 1975 horoscope calendar. She was thrilled to be listed as one of Seventy-five Women of Achievement by the *Ladies Home Journal*. Receiving awards or being one of the "1,000 Names to Drop" in a "put-on" book by Jane Trahey are part of the Trigère image. She'd be distressed if she weren't one of the designers invited to trim a Christmas tree at Saks Fifth Avenue or to create a table setting at Tiffany's. And why not? She does it all so well.

If not the center of attention, Pauline is sure to be where attention is being centered. Every decade or so Earl Blackwell puts out his *Celebrity Register,* and at a party celebrating the publication, there is Trigère happily paying thirty-five dollars for a copy for her library.

When President Gerald Ford gave his dinner in honor of the President of the French Republic and Madame Giscard d'Estaing, Pauline flew to Martinique as a guest in David Rockefeller's Grumman Gulfstream. She wore one of her decorative black and white gowns that had appeared in the all-Trigère windows before the holidays at Bergdorf Goodman. She added one accessory to the diamante-

trigère

trimmed gown—her French decoration. This was duly reported in Suzy's column.

Trigère loves to give the kind of party people talk about and read about in the newspapers, the kind of party so many wish they could give with her special flair for mixing people. Such was the cocktail-dansant she held at New York's Boat Basin celebrating son Jean-Pierre's marriage to Diane Lohr. It was a Who's Who of friends in fashion, politics, figures from the worlds of music, theatre, and art. Mollie Parnis, Bill Blass, Gustave Tassell, Giorgio di Sant'Angelo, the Wesley Simpsons, the Martin Coles, the Norman Weschslers, the Marvin Traubs, the Charles Revsons, the John Lindsays and Trigère's masseur, Joseph Rottenburger.

About the pyrotechniques of her personality, Jerry Silverman says: "Outside of being one of the great designers of the world, she's a great showman who is personally exciting. She cooks like a dream. Is one of the best ballroom dancers of today. Does numerous good deeds for the fashion industry charities. It exhilarates you to be near her."

She has been invited to become a member of the board of the first women's bank in New York. She's been asked to write a newspaper column; to host a television show. What she'd like to do, other than what she does, is to spend a week as an "observer" watching Leonard Bernstein work with an orchestra. "I'd like to take another week and see how a great chef like Bocuse operates," she says in the low voice so many find sexy. She once had the desire to be a surgeon and many compare the way she cuts into fabric to a surgeon's skill. Most of all, she would have liked to have watched Balenciaga and Vionnet in their *ateliers*.

Joseph Eula

490

If Trigère is seldom bored it is because life and people augment the *joie de vivre* she possesses in abundance. Robert Trigère once wrote an article for *Playbill* entitled "My Sister Pauline." In it he described her as "timeless . . . with the spontaneousness of the very young and the wisdom of maturity. A dynamo in action." He asked Jean-Pierre what he would have called an article if he were writing about his mother. "I'd still call it 'My Sister, Pauline' " he said, but his brother Philippe countered, "Mine would be 'My Kid Sister, Pauline.' "

Julio Wertheim, a longtime beau and the first Argentine banker to visit The People's Republic of China (in 1974) says it is impossible to describe Trigère. "Start with Pauline the Lady, Pauline the Designer, Pauline the Mother, and now Grandmother, Pauline the Speaker, Pauline the Theatre, Opera and Concert Fan."

It's very Trigère that she pouts at not being given the go-ahead by her granddaughter's parents, Melanie and Philippe Radley, to give a big party to introduce young Karen to all her friends. It's also very Trigère, however, that she had the baby brought down a few weeks after her birth to 550 Seventh Avenue, so that all her employees could admire her.

Among the employees who have been with Trigère since the beginning is Lucille Lewis, who came fresh from school in 1944. She has worked in just about every department and is now liaison between the shipping and production departments. At first her job was making shoulder pads of the football variety "out to there," then she worked the switchboard, then in the stamping department. Every time she felt frustrated in a job, Trigère just moved her into another. In Lucille's estimation, Trigère is a "beautiful person." Regardless of what you call on her for, she responds. When Lucille's women's group was trying to raise money to help save Harlem Prep, Trigère put on a fashion show, her first couture show done in Harlem. "She sent the whole line out, and those Harlem children were crazy about all those beautiful clothes." Lucille also remembers that after World War II, when baby sitters were scarce, she could take her baby son with his bottle to work and he would play in Trigère's office.

Years ago, when a valued employee, Riva Ostrow, left to start her own handbag business, Trigère gave her a word of advice. "Don't splatter yourself. Work in depth doing what you like and make the best of every single situation."

There is nothing negative about Pauline. She is Pure Positive. She is positive, too, that she would love to see Lauren Bacall play her in a film, stage play or a musical à la *Coco*. Everything is possible, because Trigère is Trigère.

trigère

TRIGÈRE ON TRIGÈRE

Francesco Scavullo

Above. "Standing on my head is better than a facial."

An interview taped directly after the 1975 summer collection for press and buyers.

Q. To what do you attribute your great zest for everything?

A. When they ask me "how do you describe Pauline?" I always say "crazy." I love to nave fun. I am grateful that I am in good health. I can work a lot, play a lot, and have this enormous stamina. I love being surrounded by stimulating people. I meet them all the time. To me, today, it's great fun and an enormous pleasure to be able to tell you I came from nowhere, and I can meet all these important people. I am not spoiled at all.

Q. Does having a sense of humor help in your business?

A. I am innately shy. I don't like to talk about myself, but I can make fun of myself. Humor makes me work, laugh, and live. I can be dead tired, put on fresh lipstick and can be raring to go. I always need twenty-four more hours in the day because I need the extravagance of life. I love to have fun.

Q. You are constantly being copied. Does it disturb you?

A. Not really. I remember a transatlantic trip on the *Queen Elizabeth* in 1947 when a short gentleman, obviously from Seventh Avenue, joined me at the railing and said, "Last year we did *such a season* with your coat, this season I didn't find one as good."

trigère

Q. What is a typical Trigère day, or is there such a thing?

A. I'm usually up at 6:30 A.M. I do yoga. My masseur comes in three times a week. On the day of a collection showing I make no appointments (except with you today), since tomorrow I am going to Phoenix, so I sorted out the clothes I plan to take early this morning. I put them on two racks. A friend who came by to pick me up to take me to work looked at them and asked, "for four days you take all that?" My problem is that I have to think first of all of my working clothes. Then there's a Mexican fiesta one night I'll be going to. I'll be selling at the store (Saks Fifth Avenue) the next day so for that I'll wear my new beautiful white suit. There's a black tie dinner for me that next night, and another small dinner party. I don't know what I'll be doing Sunday, maybe just sitting around the pool. I will, of course, edit what I take in my suitcases, but putting it on racks lets me get a better idea of the overall picture. I wake up early. I need only 5½ to 6½ hours sleep. Then I catch up with myself by going to bed early, like 10 P.M., and recharging my batteries. A typical day in New York? When I get back on Wednesday I will have to put this (summer) collection that you saw this afternoon into work. That day will be full of appointments. There will be appointments at 10:00, 11:00 and 12:00 for fabrics for fall. Once a month I might lunch at La Grenouille. Usually I eat here, sometimes a can of sardines. I gave up the cottage cheese. I need an awful lot of protein.

When I come back from this trip I will have a meeting with the staff. They will probably ask my advice. I hope they will . . . on what to buy, what amounts of fabrics. That's another hour with the staff. Perhaps between 3:00 and 4:00 P.M. I will attend to correspondence. I do come to the office with lists. I am the original list maker. What if I lose it? Once it is written down I remember. I love the backs of invitation envelopes. It has nothing to do with economy, the paper is stiffer. There is an awful lot of telephoning, social and business calls. During collection week I say "no" to everything.

Q. Suppose you are having a dinner party?

A. My cook is generally me. I will have done the soup and dessert the night before. Perhaps coming home after a party. It's relaxing. My food is always kept simple. I do not serve sixteen vegetables, or even two. One is enough. I do the table the night before. Select the color of the doilies and my helper in the house will put out the napkins to match. I do the flowers. I try to be sure I have a day when I can leave the office at 5:00 P.M. It is too much to arrive just before the guests.

494

The Washington Star

Q. Does a party end by 11:30?

A. I hope not! If anyone leaves my house before 1 A.M. I hate it. Typical days are very atypical. I come to the office. Already there is a crisis. Someone is calling me on the phone, a dress is too big or too small. I am really unruly in the way I work. Very bad for everyone. I can come back from a trip, start telling a story and I never get to finish it. When two seasons are one on top of each other (like summer and fall) it is difficult. Next week we have to see fabrics. I like to work with the pattern maker. I am also preparing a speech for the Women's Financial Association of about five hundred women on Wall Street. I do not want to speak about fashion. What they want to know is how do you do it . . . the career. I didn't know it was going to be like this. It is very difficult to say I am going to be a great actress, like Liv Ullman who says she always knew she wanted to be a great actress. The challenge is what's important. To *continue* to make it is more difficult than to make it. They won't believe me when I tell them my story. (You have to put drama into it that may not have been there.) I don't think they really believe I worked eighteen hours, Saturday and Sunday too. It was really hard work at the beginning. There was always a lack of money, till you establish your credit. Now they are happy to lend me money. But it was not always so.

Q. What do you believe is your greatest talent?

A. I have always had this ability in my hands . . . to cut . . . always. It is God's gift to me, I guess.

BIBLIOGRAPHY

Anspach, Karlyne, *The Why of Fashion* (Ames, Iowa: Iowa State University, 1967).

Ballard, Bettina, *In My Fashion* (New York: McKay, 1960).

Battersley, Martin, *The Decorative Twenties* (New York: Walker, 1970).

Battersley, Martin, *The Decorative Thirties* (New York: Walker, 1969).

Beaton, Cecil, *The Glass of Fashion* (Garden City, N.Y.: Doubleday, 1954).

Bemelmans, Ludwig, *To the One I Love the Best* (New York: Viking, 1955).

Bender, Marylin, *The Beautiful People* (New York: Coward, McCann & Geoghegan, 1967).

Bergler, Edmund, *Fashion and the Unconscious* (New York: Robert Brunner, 1953).

Brockman, Helen L, *The Theory of Fashion Design* (New York: Wiley, 1965).

Brogden, Joanne, *Fashion Design* (London: Studio Vista, 1971).

Chase, Edna Woolman, and Ilka Chase, *Always in Vogue* (New York: Doubleday, 1954).

Corinth, Kay, *Fashion Showmanship* (New York: Wiley, 1970).

Daves, Jessica, *Ready-made Miracle* (New York: G. P. Putnam's Sons, 1967).

The Duchess of Windsor, *The Heart Has Its Reasons* (New York: McKay, 1956).

Fairchild, John, *The Fashionable Savages* (Garden City: Doubleday, 1965).

Fashion Group, *Your Future in Fashion Design* (New York: Richards Rosen, rev. ed., 1966).

Flanner, Janet, *An American in Paris, Profile of an Interlude Between the Wars* (New York: Simon & Schuster, 1940).

Garland, Madge, *The Changing Form of Fashion* (New York: Praeger, 1970).

Haedrich, Marcel, *Coco Chanel, Her Life, Her Secrets* (Boston: Little, Brown, 1972).

Hawes, Elizabeth, *Fashion Is Spinach* (New York: Random House, 1938).

Hawes, Elizabeth, *It's Still Spinach* (Boston: Little, Brown, 1954).

Hawes, Elizabeth, *Why Is A Dress?* (New York: Viking, 1942).

Ireland, Patrick J., *Fashion Design Drawing* (Metuchen, N.J.: Textile Book Service, 1970).

Kolodny, Rosalie, *Fashion Design for Moderns* (New York: Fairchild, 1967).

Levin, Phyllis Lee, *The Wheels of Fashion* (Garden City, N.Y.: Doubleday, 1965).

Men's Wear, *75 Years of Fashion* (New York: Fairchild, 1965).

Poiret, Paul, *King of Fashion: The Autobiography of Paul Poiret* (Philadelphia: Lippincott, 1931).

Ray, Man, *Self Portrait* (Boston: Little, Brown, 1963).

Riley, Robert, and Walter Vecchio, *The Fashion Makers* (New York: Crown, 1967).

Schiaparelli, Elsa, *Shocking Life* (New York: Dutton, 1954).

Snow, Carmel, with Mary Louise Aswell, *The World of Carmel Snow* (New York, McGraw-Hill, 1962).

Stuart, Jessie, *The American Fashion Industry* (Boston: Simmons College, 1951).

Williams, Beryl, *Fashion Is Our Business* (Philadelphia: Lippincott, 1945).

Williams, Beryl, *Young Faces in Fashion* (Philadelphia: Lippincott, 1956).

Wolfe, Elsie de, *After All* (New York: Harper & Row, 1935).

Wolfe, Elsie de, *The World in Vogue* (New York: Viking, 1963).

Worth, Jean Philippe, translated by Ruth Scott Miller, *A Century of Fashion* (Boston: Little, Brown, 1928).

CREDITS

Incorporated. Copyright renewed 1966 by Metro-Goldwyn-Mayer Inc. (page 48) From the MGM release *The Women,* copyright 1939 Loew's Incorporated. Copyright renewed 1966 by Metro-Goldwyn-Mayer Inc. (page 47) From the MGM release *Ziegfeld Girl,* copyright 1941 Loew's Incorporated. Copyright renewed 1967 by Metro-Goldwyn-Mayer, Inc. (pages 49, 51).

Photograph on page 40 credited to Twentieth Century-Fox is covered by the following copyright: *Daddy Longlegs,* copyright 1931, Twentieth Century-Fox Film Corporation. All right reserved.

MAINBOCHER

Photographs credited to *Vogue* magazine are covered by the following copyrights: Copyright 1932 (renewed 1960), 1933 (renewed 1961), 1934 (renewed 1962), 1937 (renewed 1965), 1938 (renewed 1966), 1939 (renewed 1967), 1941 (renewed 1969), 1943 (renewed 1971), 1944 (renewed 1972), 1945 (renewed 1973), 1946 (renewed 1974), 1947 (renewed 1975), 1948, 1949, 1950, 1951, 1953, 1954, 1955, 1956, 1959, 1960, 1964, 1965, by The Conde Nast Publications Inc.

Photographs credited to *Harper's Bazaar* are covered by copyright of The Hearst Corporation.

McCARDELL

Photographs credited to *Vogue* magazine are covered by the following copyrights: Copyright 1932 (renewed 1960), 1933 (renewed 1961), 1934 (renewed 1962), 1937 (renewed 1965), 1938 (renewed 1966), 1939 (renewed 1967), 1941 (renewed 1969), 1943 (renewed 1971), 1944 (renewed 1972), 1945 (renewed 1973), 1946 (renewed 1974), 1947 (renewed 1975), 1948, 1949, 1950, 1951, 1953, 1954, 1955, 1956, 1959, 1960, 1964, 1965, by The Conde Nast Publications Inc.

Photographs credited to *Harper's Bazaar* are covered by copyright of The Hearst Corporation.

TIME cover of May 2, 1955, is reprinted by permission from TIME, The Weekly Newsmagazine. Copyright Time Inc.

NORELL

Photographs credited to *Harper's Bazaar* and *House Beautiful* are covered by copyright of The Hearst Corporation.

Photographs credited to *Vogue* magazine are covered by the following copyrights: Copyright 1932 (renewed 1960), 1933 (renewed 1961), 1934 (renewed 1962), 1937 (renewed 1965), 1938 (renewed 1966), 1939 (renewed 1967), 1941 (renewed 1969), 1943 (renewed 1971), 1944 (renewed 1972), 1945 (renewed 1973), 1946 (renewed 1974), 1947 (renewed 1975), 1948, 1949, 1950, 1951, 1953, 1954, 1955, 1956, 1959, 1960, 1964, 1965, by The Conde Nast Publications Inc.

TRIGERE

Photographs credited to *Harper's Bazaar* are covered by copyright of The Hearst Corporation.

INDEX

507